# Theological Injury

## THE MORAL INJURY PROJECT

*Theological Injury* is part of The Moral Injury Project, an ongoing writing, educational, and public-engagement initiative exploring moral injury, theological injury, caregiving, disaster response, public service, spiritual care, and the human search for meaning after suffering.

For additional resources, books, articles, training opportunities, and project updates, visit:

www.TheMoralInjuryProject.org

# Theological Injury

*Faith After Explanations Collapse*

G. C. SMITH

RESOURCE *Publications* • Eugene, Oregon

THEOLOGICAL INJURY
Faith After Explanations Collapse



Resource Publications
An Imprint of Wipf and Stock Publishers
199 W. 8th Ave., Suite 3
Eugene, OR 97401

www.wipfandstock.com

PAPERBACK ISBN: 979-8-3852-9062-8
HARDCOVER ISBN: 979-8-3852-9063-5
EBOOK ISBN: 979-8-3852-9064-2

VERSION NUMBER 07/21/26

"The questions may remain.
The scars may remain.
The mysteries may remain.
But so does God."

— G. C. Smith

# Contents

# Introduction

## *The Unfinished Sentence*

Several years ago, after a disaster, a woman sat across from me and said something I have heard many times over the years.

"I still believe in God," she said.

Then she paused.

"But I don't know what I mean by that anymore."

Her words lingered in the silence between us.

The storm had altered her life in a matter of minutes. Her home had been damaged beyond recognition. Familiar routines had disappeared, treasured possessions were gone, and the future she had imagined only days earlier suddenly seemed uncertain. Yet as we talked, it became clear that another loss was present as well. Something had happened not only to her circumstances but also to the way she understood God.

The prayers she once prayed felt different. The confidence she once carried had begun to erode. Explanations that had sustained her for years no longer seemed capable of carrying the weight of what she had experienced.

As I listened, I found myself recognizing a conversation I had heard many times before.

Over the years I have sat with people in disaster shelters after tornadoes, hurricanes, floods, and wildfires. I have listened in hospital rooms after difficult diagnoses, in churches after funerals, in nursing homes where families faced impossible decisions, in living rooms where grief had quietly taken up residence, and in recovery centers where people were trying to imagine life beyond catastrophe. Those conversations have involved disaster survivors, grieving parents, healthcare workers, pastors, chaplains, emergency responders, caregivers, and countless ordinary people whose lives had been interrupted by suffering.

The details have always been different.

The underlying experience has been remarkably similar.

People were not simply struggling with suffering.

They were struggling with what suffering had done to the way they understood God.

For much of my ministry, I assumed that the greatest spiritual challenge people faced was unbelief. I expected conversations about faith to revolve around questions of whether God existed or whether Christianity was true. Those questions certainly matter, and they deserve thoughtful attention. Yet after decades of pastoral ministry and disaster response, I have become convinced that another struggle is far more common than many of our churches recognize.

Again and again, I have met people who continue believing in God while finding themselves unable to return to the assumptions they once carried. They continue praying, worshiping, serving, and reading Scripture. They have not abandoned faith. Many remain deeply committed to the life of the church.

Yet something has shifted.

The faith they inhabit is no longer quite the faith they inherited.

The answers that once sounded reassuring now seem incomplete. The explanations that once made sense no longer seem capable of bearing the full weight of experience. Questions arise that they never expected to ask, and the confidence they once associated with mature faith begins to feel more elusive than before.

Many assume this means they are failing.

I have come to believe it may mean something quite different.

Perhaps faith is not disappearing.

Perhaps it is changing.

Looking back, I realize that some of the most important conversations of my ministry did not occur during seasons of certainty. They took place after funerals, following disasters, during long hospital stays, in the quiet aftermath of congregational crises, or at the end of exhausting deployments when people finally had enough space to speak honestly about what had been happening inside them.

Those conversations rarely began with theology.

They began with stories.

Someone described the day they lost their home.

A father spoke about the death of a child.

A nurse reflected on years spent caring for people whose suffering could not be relieved.

A pastor admitted that familiar theological answers no longer felt adequate after decades of walking beside grieving families.

A responder quietly wondered how many disasters a person could witness before something inside began to change.

Each story was unique.

Yet as I listened, I began noticing a common thread running beneath them all.

People were asking questions they often felt unable to ask anywhere else.

Not because they had stopped believing.

Because they cared deeply about what they believed.

One of the striking realities of these conversations was that very few people were asking for airtight explanations. They were not looking for philosophical arguments capable of solving the mystery of suffering. Most had already discovered that life was too complicated for easy answers.

What they longed for was something much simpler.

They wanted permission.

Permission to admit that prayer had become more complicated than it once seemed.

Permission to acknowledge disappointment without feeling guilty.

Permission to confess that they no longer understood God in quite the same way they once had.

Permission to tell the truth.

Again and again, I watched people experience relief long before they found answers. Simply discovering that someone else recognized their experience often lifted a burden they had carried for years. They realized they were not uniquely deficient. They were not secretly failing while everyone else possessed unshakable faith.

They were human.

And they were not alone.

One of the great privileges of pastoral ministry is being invited into moments that most people never see. Over the years I have been welcomed into the sacred space where polished religious language gives way to honest conversation. The public smile disappears. The rehearsed answers fade. People begin speaking from places they rarely reveal elsewhere.

Those moments have shaped this book more than any classroom, conference, or theological library ever could.

Again and again, I encountered people whose faith had not disappeared but whose understanding of faith had been profoundly altered by suffering. They continued returning to God even when they no longer understood God in the ways they once had.

At first I assumed these conversations were unusual.

Eventually I realized they were not.

They were everywhere.

Many faithful people were quietly living in this territory, often believing they were the only ones there.

That realization changed the direction of my own thinking. I began paying closer attention to the conversations that occurred after presentations, when most people had already left the room. I noticed the quiet questions asked in hallways after worship services and the hesitant confessions offered during disaster deployments when the work had finally slowed for the evening. Time after time, people lowered their voices before speaking, as though they were about to confess something shameful.

"I've never told anyone this . . . "

"I hope this doesn't sound like a lack of faith . . . "

"I probably shouldn't admit this . . . "

What followed was almost never unbelief.

It was wounded belief.

It was the testimony of people who still loved God but whose understanding of God had been profoundly reshaped by suffering. Some had experienced a single catastrophic loss. Others had been changed by years of accumulated grief, responsibility, caregiving, or repeated exposure to tragedy. Whatever the path, they eventually arrived at the same place.

They still believed.

But believing no longer felt the way it once had.

The more I listened, the more convinced I became that these conversations were describing an experience for which many of us had very little language. We knew how to speak about grief, burnout, compassion fatigue, trauma, and even moral injury. Yet there seemed to be another kind of wound, one that reached into the very framework through which people understood God, prayer, providence, justice, and hope.

That conviction became the beginning of this book.

In the years that followed, I found myself listening differently.

Instead of assuming that every spiritual struggle was simply a question of belief or unbelief, I began paying closer attention to the ways suffering reshaped people's understanding of God. I noticed that many faithful individuals were not abandoning Christianity. They were attempting to reconcile experiences they never expected with theological frameworks that no longer seemed large enough to contain them.

The changes were often subtle.

A prayer that once came naturally now felt hesitant.

A familiar Bible passage sounded different after the death of a spouse or child.

A sermon that might once have brought comfort now raised more questions than answers.

A person continued attending worship while privately wondering whether anyone else in the congregation felt as disoriented as they did.

These changes rarely happened overnight. More often they emerged gradually, almost unnoticed at first. A difficult diagnosis was followed by months of treatment. A caregiver watched someone they loved decline one day at a time. A pastor moved from one funeral to the next while quietly carrying personal grief. A disaster responder deployed repeatedly until scenes of suffering that once seemed unimaginable became almost routine.

Nothing dramatic occurred on any single day.

Instead, the questions accumulated.

The disappointments accumulated.

The losses accumulated.

Eventually, something inside began to shift.

One of the reasons this experience can be so confusing is that it often develops beneath the surface. People expect a spiritual crisis to arrive suddenly, announced by a dramatic loss of faith or an unmistakable rejection of belief. Occasionally that happens, but much more often theological disruption resembles erosion rather than explosion. The landscape changes slowly until one day a person realizes that familiar landmarks are no longer where they once were.

Looking back, I think this is one reason so many people feel isolated. They cannot identify a single moment when everything changed. They simply recognize that prayer no longer feels the same, worship no longer evokes the same response, and explanations that once seemed convincing now feel incomplete. Because the process has been gradual, they often assume it must be unique to them.

I no longer believe that.

One of the recurring discoveries of my ministry has been how many faithful people quietly carry these experiences without ever speaking about them. They volunteer in congregations, serve on committees, teach Sunday school, participate in Bible studies, deploy to disasters, care for aging parents, comfort grieving families, and continue doing the work of faith while privately wondering whether something has gone wrong inside them.

Often they are among the most dependable people in the room.

Years ago, after speaking about disaster response and moral injury, a pastor waited until nearly everyone else had left. The chairs were already being folded, conversations had ended, and volunteers were turning off the lights. Only then did he approach me.

"I thought I was the only one," he said.

He was not talking about stress.

He was not talking about exhaustion.

He was talking about faith.

For years he had carried questions that he felt unable to discuss openly. He still preached every Sunday. He still visited hospitals, led Bible studies, and officiated at funerals. Nothing about his outward ministry suggested spiritual collapse.

Yet inwardly he knew his faith had changed.

That brief conversation has stayed with me because it has been repeated so many times since. Different people have used different words, but the underlying confession has remained remarkably consistent.

"I don't pray the way I used to."

"I still trust God, but I don't understand God the way I once did."

"I believe, but I don't know what to do with these questions."

"I've never told anyone this before."

Those conversations convinced me that many churches unintentionally leave people without language for one of the most common experiences of mature faith.

We often celebrate certainty.

We know how to speak about conversion.

We know how to speak about commitment.

We know how to speak about spiritual growth.

We are often less comfortable speaking about the ways suffering changes our understanding of God.

Yet Scripture is filled with precisely those conversations.

The psalmists ask why God seems absent.

Job refuses easy explanations.

Jeremiah accuses God of abandoning him.

Habakkuk questions divine justice.

Even Jesus cries out from the cross with words of profound abandonment.

The Bible does not hide these voices.

It preserves them.

That observation gradually changed the way I understood spiritual maturity. Earlier in my ministry I assumed maturity meant possessing greater certainty. More study, more experience, and more years in ministry would naturally produce more confidence and fewer questions.

Life proved far more complicated than that.

Some questions were answered.

Others became deeper.

Some convictions became stronger.

Others became humbler.

What changed most was not simply what I believed but how I held those beliefs. Certainty gradually gave way to humility. Explanation became less important than presence. Winning theological arguments seemed less significant than walking faithfully beside people whose lives had been shattered.

That transformation did not happen because I set out to change my theology.

It happened because I kept meeting people whose experiences refused to fit neatly within the explanations I already possessed.

Again and again, they taught me that faith is often more resilient than our theological systems.

They also taught me that suffering frequently changes theology before it changes belief.

That realization eventually led me to the phrase that gives this book its central theme.

I began thinking of these experiences as theological injury—not because theology is unimportant, but because theology matters deeply. The ways we understand God shape how we pray, how we hope, how we grieve, how we endure disappointment, and how we interpret our lives. When those understandings are wounded, the injury reaches far beyond the intellect.

It touches the heart.

It touches relationships.

It touches the soul.

And for many faithful people, it changes the journey of faith forever.

As I continued reflecting on these conversations, I realized that one of the greatest difficulties people faced was not simply the experience itself but the absence of language for it. Human beings naturally seek words for what they are living. We know how to speak about physical injury because everyone understands what happens when a body is wounded. Increasingly, we have learned to recognize emotional trauma, compassion fatigue, burnout, and moral injury. Those terms have given people permission to acknowledge experiences that previous generations often carried in silence.

Yet many of the people I encountered were describing something different.

Their deepest struggle was not primarily emotional, although emotions were certainly involved. It was not merely psychological, although suffering always affects the mind. It was not simply moral, though moral questions often surfaced as well.

Something had happened to the way they understood God.

The more I listened, the more convinced I became that this experience deserved to be named.

That is why I have chosen the phrase theological injury.

No phrase is perfect. Every attempt to describe human experience has limitations. Yet this language seems to capture something important. It recognizes that suffering can wound not only our emotions and our bodies but also the theological framework through which we understand the world. Long-held assumptions about prayer, providence, justice, divine action, protection, and suffering may no longer seem capable of bearing the weight of lived experience.

The injury is not merely intellectual.

It is profoundly personal.

People discover that explanations which once brought comfort now feel inadequate. Images of God that once seemed clear become more difficult to reconcile with what they have witnessed. Questions arise that cannot simply be dismissed because they emerge not from curiosity alone but from grief, responsibility, love, and loss.

In many ways, theological injury resembles grief.

Something has been lost.

Sometimes it is confidence.

Sometimes it is a cherished assumption.

Sometimes it is the expectation that life will unfold according to patterns we believed we understood.

Sometimes it is an image of God that no longer seems large enough to encompass what we have experienced.

That loss deserves to be acknowledged.

One of the surprising discoveries of my own journey has been that many faithful people interpret this experience as failure when it may actually represent growth. Earlier understandings of God often serve us well for a season. They provide structure, guidance, and reassurance. Yet life has a way of introducing realities that exceed the capacity of those earlier frameworks. Suffering, prolonged caregiving, repeated exposure to tragedy, institutional betrayal, and profound disappointment frequently confront us with questions we never imagined asking.

The old answers are not necessarily false.

They are simply no longer sufficient.

That distinction matters.

A child eventually outgrows clothing that once fit perfectly. The clothing was not defective. The child simply grew. In a similar way, many believers discover that the theological frameworks that sustained them earlier in life require deepening as experience becomes more complex. The process can feel unsettling because growth often involves letting go of forms that once provided security.

Looking back, I realize that much of my own ministry involved accompanying people through precisely that transition. Rarely did I encounter individuals who wanted to discard faith altogether. More often, they were searching for a faith spacious enough to hold both belief and unanswered questions, both hope and grief, both trust and mystery.

They were looking for a faith capable of telling the truth.

Over the years I have become convinced that this search is far more common than many churches recognize. Outwardly, congregations often appear confident and settled. Inwardly, many people carry quiet questions they have never voiced aloud. They wonder whether prayer still matters after years of unanswered requests. They wonder how to reconcile repeated tragedy with the goodness of God. They wonder why certain theological explanations that once sounded persuasive now feel strangely hollow.

Many assume everyone else possesses a certainty they themselves have somehow lost.

Again and again, I have discovered the opposite.

The person sitting beside them in worship may be carrying similar questions.

The pastor leading the service may have wrestled with many of the same uncertainties.

The disaster responder offering comfort may have spent years asking difficult questions after witnessing extraordinary suffering.

The caregiver quietly praying beside a hospital bed may understand theological disruption more deeply than anyone realizes.

The territory is far less lonely than it appears.

That conviction lies near the heart of this book.

I am not writing because I have solved the mystery of suffering. I have not. I am not writing because I possess explanations capable of resolving every difficult question. I do not. Nor am I attempting to defend a particular theological system or persuade readers that every experience can be neatly understood.

I am writing because I believe people deserve companionship while they navigate this landscape.

They deserve language that helps them recognize what they are experiencing.

They deserve the reassurance that faithful people have walked this road throughout the history of Scripture and the history of the church.

Most of all, they deserve to know that questions do not automatically separate them from God.

If anything, the biblical story suggests the opposite.

Again and again we encounter men and women whose deepest prayers emerge not from certainty but from confusion, lament, disappointment, and longing. Their questions are preserved not as evidence of failure but as testimony to a relationship that continued even when understanding did not.

That observation has become one of the anchors of my own faith.

I no longer believe that mature faith is measured primarily by the absence of questions.

I believe it is often revealed by the willingness to remain in relationship with God while those questions continue to unfold.

That kind of faith is quieter than the certainty many of us admired when we were younger.

It is also stronger.

It has survived contact with reality.

And it is the kind of faith this book seeks to explore.

If you have picked up this book because your faith no longer feels the way it once did, I hope you will discover that you are not alone.

If you are reading because someone you love is struggling, I hope these pages will help you listen with greater patience and greater compassion. One of the gifts we can offer another person is not the certainty of our answers but the willingness to remain present while difficult questions are being lived.

If you are a pastor, chaplain, healthcare professional, counselor, disaster responder, caregiver, or spiritual director, I hope this book provides language for conversations you have probably already been having. You may discover that many of the people who come seeking help are not asking for philosophical arguments as much as they are asking whether anyone else has ever stood where they now find themselves.

This book is not a map that eliminates every mystery.

It is a companion for the journey.

The chapters that follow explore prayer, suffering, lament, silence, moral injury, disaster response, caregiving, hope, faith, wisdom, and grace. Along the way we will encounter people whose assumptions have been shaken, whose understanding of God has changed, and whose faith has been wounded without disappearing. We will consider voices from Scripture, theology, psychology, pastoral ministry, and the lived experience of ordinary believers who discovered that faith sometimes grows in unexpected ways.

As the years have passed, I have become less interested in defending certainty and more interested in recognizing faithfulness. I have watched too many people continue loving after heartbreaking loss, continue praying after long seasons of silence, continue serving after profound disappointment, and continue seeking God when much of what they once assumed no longer seemed adequate. Those are the people who have become my teachers.

They have convinced me that faith is often far more resilient than we imagine.

One of the recurring themes throughout this book is that suffering frequently changes our understanding of God before it changes our belief in God. We may continue praying while praying differently. We may continue trusting while trusting more humbly. We may continue believing while discovering that many of our earlier explanations have become too small for the realities we now face.

That realization can feel frightening.

It can also become the beginning of a deeper and more honest spiritual life.

I have come to believe that many people spend years trying to recover the faith they once possessed when, in fact, God may be inviting them into a faith they have not yet imagined. The journey is rarely easy. It often involves grief because something real has been lost. Yet grief is not always the final chapter of the story. Sometimes it becomes the doorway to wisdom, compassion, humility, and a deeper awareness of God's presence.

That is certainly what I have witnessed.

Again and again, the people who have most shaped my understanding of faith have not been those who seemed untouched by suffering. They have been people who carried scars without allowing those scars to become the whole story. They learned to pray with unanswered questions, to hope while living with uncertainty, and to continue loving even after disappointment. Their faith became quieter than it once was, less interested in easy explanations and more willing to trust the God who remained present when explanations did not.

Those lives have given me hope.

They have also reminded me that Christianity has always been a faith shaped by people who walked through wilderness before they reached promise, exile before they returned home, lament before they sang again, and death before resurrection. Scripture never suggests that faith eliminates suffering. Instead, it repeatedly reveals a God who meets people within suffering and continues walking with them through it.

That is the God I have encountered in hospital rooms and disaster shelters, at gravesides and recovery centers, in congregational conflicts and quiet conversations long after everyone else had gone home. Rarely has God appeared through dramatic explanations. More often, God's presence has become visible through faithful companions, unexpected kindness, quiet courage, and the grace that somehow enables people to take one more step when they believed they had no strength left.

Looking back across the years, I realize that this book grew out of thousands of conversations rather than a single moment of inspiration. Some conversations lasted only a few minutes. Others unfolded over months or years. Together they taught me that many faithful people live within a sentence they never quite finish.

"I still believe . . . "

Then comes the pause.

A pause filled with grief.

A pause filled with disappointment.

A pause filled with questions.

A pause filled with hope.

The sentence remains unfinished not because faith has ended, but because the journey is still unfolding.

Perhaps that is where genuine faith has always lived—not at the end of every question, but in the willingness to continue the conversation with God even when many questions remain.

That is the journey we will explore together.

It begins with an unfinished sentence.

"I still believe . . .

. . . but."

## *Chapter 1*

# I Still Believe, But . . .

Several years ago, during a disaster response, I sat with a survivor whose life had been changed in a matter of minutes. The details were familiar: a sudden catastrophe, a home damaged beyond repair, and a future that no longer looked the way it had looked the day before.

We talked for a long time about insurance, housing, family, and the exhausting work of figuring out what came next. As often happens in disaster response, the conversation gradually moved beyond practical concerns. We began talking about loss, uncertainty, and the strange disorientation that follows an event capable of dividing life into before and after. Eventually, we began talking about faith.

At one point the survivor grew quiet and stared out the window.

"I still believe in God," the person said.

Then there was a long pause.

"But . . . "

The sentence was never completed because it did not need to be. The unfinished word carried the weight of everything that had changed. I could almost hear the rest of the sentence.

I still believe in God, but I do not understand what happened.

I still believe in God, but prayer feels different now.

I still believe in God, but the explanations I used to trust no longer seem to work.

I still believe in God, but I have questions I never had before.

Over the years I have heard versions of that unfinished sentence from disaster survivors, grieving parents, caregivers, healthcare workers, clergy, chaplains, and responders. The details differ, but the pattern remains remarkably similar. These individuals have not abandoned faith. In many cases they still attend worship, continue praying, read Scripture, and identify themselves as Christians. Yet something important has changed. The faith they once carried no longer fits quite the same way. Assumptions that once seemed reliable no longer feel secure, and explanations that once provided comfort no longer seem adequate.

They still believe.

But.

That small word often marks the beginning of a profound spiritual journey.

For some people the experience is frightening because they assume something has gone wrong. They wonder whether they are losing faith, worry that their questions indicate weakness, and sometimes fear they have disappointed God. In reality, something very different may be happening. Their faith may not be disappearing. It may be changing.

For many years Christian communities have tended to think about faith and doubt as opposites. Faith occupies one side and doubt the other. More faith supposedly means less doubt, while more doubt means less faith. Real life is rarely that simple. Many of the people I have encountered continue believing even while carrying substantial questions. They continue praying while struggling with prayer. They continue trusting God while wrestling with disappointment, confusion, anger, or grief. The tension is not always faith versus unbelief. More often, it is faith versus certainty.

Those are not the same thing.

One of the central arguments of this book is that theological injury occurs when experiences of suffering disrupt previously held assumptions about God, prayer, providence, protection, justice, or meaning. The person still believes, but belief now exists alongside questions that cannot easily be answered. The result is not necessarily unbelief. More often, it is wounded faith.

Over time I began noticing that these conversations were not isolated. A grieving parent would ask a difficult question after a funeral. A disaster survivor would express disappointment with God after losing a home. A caregiver would quietly admit that prayer no longer felt the way it once had. A pastor would confess uncertainty about theological answers they had preached for years. Each story was different, but the questions were remarkably similar. Again and again, people described experiences that did not fit neatly into the categories churches often provide for understanding faith. They had not stopped believing. They had not rejected God. They had not abandoned Christianity. Yet the faith they once carried had been disrupted—not destroyed, but disrupted.

Eventually I began wondering whether these experiences represented something larger than individual struggles. Perhaps they were describing a recognizable spiritual reality.

Researchers studying religion and spirituality have observed similar patterns. Psychologist Kenneth Pargament and other scholars have spent decades examining how people use faith to navigate suffering, crisis, and major life disruptions. Their research suggests that spiritual struggle is not unusual among religious people. Periods of questioning, disappointment, conflict, and uncertainty often emerge precisely when individuals are trying to make sense of painful experiences.

I find that observation reassuring—not because it solves the problem, but because it reminds us that wounded faith is not rare. Many believers assume they are alone. They assume their questions indicate failure and that everyone else possesses a stronger faith. The evidence suggests otherwise. Questions are common. Spiritual struggle is common. The disruption of previously held beliefs is common.

What is uncommon is our willingness to talk honestly about these realities.

Several years ago, after speaking about moral injury and disaster response, a pastor approached me following a presentation. He waited until most people had left the room. Chairs were being stacked, conversations were ending, and people were gathering coats and heading toward the exits. Then he said something I have never forgotten.

"I thought I was the only one."

He was not talking about burnout or stress. He was talking about faith.

Years of ministry had left him carrying questions he felt unable to discuss openly. He still believed. He still served. He still preached. Yet he no longer experienced faith in the same way he once had. That conversation lasted only a few minutes, but I have had versions of it many times since. The people and circumstances have been different, but the underlying theme has remained remarkably consistent. Something happened. The experience changed them. Now they were trying to understand what had happened to their faith.

One reason these conversations remain hidden is that many believers have never been given permission to imagine faith and questioning existing together. In some Christian communities, certainty becomes one of the primary markers of spiritual maturity. Strong faith is associated with confidence. Mature believers are expected to possess answers, while doubt is treated as something to overcome as quickly as possible. The intention is usually good. Churches want to encourage trust. Pastors want to strengthen faith. Parents want their children to develop confidence in God.

Yet the unintended consequence is that many people become frightened by their own questions. When suffering disrupts their assumptions, they conclude that something must be wrong. If faith is supposed to produce certainty, then uncertainty feels like failure. If mature believers are expected to possess answers, then unanswered questions feel like weakness. Instead of speaking honestly about their struggles, many people learn to hide them.

I have seen this repeatedly in both ministry and disaster response.

Several years ago, a longtime church member approached me after worship. This was someone who had spent decades in the life of the church—teaching classes, serving on committees, attending Bible studies, and participating faithfully in congregational life. After a few moments of conversation, the person lowered their voice and asked a question that seemed to carry years of hesitation.

"Is it normal to have questions about God after something like this?"

The question itself was not surprising. The fear behind it was. The individual was not asking whether questions existed. The individual was asking whether questions were permissible.

That distinction matters.

Human beings naturally ask questions after suffering because suffering disrupts expectations. Questions arise because grief forces us to confront realities we would rather avoid and because the world no longer feels as predictable as it once did. The remarkable thing is not that people ask questions. The remarkable thing is that so many believers feel ashamed for having them.

Again and again, I have encountered people who assume that questioning reflects spiritual failure. A disaster survivor wonders whether disappointment with God indicates weak faith. A caregiver worries that frustration during prayer reflects a lack of trust. A pastor feels guilty for struggling with theological explanations that once seemed convincing. A responder quietly wonders whether years of exposure to tragedy have somehow damaged belief.

What many of these individuals need most is not correction. They need reassurance. They need someone to tell them that questions are not unusual, uncertainty is not uncommon, and faithful people have always wrestled with experiences they could not fully understand.

Scripture repeatedly demonstrates this reality. The Psalms are filled with questions.

"How long, O Lord?"

"Why do you hide your face?"

"Why have you forgotten me?"

These are not the questions of unbelievers. They are the questions of believers attempting to remain in relationship with God amid experiences that seem impossible to explain. The same pattern appears throughout Scripture. Job questions. Jeremiah questions. Habakkuk questions. The psalmists question. Even Jesus cries out from the cross.

The presence of questions does not indicate the absence of faith. In many cases, it demonstrates the persistence of faith. People continue asking because they continue caring. They continue wrestling because the relationship still matters. The person who has completely abandoned God rarely argues with God. Arguments belong to relationships. Lament belongs to relationships. Questions belong to relationships.

This insight changed the way I think about spiritual struggle. For many years I assumed that the goal of faith was certainty. The longer I spend alongside suffering, the more convinced I become that certainty is often overrated. Certainty feels secure, reassuring, and strong. Yet certainty can become surprisingly fragile when confronted by realities it cannot explain.

Faith is different.

Faith can survive unanswered questions.

Faith can survive disappointment.

Faith can survive confusion.

Faith can survive seasons in which explanations collapse.

Several years ago, I witnessed this reality in a hospital room.

A family had gathered around the bed of a loved one whose life was nearing its end. They had prayed faithfully for healing. Their congregation had prayed. Friends had prayed. Hope had remained remarkably strong even as the medical situation became increasingly difficult. When I entered the room that afternoon, the family was exhausted—not physically, but spiritually. It was the kind of exhaustion that develops when hope and disappointment have been living side by side for a very long time.

For a while we talked about ordinary things—family memories, favorite stories, and the small details that become precious when time feels short. Then the conversation shifted. One family member finally voiced what everyone else seemed to be carrying.

"I don't know what to do with all of this."

The statement hung quietly in the air. No one asked for a theological explanation. No one wanted a lecture about suffering. No one needed a carefully constructed defense of God. What they needed was permission to tell the truth. The truth was that they still loved God. They still prayed. They still believed. The truth was also that they were confused, disappointed, tired, and increasingly unsure how to reconcile their experience with what they thought they understood about prayer.

As I listened, I found myself thinking about how often faith communities underestimate the spiritual impact of prolonged suffering. We are usually prepared for crisis. We are less prepared for endurance. A sudden tragedy can shatter assumptions, but a long season of suffering can slowly erode them—day after day, month after month, prayer after prayer. Theological injury frequently develops this way, not through a dramatic loss of belief, but through the gradual accumulation of unanswered questions.

That afternoon nobody in the room announced that they had stopped believing in God. In fact, quite the opposite. What they were struggling to understand was how belief was supposed to function in circumstances like these. How should prayer be understood when healing does not occur? How should hope be understood when outcomes remain unchanged? How should faith be understood when experience refuses to cooperate with expectation?

Those are not the questions of unbelievers. They are the questions of people trying desperately to remain faithful.

Again and again, I have encountered similar questions among pastors, caregivers, healthcare workers, responders, and grieving families. These are rarely people abandoning faith. More often, they are discovering that faith and certainty are not the same thing. Faith ultimately depends less upon complete understanding than upon relationship. A marriage does not survive because each person understands everything about the other, nor does a friendship endure because every question has been resolved. Relationships survive because commitment remains even when understanding is incomplete.

Perhaps faith works similarly.

Perhaps mature faith is not the absence of questions. Perhaps mature faith is the willingness to remain in relationship with God while carrying questions that have not yet been answered. If that is true, then many people experiencing theological injury are not failing. They are learning a different form of faith—a more complicated faith, a less certain faith, a faith shaped by experience rather than assumption, and a faith that has lost some answers while discovering greater honesty. Painful as that transition may be, it may also become one of the most important spiritual journeys a person ever undertakes.

The distinction between faith and certainty eventually led me to another realization. Faith and theology are closely related, but they are not identical. For much of my life I assumed they rose and fell together. If theology became uncertain, faith must be weakening. If familiar answers stopped working, something must be wrong. Many Christians have been taught, explicitly or implicitly, to think this way. Certainty becomes a sign of spiritual health. Confidence becomes evidence of faithfulness. Questions become evidence of failure.

Yet the lives of real people rarely fit those categories.

Nor does Scripture.

Several months after another disaster deployment, I spoke with a survivor whose recovery appeared, at least from the outside, to be progressing well. Temporary housing had been secured. Insurance claims were moving forward. Daily life had begun settling into a new routine. Yet something remained unsettled.

As we talked, the survivor described feeling disconnected from the faith that had once provided comfort.

"I still pray," the person said. "I just don't know what I think anymore."

The statement stayed with me because it captured a tension I had heard many times before. Prayer remained. Faith remained. The relationship with God remained. What had changed was something else: the framework, the assumptions, the understanding, the theology.

For many people, theological injury begins there—not with the loss of faith, but with the loss of certainty. That distinction may seem small, but it is not. A person can continue trusting God while no longer trusting previous explanations about God. A person can continue praying while questioning how prayer works. A person can continue believing while struggling to understand suffering.

Some of the most faithful people I know carry exactly those questions.

Years of ministry and disaster response have convinced me that suffering often challenges theology before it challenges faith. The questions people ask are rarely abstract. They emerge from lived experience. A parent struggles to understand the death of a child. A caregiver wrestles with unanswered prayer. A responder tries to make sense of repeated tragedy. A pastor wonders whether explanations that once seemed sufficient can still bear the weight of reality. The issue is not indifference. The issue is meaning.

Human beings naturally try to make sense of what happens to them. When existing explanations fail, new understanding becomes necessary. The process is rarely comfortable. More often, it feels like grief because something is genuinely being lost. Sometimes it is an assumption.

Sometimes it is an expectation. Sometimes it is an image of God that no longer seems capable of carrying the weight of experience.

Many believers describe this season in language usually associated with mourning. They speak of disappointment, confusion, disorientation, and sometimes even betrayal—not necessarily because they have concluded that God abandoned them, but because the God they thought they understood no longer seems quite so understandable. This experience can be frightening, particularly for people who have spent years building their lives around faith. A pastor discovers questions never expected. A nurse finds it increasingly difficult to reconcile certain theological claims with what is witnessed daily. A caregiver wonders why prayers seem unanswered. A responder struggles to understand how repeated tragedy fits within a theology of providence.

The questions emerge not because these individuals care less about God. More often, they emerge because they care deeply. Theological injury is frequently born from engagement rather than indifference. The people most affected are often those who have taken faith seriously. They expected faith to help them make sense of life. They expected prayer to provide reassurance. They expected certain theological convictions to remain reliable.

Then life became more difficult to understand.

One of the gifts of Scripture is that it repeatedly acknowledges this reality. The Bible contains remarkably few examples of uncomplicated faith. Abraham questions. Moses protests. Jeremiah argues. Habakkuk complains. Job demands answers. The psalmists lament. Even the disciples struggle repeatedly to understand what God is doing. The biblical story is not populated by people who never questioned. It is populated by people who continued engaging God amid uncertainty.

That observation has become increasingly important to me over the years. The opposite of faith is not questioning. The opposite of faith is disengagement. The wounded believer who continues wrestling with God remains engaged. The grieving parent who continues praying remains engaged. The responder who continues searching for meaning remains engaged. The caregiver who continues bringing confusion before God remains engaged. The relationship persists even when certainty does not.

Again and again, I have encountered people whose theology was wounded while faith remained alive. The questions were real. The uncertainty was real. The disruption was real. Yet beneath all of it, relationship endured. Trust endured. Hope endured. Sometimes only barely, but it endured.

That may be one of the most important things we can say about theological injury. It is not always the story of faith being lost. Often it is the story of faith struggling to survive after its previous explanations have collapsed.

That is why I have chosen the phrase theological injury. The phrase is imperfect. Every phrase is. Yet it names something I believe many people experience and relatively few people discuss. We know what it means to speak about physical injury. We understand emotional injury. Increasingly, we understand psychological injury and moral injury. Yet suffering can also wound theology. It can wound assumptions about prayer, providence, justice, suffering, and divine action.

The injury is not merely intellectual.

It is deeply personal.

A person loses confidence in explanations that once provided comfort. They discover that answers which once seemed convincing no longer satisfy. They find themselves standing in unfamiliar territory, carrying questions they never expected to ask. The wound often remains invisible. A person may still attend church, still pray, still read Scripture, and still serve. Outwardly, very little appears different. Yet inwardly an important shift has occurred.

The map no longer matches the terrain.

Because churches often lack language for this reality, many people assume they are facing it alone. They are not. One of the goals of this book is to provide language for an experience that many faithful people struggle to describe. Another is to offer companionship—not answers to every question, not explanations for every tragedy, and not certainty restored, but something more modest and perhaps more important: the assurance that wounded faith is still faith, that questions do not automatically signal failure, and that others have walked this road before.

Several years ago, after a presentation on disaster response and moral injury, a woman waited until nearly everyone else had left the room. Chairs were being stacked, conversations were ending, and people were gathering coats and heading toward the exits. When she finally approached, she spoke softly.

"I've never told anyone this."

Then she described a loss that had occurred years earlier. The details are not important here. The grief was. For years she had carried questions she felt unable to voice in church—questions about God, questions about prayer, and questions about why certain things had happened while others had not.

What struck me was not the questions themselves. I had heard similar questions many times before. What struck me was what she said next.

"I still believe," she told me.

Then she paused.

"But I don't believe the way I used to."

There it was again: the sentence I had heard in so many forms over so many years. Not unbelief. Not rejection. Not abandonment. Change. Something had happened. Something had been wounded. Yet something had also remained.

That distinction lies at the heart of this book.

Much of Christian writing about doubt focuses on whether faith survives. That is an important question. But many people experiencing theological injury are asking a different one. What happens when faith survives, but not unchanged? What happens when a person continues believing, yet no longer experiences belief in the same way? What happens when old assumptions collapse but relationship endures?

Those questions describe the experience of countless people—pastors, caregivers, healthcare workers, responders, chaplains, parents, survivors, and ordinary believers trying to make sense of extraordinary circumstances. Many of them do not need arguments proving God's existence. They already believe. What they need is language: language for the disruption, language for the grief, language for the questions, and language for the strange experience of remaining faithful while feeling fundamentally changed.

Years later, I still remember the survivor staring out the window.

"I still believe in God," the person said.

Then came the pause.

"But . . . "

The sentence was never completed because it did not need to be.

Over the years I have come to believe that countless people live inside that unfinished sentence. They still believe. They still pray. They still hope. Yet something has changed. Something has been wounded. Something no longer fits the way it once did.

This book is an exploration of that territory—not the territory beyond faith, but the territory within faith; the territory where belief survives but certainty does not; the territory where theology struggles to catch up with experience; the territory where many faithful people quietly live.

The rest of this book lives inside that unfinished sentence.

*CHAPTER 2*

# Faith and Theology Are Not the Same Thing

Several years ago, I sat with a pastor who was nearing retirement. He had served faithfully for decades. He had baptized children who were now adults, buried members he had known for most of his ministry, preached thousands of sermons, led countless meetings, visited hospital rooms, stood beside grieving families, and accompanied people through some of the most important moments of their lives. By every outward measure, he had been successful.

Yet on this particular afternoon, he seemed troubled.

We were talking about ministry, aging, and the changing nature of faith when he suddenly stopped speaking. For a few moments he stared into his coffee cup before finally saying something that seemed difficult to admit.

"I'm not sure I believe some of the things I used to believe."

The statement hung in the air.

Had he stopped believing in God? No. Had he abandoned Christianity? No. Had he lost interest in prayer, worship, or Scripture? Again, no. In fact, he continued speaking about God with deep affection. He remained active in the church and spoke openly about his gratitude for many years of ministry.

Yet something had changed.

As our conversation continued, it became clear that what had shifted was not faith itself. It was theology.

Years of ministry had exposed him to suffering he could not easily explain. He had prayed for people who died. He had watched good people endure devastating losses. He had witnessed marriages collapse, children suffer, communities fracture, and faithful believers experience tragedies for which he could find no satisfying explanation. Over time, some of the theological assumptions he carried earlier in life no longer seemed adequate. Certain answers no longer answered. Certain explanations no longer explained.

What struck me most was that he interpreted this change as a threat to faith.

Many people do.

When long-held theological assumptions begin to shift, it can feel as though the entire structure of belief is collapsing. People often assume that if they no longer understand God the way they once did, they must be losing God altogether.

Yet faith and theology are not identical. They are deeply connected, but they remain distinct. Faith involves trust, relationship, commitment, and orientation toward God. Theology involves the ways we understand, interpret, explain, and describe God. Faith asks, "Do I trust God?" Theology asks, "How do I understand God?" Faith is relational. Theology is interpretive. Faith is lived. Theology is articulated.

Both matter.

Yet confusing them can create unnecessary suffering.

When people assume faith and theology are identical, any challenge to a theological belief feels like a challenge to faith itself. Questions become dangerous. Uncertainty becomes threatening. Experiences that do not fit existing theological frameworks can produce profound anxiety, particularly during periods of suffering.

Most of us do not spend much time examining our theology when life is going well. Assumptions often remain invisible until experience challenges them. We carry ideas about prayer, providence, justice, suffering, blessing, and divine action without giving them much conscious attention.

Then something happens.

A diagnosis arrives. A child dies. A marriage ends. A disaster strikes. A prayer goes unanswered.

Suddenly assumptions that once felt solid begin to crack.

Often the experience feels like a crisis of faith.

Sometimes it is.

But sometimes it is something else.

Sometimes it is a crisis of theology.

Many people who believe they are losing faith are actually losing confidence in explanations that no longer fit their experience. What is being questioned is not necessarily God. What is being questioned is a particular understanding of God.

The difference matters.

One can continue trusting God while questioning previous assumptions about God. In fact, many of the people I have encountered through ministry and disaster response have done exactly that. Their faith survived. Their theology changed.

Understanding the difference between those two realities often becomes the first step toward healing.

The conversation with that retired pastor stayed with me long after we finished our coffee. Part of what made it memorable was that he was not describing a loss of faith. He still prayed. He still worshiped. He still spoke about God with affection and gratitude. Yet some of the theological assumptions that had guided him earlier in life no longer seemed capable of carrying the weight of experience.

The longer I reflected on that conversation, the more I realized how much of our theology is inherited long before it is examined.

Most people do not develop their understanding of God through formal theological study. We absorb it gradually through family stories, Sunday school lessons, sermons, hymns, personal experiences, and the faith communities that shape us. Over time these assumptions become so familiar that we rarely notice them. They simply become part of how the world works.

When people hear the word theology, they often think about formal doctrines. Yet much of the theology that guides daily life exists beneath the surface. It appears less as doctrine than as expectation.

God protects faithful people.

Prayer changes outcomes.

Suffering eventually makes sense.

Obedience leads to blessing.

If we trust God, things will somehow work out.

Most believers would never state these assumptions quite so simply. Yet versions of them often shape how people understand life and faith. The assumptions themselves are not the problem. The problem is that many remain unexamined until life challenges them. For years they function quietly in the background. They help us make sense of the world. They provide coherence. They offer reassurance.

Then reality refuses to cooperate.

The conversation with that retired pastor stayed with me long after we finished our coffee. Part of what made it memorable was that he was not describing a loss of faith. He still prayed. He still worshiped. He still spoke about God with affection and gratitude. Yet some of the theological assumptions that had guided him earlier in life no longer seemed capable of carrying the weight of experience.

The longer I reflected on that conversation, the more I realized how much of our theology is inherited long before it is examined. Most people do not develop their understanding of God through formal theological study. We absorb it gradually through family stories, Sunday school lessons, sermons, hymns, personal experiences, and the faith communities that shape us. Over time these assumptions become so familiar that we rarely notice them. They simply become part of how the world works.

When people hear the word theology, they often think about formal doctrines. Yet much of the theology that guides daily life exists beneath the surface. It appears less as doctrine than as expectation: God protects faithful people. Prayer changes outcomes. Suffering eventually makes sense. Obedience leads to blessing. If we trust God, things will somehow work out.

Most believers would never state these assumptions quite so simply. Yet versions of them often shape how people understand life and faith. The assumptions themselves are not the problem. The problem is that many remain unexamined until life challenges them.

For years they function quietly in the background, helping us make sense of the world, providing coherence, and offering reassurance. Then reality refuses to cooperate.

A diagnosis arrives. A child dies. A marriage ends. A disaster strikes. A prayer goes unanswered.

Suddenly assumptions that once felt solid begin to crack.

Often the experience feels like a crisis of faith. Sometimes it is. But sometimes it is something else entirely. Sometimes it is a crisis of theology.

Many people who believe they are losing faith are actually losing confidence in explanations that no longer fit their experience. What is being questioned is not necessarily God. What is being questioned is a particular understanding of God.

The difference matters because a person can continue trusting God while questioning previous assumptions about God. In fact, many of the people I have encountered through ministry and disaster response have done exactly that. Their faith survived even as their theology changed. Understanding the distinction between those two realities often becomes the first step toward healing.

I remember conducting a funeral for a young man whose death devastated an entire community. The sanctuary was full. Friends, classmates, coworkers, and family members filled nearly every pew, and the grief in the room felt almost tangible.

Afterward people lingered throughout the church. Small conversations unfolded in hallways and around tables in the fellowship hall, and no one seemed eager to leave.

Eventually a family member approached me and quietly asked, "Why would God allow this?"

It was not a philosophical question.

It was grief speaking.

The individual was not looking for an explanation that would somehow make the loss acceptable. No explanation could do that. The question emerged because an assumption had collided with reality. This is not supposed to happen. Good people are not supposed to die like this. Faithful families are not supposed to experience this kind of pain. The world is not supposed to work this way.

When assumptions collide with experience, theological injury often begins.

Sometimes the collision occurs suddenly, as it did that day. More often it develops gradually. A caregiver prays for healing that never comes. A pastor watches a congregation fracture despite years of faithful leadership. A parent struggles with unanswered prayers for a child. A health-care worker witnesses suffering that seems random and relentless. A responder moves from one catastrophe to another.

The experiences accumulate. Questions emerge. Theological frameworks begin straining under the weight of reality.

For many people, the most difficult discovery is not that suffering exists. Most people already know that. The difficult discovery is that suffering often refuses to cooperate with our explanations.

This is not a modern problem. Scripture repeatedly wrestles with the same reality.

The book of Job begins with assumptions about justice, reward, and the moral order of the universe. Job's friends are convinced that suffering must fit within their existing theological framework. If suffering exists, someone must have done something wrong. The system must remain intact.

The entire book exposes the inadequacy of that explanation.

Job's friends defend certainty.

Job tells the truth.

By the end of the story, certainty emerges far more wounded than faith.

The same pattern appears in Habakkuk. The prophet looks at violence, injustice, and suffering and asks questions that sound remarkably contemporary. How long? Why does evil continue? Where is God? What is happening?

Habakkuk's questions do not emerge from unbelief. They emerge from the collision between inherited assumptions and lived reality.

Jeremiah experiences similar struggles. So do many of the psalmists. Again and again, Scripture portrays faithful people wrestling with theological expectations that no longer seem capable of explaining what they are experiencing.

That observation matters because many modern believers assume their questions are unusual.

They are not.

What is unusual is how little we discuss them.

Several years ago, after leading a workshop on moral injury and faith, a participant approached me during a break. The individual described growing up in a church where faith was presented primarily as certainty. Questions were discouraged. Doubt was viewed with suspicion. Strong believers were expected to possess confidence and clarity.

Then life happened.

A death in the family. A serious illness. Financial struggles. Relationships that became strained.

The participant described feeling as though the entire theological framework of childhood had begun collapsing.

"I thought I was losing faith," the person told me.

Then came a sentence I have heard many times.

"But now I wonder if I was losing something else."

I think many people eventually arrive at that realization. What is being lost is not necessarily faith. Sometimes it is an explanation. Sometimes it is an expectation. Sometimes it is an image of God that can no longer carry the weight of experience.

The loss can feel profound because theological assumptions help people navigate life. They provide meaning, coherence, and a sense of order in a world that often feels unpredictable. When those assumptions begin to fail, people can feel profoundly disoriented. The map no longer matches the terrain. The explanations no longer fit the experience. The world no longer feels as understandable as it once did.

That disorientation is one of the reasons theological injury can be so painful. Yet it may also create an unexpected opportunity. Sometimes the collapse of inadequate explanations becomes the beginning of deeper understanding. Sometimes old assumptions must be questioned before faith can mature. Sometimes certainty must loosen its grip before trust can deepen.

I wish I could say these questions have always felt comfortable to me.

They have not.

Years of disaster response forced me to revisit assumptions I once carried without much examination. I have prayed with families whose loved ones did not survive. I have stood in shelters filled with people whose lives changed overnight. I have listened to parents, spouses, and survivors ask questions that had no satisfying answers. More than once I found myself wrestling with those same questions after deployments ended—not because I stopped believing in God, and not because faith suddenly became unimportant, but because experience exposed the limitations of explanations that once seemed adequate.

One of the hidden realities of disaster work is that it often wounds theology before it wounds emotion. Responders expect exhaustion. They expect stress. They expect grief. What many do not expect is the way repeated exposure to suffering can challenge assumptions about providence, prayer, justice, and divine action.

Those experiences did not lead me away from faith.

They led me toward deeper questions.

Over time I came to realize that deeper questions are not necessarily evidence of weaker faith. Sometimes they are evidence of faith refusing to settle for explanations that no longer fit reality.

James Fowler observed that mature faith often grows in complexity rather than certainty. Experiences that challenge earlier assumptions may feel threatening, yet they can become part of spiritual development rather than evidence of decline. What many people interpret as regression may actually be growth.

The process is rarely comfortable.

But it may be necessary.

That possibility may be one of the most difficult truths for believers to accept. When a theological explanation collapses, it rarely feels like an intellectual adjustment. It feels personal. What is being challenged is not merely an idea but a way of understanding God, prayer, suffering, and the world itself.

Because theology often functions as a map for navigating life, the loss of that map can feel frightening. For many people, the immediate assumption is that faith itself is disappearing.

Yet that is not always what is happening.

Years ago, I sat with a caregiver who had spent many months caring for a seriously ill family member. Medical appointments, medications, sleepless nights, difficult decisions, and the emotional strain of watching someone you love suffer had gradually consumed daily life.

Throughout that period, the caregiver prayed faithfully—not occasionally, but daily, sometimes hourly. Healing was requested. Strength was requested. Wisdom was requested. Comfort was requested. Yet as the illness progressed, the caregiver found it increasingly difficult to reconcile experience with expectation.

At one point the person said something I have never forgotten.

"I don't know what prayer means anymore."

The sentence was heartbreaking because of what it revealed. The caregiver did not say, "I don't believe in God anymore." The caregiver did not say, "I have abandoned faith." The caregiver did not say, "I am finished with Christianity."

Prayer still mattered.

God still mattered.

Faith still mattered.

What no longer made sense was the framework through which those realities had previously been understood.

That distinction appears repeatedly in conversations about theological injury. People often describe themselves as losing faith when they are actually losing confidence in a particular explanation of faith. They assume the entire structure is collapsing because one part of the structure has become unstable.

Yet faith and theology do not always change at the same pace. Sometimes theology changes first. Sometimes experience forces questions theology has not yet learned how to answer. Sometimes reality exposes weaknesses in assumptions that have remained unexamined for years.

The resulting disorientation can feel overwhelming.

Beneath many theological struggles lies a deeper fear:

What if questioning my understanding of God leads me away from God?

It is a reasonable fear.

It is also one that Scripture repeatedly challenges.

The biblical story contains numerous examples of people whose understanding of God changed dramatically over time. Abraham's understanding changed. Moses' understanding changed. Elijah's understanding changed. Peter's understanding changed. The disciples repeatedly discovered that God was larger, stranger, and less predictable than they had assumed. Growth often required letting go of previous assumptions. The process was not comfortable, but it was transformative.

Life itself often becomes the catalyst for that transformation. The young parent who once believed suffering always had an explanation encounters a tragedy that defies explanation. The pastor who assumed faithful ministry would produce predictable outcomes discovers that congregations are more complicated than formulas allow. The responder who expected meaningful closure discovers that some losses remain unresolved. The caregiver who expected healing discovers that healing does not always arrive.

Experience expands the questions.

Theology must eventually expand as well.

Unfortunately, many faith communities provide people with certainty when what they ultimately need is resilience. Certainty works well as long as reality cooperates. Resilience becomes necessary when it does not. A faith built primarily upon certainty may struggle when certainty becomes impossible. A faith rooted in relationship, however, can survive unanswered questions, disappointment, ambiguity, and the painful recognition that God may be larger than our explanations.

This realization has become increasingly important to me in disaster response. Disasters strip away illusions of control. They challenge expectations and force people to confront realities they would never have chosen. Again and again, I have watched survivors wrestle with questions that emerged not because they lacked faith, but because their experiences exceeded the capacity of their existing theological frameworks.

The same thing happens in hospitals.

The same thing happens at funerals.

The same thing happens in congregational crises.

The same thing happens in ordinary lives disrupted by extraordinary circumstances.

Eventually a person reaches a crossroads. One path involves clinging ever more tightly to explanations that no longer fit reality. The other involves acknowledging the mismatch and beginning the difficult work of rethinking what is no longer working.

The second path is rarely easy. It often feels like loss—the loss of certainty, the loss of assumptions, and the loss of explanations that once provided comfort. Yet it may also create space for something new: a deeper faith, a more honest faith, a faith less dependent upon answers and more dependent upon trust, a faith willing to admit what it does not know, and a faith capable of living with mystery.

This is where many people misunderstand theological injury. They assume the goal is to return to previous certainty. Often that is impossible. Life has changed. Experience has changed. The questions have changed. Returning to earlier assumptions may no longer be possible—or even desirable.

The goal is not regression.

The goal is growth.

Not the growth of certainty.

The growth of faith.

Theology will always matter. How we understand God shapes how we live, pray, serve, and hope. Yet theology is healthiest when it remains humble enough to recognize its limits. God is always larger than our explanations of God.

That truth can feel threatening at first.

Eventually, it can become liberating.

If God is larger than our explanations, then the failure of an explanation does not necessarily mean the failure of God. The collapse of certainty does not necessarily mean the collapse of faith. The loss of an answer does not necessarily mean the loss of hope. Sometimes what feels like the end of faith is actually the beginning of a deeper encounter with the God who was never fully contained by our explanations in the first place.

Years after our conversation, I still think about that retired pastor sitting across from me. The afternoon sun was beginning to fade through the café window, and our coffee cups had long since gone cold. As he gathered his coat, he smiled and repeated something he had said earlier.

"I don't think I know as much as I used to think I knew."

For a moment he looked almost embarrassed by the admission. Then he smiled again.

"But I trust God more than I used to."

That sentence has remained with me because it captures the central distinction of this chapter. Earlier in life, he possessed more certainty. Now he possessed more humility. Earlier in life, he had more answers. Now he had more trust. The change had not come because he abandoned God. It had come because life taught him that God was larger than the explanations he once relied upon.

Perhaps that is one of the hidden gifts of theological injury. It reveals the difference between God and our understanding of God. The distinction can feel frightening at first. Eventually, however, it becomes liberating, because the loss of an explanation is not the loss of God. The collapse of certainty is not the collapse of faith. Sometimes it is the beginning of a deeper journey into the mystery, humility, and trust that mature faith has carried all along.

## *Chapter 3*

# Naming the Wound

Several years ago, after a presentation on disaster response and moral injury, a woman waited until most people had left the room. The session had ended nearly twenty minutes earlier. Chairs were being folded, conversations were winding down, and volunteers were gathering materials and preparing to leave. Yet she remained near the back of the room, watching people drift toward the exits.

Eventually she approached.

"I think something happened to my faith," she said.

Her voice was quiet, almost hesitant.

"What do you mean?" I asked.

For a moment she seemed unsure how to answer.

"I don't know," she said. "That's the problem."

Then she began describing the previous several years of her life: a serious illness in the family, a difficult death, financial struggles, the loss of a close friendship, and several disappointments that had arrived in quick succession. None of the events alone seemed sufficient to explain what she was feeling. Together, however, they had changed something.

As she spoke, I noticed that she never once said she had stopped believing in God. In fact, quite the opposite. She still attended church, still prayed, still read Scripture, and still considered herself a Christian. Yet something felt different. Prayer felt different. Worship felt different. Certain sermons frustrated her. Certain theological explanations irritated her. Questions she had once pushed aside now seemed impossible to ignore.

Most unsettling of all, she could not explain what was happening. She knew something had changed. She simply lacked language for it.

That conversation stayed with me because I have heard versions of it many times over the years—not only from disaster survivors, responders, and clergy, but from ordinary believers trying to make sense of experiences that no longer fit comfortably within the theological frameworks they once trusted. Often they struggle to describe what they are experiencing. They know they are not where they once were. They know certain answers no longer work. They know old assumptions feel less convincing. Yet they cannot quite identify what has happened.

Part of the difficulty is that we generally recognize wounds only when we know what to call them. A person with a broken arm knows something is wrong. A grieving individual recognizes grief. Someone experiencing burnout may eventually learn to identify exhaustion, cynicism, and emotional depletion. Naming a wound does not remove it, but naming it helps us understand it.

Theological injury is often different. Many people experience it long before they have language for it, and the result can be deeply confusing. Without language, people frequently misinterpret their experience. They assume they are losing faith. They assume they are backsliding spiritually. They assume they have become cynical. They assume they are disappointing God. Sometimes they conclude they are simply broken.

What if something else is happening?

What if the experience is not the collapse of faith but the disruption of theological assumptions? What if the discomfort they feel is not evidence of spiritual failure but evidence that their understanding of God is struggling to catch up with experience?

That possibility changes the conversation because once a wound has a name, it can be examined, understood, and cared for.

The longer I work with caregivers, clergy, healthcare professionals, disaster responders, and survivors, the more convinced I become that theological injury often goes unrecognized precisely because it rarely arrives dramatically. Most people do not wake up one morning and announce that their theology has been wounded.

The process is usually gradual.

Questions accumulate.

Disappointments accumulate.

Experiences accumulate.

Over time something begins shifting.

The person who once prayed with confidence now prays with hesitation. The individual who once found comfort in certain explanations now finds them unsatisfying. The believer who once felt reassured by familiar answers now feels strangely disconnected from them.

The change may be subtle at first. A person notices irritation when hearing a particular sermon. Another feels uncomfortable with explanations that once seemed comforting. Someone else begins avoiding conversations about suffering because the usual responses no longer ring true.

Small changes.

Easy to dismiss.

Easy to overlook.

Yet they often signal something important.

Years ago, I began noticing a recurring pattern in conversations following disaster deployments. Responders would rarely begin by discussing theology. Instead, they talked about exhaustion, frustration, disappointment, helplessness, and situations they could not fix. They described losses they could not prevent and outcomes they could not change. At first glance these appeared to be emotional struggles, and often they were.

Yet as conversations continued, another layer frequently emerged. Questions about God. Questions about prayer. Questions about justice. Questions about suffering. Questions about why some people seemed protected while others were not. Questions about why tragedy appeared so random.

The emotional struggle often revealed a theological struggle beneath it.

The wound was not only emotional.

It was theological.

I wish I could say I recognized this dynamic immediately in my own experience.

I did not.

There were seasons in disaster response when I found myself increasingly impatient with answers I once offered confidently. After enough conversations with grieving families, enough shelter visits, and enough prayers spoken beside losses that could not be repaired, I began noticing a subtle shift. Certain explanations still contained truth, but they no longer felt complete. Experience had complicated them.

At first I assumed the change reflected fatigue.

Later I began wondering whether something deeper was occurring.

Looking back, I believe I was encountering theological injury before I had language for it.

This is one reason theological injury can be difficult to recognize. Its symptoms often appear in places we do not expect.

Not all theological injury sounds theological.

Sometimes it sounds like frustration.

Sometimes it sounds like fatigue.

Sometimes it sounds like disappointment.

Sometimes it sounds like silence.

Several years ago, a pastor told me that one of the first signs something had changed was that sermons became harder to preach. Not because he had stopped believing. Not because he no longer cared about Scripture. Not because he was planning to leave ministry. The difficulty was something else.

Certain answers no longer felt honest.

For years he had relied upon explanations that seemed both theologically sound and pastorally helpful. Yet after decades of ministry, hospital visits, funerals, congregational crises, and private conversations with people carrying profound suffering, some of those explanations no longer felt capable of carrying the weight they were being asked to bear.

"I still believe what I preach," he told me, "I just don't preach it the same way anymore."

That statement captures something important about theological injury. Often the first symptom is not disbelief. It is discomfort. A person begins feeling uneasy with answers that once seemed reassuring. Explanations that once brought comfort now feel incomplete. Certain theological claims may still contain truth, yet they no longer feel sufficient for the realities a person has encountered.

The individual may not know how to articulate the change. They simply sense a growing tension between experience and explanation, and that tension often produces confusion.

Years ago, a healthcare professional described feeling increasingly frustrated during worship services. The frustration surprised her because she remained deeply committed to her faith. She continued attending church, praying, and reading Scripture. Yet she found herself reacting strongly whenever someone suggested that suffering always happens for a reason.

After years of caring for critically ill patients, the statement no longer felt comforting.

It felt inadequate.

She had witnessed too much suffering, too many losses, and too many unanswered questions. The issue was not that she rejected God. The issue was that her experience had complicated her understanding of how God works in the world.

That distinction appears repeatedly in conversations about theological injury. The symptoms are often subtle. Some people find themselves becoming impatient with simplistic answers. Others discover that prayer feels different than it once did. Some notice growing anger when discussing suffering. Others experience a sense of distance from God that they struggle to explain. Still others find themselves asking questions they never expected to ask.

Why did this happen?

Where was God?

Why wasn't this prevented?

Why do some prayers seem unanswered?

Why do faithful people suffer?

Why does tragedy appear so random?

These questions are not necessarily signs of failing faith. More often, they are signs that faith is struggling to integrate experiences that no longer fit previous assumptions.

Researchers who study religious and spiritual struggle have observed similar patterns. Kenneth Pargament's work suggests that spiritual struggle frequently emerges when people attempt to reconcile painful experiences with existing beliefs about God and the world. Julie Exline's research likewise demonstrates that disappointment, doubt, anger, confusion, and perceived distance from God are remarkably common among religious individuals navigating suffering and loss.

What strikes me about this research is not that such struggles exist.

It is how normal they appear to be.

Many people assume they are alone.

The evidence suggests otherwise.

Theological injury may feel isolating.

Yet it is far from uncommon.

For some people, the symptoms become surprisingly recognizable once they are named. Prayer feels different than it once did. Sermons that previously brought comfort now create irritation. Familiar explanations sound incomplete. Questions about suffering become harder to dismiss. Worship feels more complicated. A person may find themselves carrying disappointment, confusion, or even anger while continuing to believe.

None of these experiences automatically indicate failing faith. More often, they indicate that faith is struggling to make sense of experiences that no longer fit earlier assumptions.

In fact, one of the most challenging aspects of theological injury is that it often develops in highly faithful people. The individuals most affected are frequently those who have taken faith seriously. They prayed sincerely. They served faithfully. They trusted deeply. They expected faith to help them make sense of life.

Then life became more difficult to understand.

The resulting struggle can feel deeply personal. Some people describe disappointment with God. Others describe confusion. Some speak about anger. Others talk about grief.

Grief is an especially important word.

Many people experiencing theological injury are grieving something—not necessarily the loss of faith, but the loss of certainty, the loss of assumptions, and the loss of explanations that once made the world feel coherent.

The loss can be profound because theological frameworks do more than explain God. They help people organize reality. They provide meaning. They create a sense of order. When those frameworks begin to crack, people can feel disoriented in ways that are difficult to describe.

The map no longer matches the terrain.

The explanations no longer fit the experience.

The world no longer feels as understandable as it once did.

For many people, this period can feel profoundly unsettling because the symptoms rarely arrive all at once. Instead, they emerge gradually. A person notices that prayer has become more difficult—not impossible, but different. The words still come, yet the confidence behind them has changed. Prayers that once felt straightforward now carry hesitation, and questions linger beneath the surface.

Others discover that worship affects them differently than it once did. Certain hymns suddenly feel more poignant. Certain sermons create discomfort rather than reassurance. Statements that once sounded comforting now seem incomplete.

Sometimes the change appears in conversation. A person finds themselves increasingly reluctant to offer easy explanations for suffering. They hesitate before saying things they once would have spoken with confidence. They listen differently. They speak differently. They become less interested in answers and more interested in honesty.

Still others notice emotional reactions they did not expect. Anger emerges when discussing tragedy. Frustration appears when someone offers a simplistic explanation for complex suffering. A sense of distance from God develops, even while faith remains important.

These experiences can be alarming because they often seem inconsistent. One day faith feels strong. The next day uncertainty feels overwhelming. One moment prayer feels meaningful. The next moment it feels frustrating. A person may wonder whether they are moving backward spiritually.

In reality, they may be moving through a process of theological adjustment.

Many believers assume that mature faith should become increasingly certain. Experience often suggests otherwise. The longer people live, the more complexity they encounter. The more suffering they witness, the more exceptions they discover. The more deeply they engage real human lives, the more difficult simple explanations become.

As a result, mature faith often looks different than early faith. It may contain fewer certainties and more humility. It may speak less confidently about things it cannot know. It may become more comfortable with mystery and more cautious about easy answers.

That transition can feel like loss because something is being relinquished—an assumption, an expectation, or a framework that once seemed adequate. Yet what emerges on the other side is not necessarily weaker faith.

Often it is more honest faith.

A faith that has learned to survive uncertainty.

A faith that has learned to remain in relationship with God even when explanations are unavailable.

A faith that continues walking forward without demanding that every question be answered first.

This is why theological injury often feels lonely.

People know something has changed.

They simply do not know what to call it.

Fortunately, Scripture provides companions for this journey. Job experiences theological injury when suffering destroys assumptions about fairness and reward. Habakkuk experiences theological injury when reality refuses to align with his understanding of divine justice. Jeremiah experiences theological injury when faithfulness fails to produce the outcomes he expected. The psalmists repeatedly express confusion, disappointment, anger, and bewilderment.

Again and again, faithful people discover that experience has complicated theology. The Bible does not hide those struggles. It preserves them.

That observation has become increasingly important to me. Many churches teach people how to believe. Far fewer teach people what to do when belief becomes complicated. Many communities provide language for certainty. Far fewer provide language for disruption. Many celebrate confidence. Far fewer acknowledge confusion.

Yet Scripture appears remarkably comfortable with wounded faith—not because suffering is good or questions are pleasant, but because they are real, and faithful people have always encountered them.

The longer I reflect on these conversations, the more convinced I become that one of the most painful aspects of theological injury is not the wound itself. It is the confusion surrounding the wound. People often know something has changed long before they understand what has changed. They sense a growing distance from answers that once seemed reassuring. They notice discomfort during conversations that once felt comforting. They find themselves struggling with assumptions they previously accepted without question, yet they cannot explain why.

Without language, the experience can feel deeply isolating.

Years ago, after a difficult deployment, I found myself talking with a responder who had spent years moving from one disaster to another. The individual had seen communities destroyed by tornadoes, families displaced by floods, and survivors trying to rebuild lives that had changed in a matter of minutes.

At one point the responder paused and said something I have never forgotten.

"I don't think God has changed," the person said. "I think my understanding of God has changed. But I don't know what to do with that."

The statement captured something I had been hearing for years. The person was not describing unbelief. The person was describing disorientation. A framework that once felt reliable no longer seemed capable of carrying the weight of experience.

What made the conversation memorable was not the question itself.

It was the relief that followed when the experience finally had a name.

Not an answer.

A name.

Sometimes naming a wound is more important than immediately trying to solve it. A physician does not heal an illness by pretending it does not exist. A counselor does not help a grieving person by refusing to acknowledge grief. In the same way, theological injury cannot be addressed if it remains unnamed.

Recognition becomes the beginning of understanding. Understanding becomes the beginning of care. Care becomes the beginning of healing.

I have seen this happen repeatedly. A pastor realizes that frustration with certain sermons is connected to unresolved theological questions. A caregiver discovers that disappointment with prayer does not automatically mean a loss of faith. A healthcare worker recognizes that repeated exposure to suffering has affected not only emotional well-being but spiritual assumptions as well. A responder realizes that questions about justice, providence, and suffering are not signs of spiritual failure. They are signs of spiritual struggle.

There is a difference.

One of the reasons I have chosen the phrase theological injury is that it acknowledges the reality of the wound without assuming the outcome. Injury is not the same as destruction. An injured muscle can heal. An injured relationship can recover. An injured understanding can develop in new ways. The word itself creates space for hope—not certainty, but hope.

That distinction matters.

Many people experiencing theological injury fear that the presence of questions means faith is disappearing. Yet some of the most faithful people I have encountered carry significant questions. They continue praying. They continue worshiping. They continue serving. They continue seeking God. The questions remain.

So does the faith.

In fact, I have increasingly come to believe that mature faith often looks different than people expect. It is usually less certain than earlier faith and often more humble. It tends to speak with fewer declarations and more curiosity. It is less interested in winning arguments and more interested in remaining in relationship with God.

That kind of faith may appear weaker from the outside.

I suspect it is often stronger.

Not because it has more answers.

Because it has learned how to live without them.

The woman who approached me after that presentation eventually said something that captured the heart of the issue.

"I don't know what happened," she told me. "I just know I don't experience faith the way I used to."

At the time, she lacked language for that experience.

Many people do.

Perhaps that is why naming the wound matters. Not because naming it solves it or removes it, but because naming it allows us to recognize that something real has occurred. A wound that remains unnamed often becomes a source of confusion. A wound that is recognized can become a source of understanding. And understanding is often where healing begins.

The woman and I talked for nearly an hour. By the time the conversation ended, she had not found answers to every question. Neither of us expected that. What she found instead was language—a way of describing what she had been experiencing, a way of understanding that she was not alone, and a way of recognizing that her questions were not necessarily evidence of failing faith. Sometimes they were evidence of a wounded theology struggling to make sense of a changed world.

As she prepared to leave, she paused at the doorway. Most of the chairs had been stacked by then. The room was nearly empty. One bank of lights had already been turned off, leaving half the room in shadow. Volunteers were gathering the last remaining materials and preparing to lock the building.

She rested her hand on the doorframe and smiled.

"I thought I was the only one."

I have heard that sentence many times over the years—from pastors, responders, caregivers, survivors, healthcare workers, and ordinary believers trying to understand changes they could not explain.

Perhaps one of the most important things we can say about theological injury is that it often feels isolating while being surprisingly common.

People experience it quietly. They carry it privately. They assume nobody else understands.

Yet countless faithful people have walked this road before. Job walked it. Jeremiah walked it. Habakkuk walked it. The psalmists walked it. Many faithful people continue walking it today.

The first step toward healing is often recognizing that the wound has a name.

And that you are not walking through it alone.

## *Chapter 4*

# When Prayer Stops Working the Way We Thought

Several years ago, after a disaster deployment, I sat with a woman whose life had been changed in a matter of days. The storm itself had passed. Emergency response operations were underway. Volunteers had arrived. Supplies were being distributed. Recovery planning had begun. Yet none of those developments altered the reality she now faced. Her home was gone. Photographs collected across decades were gone. Family heirlooms were gone. The ordinary routines that had once structured daily life had disappeared almost overnight.

For nearly an hour we talked about practical concerns—housing, insurance, family, and recovery. The conversation followed a pattern familiar to anyone who has spent time in disaster response. Eventually she looked at me and asked, "Can I tell you something?"

"Of course," I replied.

She hesitated for a moment before continuing.

"I prayed that this wouldn't happen."

The statement was simple, yet it carried enormous weight. She was not asking a question about weather patterns, emergency management, or disaster preparedness. She was wrestling with something far more personal. She had prayed, and the storm had come anyway.

For many people, theological injury begins in precisely that space—not in atheism, unbelief, or rebellion, but in disappointment. More specifically, it begins in disappointment connected to prayer.

One of the most difficult realities of faith is that nearly every believer eventually encounters prayers that seem unanswered. The circumstances vary from person to person. A parent prays for a child's safety. A spouse prays for healing. A caregiver prays for recovery. A congregation prays for reconciliation. A responder prays for protection. A family prays for one more year, one more month, or one more day.

Sometimes the hoped-for outcome arrives. Sometimes it does not.

The problem is not simply that prayers go unanswered. The deeper problem is that unanswered prayer often disrupts assumptions we did not realize we were carrying. Most believers possess an understanding of how prayer works. Those understandings may never be stated explicitly, yet they quietly shape expectations. We assume prayer matters. We assume God listens. We assume God cares. We assume divine action somehow intersects with human need.

These assumptions are not unreasonable. Scripture repeatedly encourages prayer. Jesus teaches his followers to pray. The Psalms are filled with prayers of every imaginable kind, and the history of faith is inseparable from the practice of prayer itself.

The challenge emerges when experience refuses to cooperate with expectation. A prayer for healing is followed by death. A prayer for protection is followed by disaster. A prayer for reconciliation is followed by separation. A prayer for relief is followed by continued suffering. In those moments, many people begin asking questions they never imagined they would have to ask.

Did God hear me?

Did I pray incorrectly?

Did I lack faith?

Does prayer actually change anything?

If God could have acted, why didn't God act?

These questions are rarely theoretical. They emerge from lived pain rather than abstract theology.

Several years ago, a pastor shared the story of a member of his congregation who had spent months praying for a spouse undergoing cancer treatment. Family members prayed. Friends prayed. The church prayed. Prayer chains formed. Meals were delivered. Support flowed from every direction.

Yet the illness progressed.

Eventually the spouse died.

In the months that followed, the surviving partner continued attending worship, continued reading Scripture, and continued identifying as a Christian. Yet prayer became different. It was not impossible, but it had become complicated. The individual no longer doubted God's existence. Instead, trusting prayer itself had become difficult.

That distinction matters because many people assume theological injury begins when faith disappears. More often it begins when expectations collapse. A person still believes in God. They simply no longer understand prayer the way they once did.

The resulting confusion can feel deeply isolating. Churches understandably celebrate stories of answered prayer. Testimonies often highlight dramatic interventions, unexpected recoveries, and remarkable outcomes. Those stories are meaningful and deserve to be told.

Yet many believers quietly carry another set of stories. They remember the surgery that failed, the reconciliation that never happened, the child who was not protected, the diagnosis that did not improve, the disaster that was not prevented, and the prayer that appeared to receive no answer.

These experiences seldom receive the same attention. As a result, people often conclude they are alone in their disappointment.

They are not.

One of the most striking observations from years of ministry and disaster response is how many faithful people carry unresolved questions about prayer—not because they have abandoned faith, but because life has become more complicated than the theological explanations they once trusted. For some, the disappointment produces anger. For others it produces confusion. For still others it produces silence. Many simply stop talking about prayer altogether, not because they no longer care, but because they no longer know what to say.

Theological injury frequently develops in precisely that space between expectation and experience, between what we believed prayer would do and what actually happened.

One of the reasons unanswered prayer can be so disruptive is that many of our assumptions about prayer are formed long before they are examined. Most believers do not begin with a carefully constructed theology of prayer. Instead, they inherit one through sermons, Bible studies, testimonies, devotional books, conversations with trusted Christians, and personal experience. Over time these assumptions become so familiar that they feel almost self-evident.

Prayer changes things.

God answers prayer.

Ask and you shall receive.

Seek and you shall find.

Knock and the door will be opened.

All of those statements emerge from Scripture. The difficulty arises when believers encounter experiences that seem inconsistent with how they understand those promises. A parent prays fervently for a child and receives devastating news. A congregation prays for healing and instead gathers for a funeral. A family prays for protection and loses their home. A caregiver prays for recovery and watches a loved one decline.

The resulting questions are not primarily intellectual. They are relational.

If prayer is conversation with God, unanswered prayer can feel like a conversation in which one voice suddenly becomes difficult to hear. That perception often creates a profound sense of disorientation.

Years ago, during a conversation with a healthcare professional, I heard this struggle expressed with unusual honesty.

"I still pray," she told me. "I just don't know what I expect anymore."

The statement stayed with me because it captured a reality I have encountered repeatedly. She had not stopped believing in prayer, nor had she stopped believing in God. Yet years of witnessing suffering had complicated the expectations she once carried about how prayer worked. Theological injury often emerges at exactly that point—not when prayer disappears, but when certainty about prayer disappears.

There were seasons in disaster response when I became increasingly cautious about what I said regarding prayer. Early in ministry, I often felt pressure to explain. People were hurting, and explanations seemed helpful. Yet after enough conversations with grieving families, enough shelter visits, enough hospital rooms, and enough prayers offered beside losses that could not be repaired, I found myself speaking more carefully.

It was not that I believed less in prayer. If anything, prayer became more important. What changed was my confidence in simplistic explanations.

The more suffering I witnessed, the more convinced I became that prayer is deeper and more mysterious than many of us imagine. Experience did not diminish faith in prayer. It diminished certainty about how prayer works.

Researchers who study religion and spirituality have long observed that prayer can become a source of struggle as well as comfort. Kenneth Pargament's work suggests that many believers experience spiritual distress when deeply held expectations about God's activity appear inconsistent with lived experience. People often find themselves attempting to reconcile what they believe about God with outcomes they neither expected nor wanted.

What makes this process so difficult is that disappointment with prayer is often accompanied by guilt. People wonder whether they lacked faith, prayed incorrectly, asked for the wrong thing, or somehow disappointed God. I have heard each of those concerns repeatedly over the years, and what strikes me is how often people assume responsibility for outcomes they could never control.

The parent whose child was not healed wonders whether they should have prayed more. The spouse who loses a partner wonders whether they lacked sufficient faith. The caregiver who receives no miracle wonders whether they somehow failed God. These burdens can become extraordinarily heavy.

Yet Scripture rarely describes unanswered prayer in those terms. The Bible contains numerous examples of faithful people whose prayers did not receive the answers they desired. David prays and grieves. Jeremiah cries out repeatedly. Habakkuk pleads for understanding. The psalmists ask questions that often remain unresolved.

Perhaps the most striking example comes from Jesus himself. In the Garden of Gethsemane, Jesus prays that the cup might pass from him. The prayer is honest, direct, and deeply human.

Yet the suffering remains.

That scene deserves careful attention because the unanswered prayer in Gethsemane is not evidence of weak faith, divine indifference, or the failure of prayer itself. The prayer remains part of a faithful relationship even though the desired outcome does not occur.

That observation challenges many assumptions people carry about prayer. We often evaluate prayer by outcomes. Scripture frequently evaluates prayer by relationship.

Those are not the same thing.

The distinction became increasingly important to me during years of disaster response. Again and again, I encountered people whose understanding of prayer had been wounded by experience. Survivors prayed for protection. Families prayed for healing. Responders prayed for favorable outcomes.

Sometimes those prayers seemed to be answered in ways that were obvious and deeply meaningful.

Sometimes they were not.

The difficulty was not merely the absence of a desired outcome. The difficulty was what that absence appeared to imply. People wondered whether God had stopped listening, become distant, or whether prayer still mattered at all. In many cases, the deepest wound was not the event itself but the meaning attached to the event. One person concluded that unanswered prayer meant abandonment. Another concluded it meant failure. Still another concluded it meant God no longer cared.

Theological injury often develops in those interpretations. Not simply because suffering occurs, but because suffering begins reshaping the way people understand God's relationship to their lives.

That is why conversations about unanswered prayer require such care. The issue is rarely theological in a purely academic sense. The issue is relational. People are trying to understand what a painful experience means about God, about themselves, and about the relationship between them.

Those are not small questions.

They reach to the heart of faith itself.

Several years ago, after a community presentation, a man approached me with a question he had been carrying for a long time. He waited until most of the room had emptied before speaking. That alone told me something. People rarely wait until everyone else has left to ask easy questions.

"My wife died eight years ago," he said.

Then he paused.

"We prayed every day."

For a few moments neither of us said anything. Eventually he continued.

"People told me God answered the prayer. They said the answer was just no."

He looked down at the floor before speaking again.

"I know they're trying to help. But honestly, that answer has never helped me."

I have thought about that conversation many times over the years because it illustrates something important. Many attempts to explain unanswered prayer are offered with good intentions. Most are attempts to comfort. Most are attempts to protect faith. Most are attempts to make sense of suffering. Yet explanations offered too quickly can sometimes deepen theological injury rather than heal it.

A grieving parent asks why a child died. A survivor asks why a disaster destroyed one home and spared another. A caregiver asks why years of prayer seemed to change nothing. Before grief has even been allowed to speak, explanations begin arriving.

"God needed another angel."

"Everything happens for a reason."

"God never gives us more than we can handle."

"The answer was no."

"God has a better plan."

Most people who offer such statements are trying to help. The problem is that suffering often exposes the limits of explanations. A statement that sounds reassuring in theory can feel painfully inadequate in the presence of actual grief.

One of the recurring themes in Scripture is that faithful people are rarely rushed toward explanation. Job's friends spend much of the book trying to explain suffering. Their explanations become increasingly elaborate. Yet by the end of the story, certainty appears far less trustworthy than compassion. The friends speak often. Job tells the truth.

The distinction matters because many wounded believers do not initially need answers. They need permission—permission to tell the truth about disappointment, permission to acknowledge confusion, permission to admit anger, permission to say that prayer has become complicated, and permission to grieve expectations that have collapsed.

Perhaps this is one reason lament occupies such an important place in Scripture. Lament is what faith sounds like when explanations fail. It is the language believers use when suffering refuses to cooperate with theology, when prayers seem unanswered, and when certainty gives way to confusion. Far from representing the absence of faith, lament often represents faith refusing to let go of God.

The lament psalms do not resolve every question. They keep the conversation alive. In that sense, lament may be one of the most honest forms of prayer found in Scripture. They are remarkable not because they solve suffering—they do not—but because they refuse to pretend. Again and again, the psalmists bring confusion directly before God.

"How long, O Lord?"

"Why have you hidden your face?"

"Why do you stand far away?"

"Will you forget me forever?"

These are not the prayers of unbelievers. They are the prayers of people who continue bringing their questions into relationship with God.

That observation has become increasingly important to me because the opposite of faith is not questioning. The opposite of faith is disengagement. The person who continues bringing disappointment before God remains engaged. The person who continues praying through confusion remains engaged. The person who continues wrestling with unanswered prayer remains engaged. The relationship persists even when certainty does not.

Years ago, during a particularly difficult period of disaster response, I found myself reflecting on the prayers I had heard in shelters, recovery centers, and temporary housing sites. Some were prayers of gratitude. Some were prayers of fear. Some were prayers of exhaustion.

Many were prayers without answers.

People prayed for loved ones they could not locate. People prayed for homes that had already been destroyed. People prayed for outcomes that would never arrive.

And yet they continued praying.

That reality challenged assumptions I carried about prayer. I had often thought of prayer primarily in terms of results. Disaster survivors taught me to think about prayer differently. Sometimes prayer is not a strategy for changing circumstances. Sometimes prayer is the act of remaining in relationship when circumstances refuse to change.

The distinction may seem subtle.

It is not.

One understanding of prayer measures success by outcomes. The other measures faithfulness by relationship. Most believers eventually discover that both dimensions matter. We pray because we hope. We pray because we trust. We pray because Scripture invites us to pray. We pray because God cares.

Yet many faithful people eventually reach a point where they can no longer sustain a theology of prayer built entirely upon visible results. Life becomes too complicated. The exceptions become too numerous. The losses become too significant.

At that point, faith faces a choice.

Either prayer must be abandoned.

Or prayer must be understood more deeply.

I have watched many people choose the second path. Not quickly, not easily, and never without struggle, but gradually they continue praying even when they no longer understand everything about prayer. They continue trusting even when outcomes disappoint them. They continue bringing questions before God even when answers remain elusive.

What emerges is often a different kind of faith—less certain, more humble, less confident in explanations, and more deeply rooted in relationship.

That transformation can feel like loss while it is happening. In some ways, it is. The person is grieving an earlier understanding of prayer—an expectation, an assumption, or a certainty. They are letting go of ideas that once made the world feel more predictable, relinquishing explanations that once provided comfort.

The grief is real because something real has been lost. Many people experiencing theological injury do not simply mourn an unanswered prayer. They mourn the understanding of prayer they carried before disappointment arrived. They mourn the confidence that outcomes would make sense. They mourn the expectation that faithful prayer would reliably produce understandable results.

The loss can feel profound because prayer occupies such a central place in the life of faith. Prayer is not merely a religious practice. For many believers, it is one of the primary ways they experience relationship with God. When prayer becomes complicated, the relationship itself can feel unsettled.

Yet again and again, I have watched people discover that something survives the disappointment. Trust survives. Hope survives. Relationship survives. Sometimes only barely, but it survives.

The woman whose home had been destroyed eventually said something near the end of our conversation that I have never forgotten.

"I don't think I'll ever understand why this happened," she said.

Then she looked out the window for a moment before continuing.

"But I still find myself talking to God about it."

There was no triumph in her voice. No dramatic resolution. No easy answer. There was only honesty. The storm had come. The loss was real. The questions remained. Yet so did the conversation.

I have come to believe that this distinction matters more than many of us realize. Faith is often portrayed as certainty, and prayer is often portrayed as confidence. Yet some of the deepest faith I have encountered has emerged among people who possessed very little certainty and who prayed with more questions than answers. The disaster survivor who still speaks to God despite disappointment, the caregiver who continues praying despite exhaustion, the grieving spouse who continues showing up to worship despite unanswered questions, and the responder who continues seeking God amid repeated exposure to suffering rarely describe themselves as possessing extraordinary faith.

Yet I often think they do.

Not because they have resolved every question, but because they have remained in relationship despite unresolved questions.

That may be one of the most important lessons theological injury teaches. The goal is not always to recover the certainty we once possessed. Sometimes certainty has been replaced by something more durable—something capable of surviving disappointment.

A faith that depends entirely upon favorable outcomes will eventually struggle. Life is too complicated. Loss is too common. Suffering is too real.

A faith rooted in relationship can endure what explanations often cannot.

As we finished talking, volunteers were beginning to close the recovery center for the evening. Folding tables were being stacked against the wall. Boxes of supplies were being organized for the next day. Outside, the late-afternoon light was beginning to fade.

The woman gathered her things and prepared to leave. Before walking away, she smiled gently and shook her head.

"I guess I'm still praying."

The statement was almost humorous, almost surprised, as though she had just discovered something about herself.

I watched her walk toward the exit and found myself thinking about how often faith survives in forms we do not immediately recognize. Sometimes it survives not as certainty but as persistence, not as confidence but as honesty, and not as answers but as relationship.

Theological injury often begins when prayer no longer works the way we thought it would. Yet the story does not necessarily end there. Sometimes, beneath the disappointment, beneath the confusion, and beneath the unanswered questions, something remains.

The conversation continues.

And that may be one of the deepest forms of faith we will ever know.

## *Chapter 5*

# The God We Thought We Knew

Several years ago, I sat with a man whose life had been divided into two distinct periods. There was the life before, and there was the life after.

Before the diagnosis, he rarely thought much about theology. He attended church regularly, served in leadership, prayed before meals, volunteered when needed, and generally lived what most people would consider a faithful life. God occupied a meaningful place in his world, but faith largely operated in the background. It was present, dependable, and familiar.

Then his wife became ill.

At first there was optimism. The doctors were encouraging. The treatments seemed promising. Family members organized prayer chains. Friends brought meals. Congregations added her name to prayer lists. People spoke confidently about healing.

For a time, he spoke that way as well.

Then the treatments stopped working. The disease progressed. The prayers intensified. The outcome did not change.

Months later, after her death, he sat quietly in a church fellowship hall long after everyone else had gone home.

"I still believe in God," he told me.

Then he stared into his coffee for a moment before adding, "I just don't know what to do with the God I thought I knew."

His words stayed with me, not because they were unusual, but because they were remarkably common. Over the years I have heard countless variations of the same confession. A disaster survivor stands in the remains of a home and wonders why divine protection seemed absent. A parent loses a child despite years of faithful prayer. A caregiver watches suffering continue long after every reasonable request for relief has been offered. A responder witnesses devastation repeatedly and struggles to reconcile what they see with what they once believed about God's presence in the world.

Again and again, the question beneath the question sounds remarkably similar:

What happened to the God I thought I knew?

For many people, theological disruption does not begin with the loss of belief. It begins with the loss of assumptions.

Most of us carry assumptions about God whether we realize it or not. We assume certain things about how God works. We assume certain things about prayer, providence, protection, justice, and suffering. Rarely do we write these assumptions down. We absorb them over time through sermons, Bible studies, family conversations, personal experiences, and years of participation in faith communities. Eventually they become part of the theological air we breathe.

As long as life unfolds in ways that broadly align with those assumptions, we seldom notice them.

Then something happens.

Suddenly assumptions we never examined become impossible to ignore.

One of the most common assumptions involves divine protection. Most believers understand intellectually that faithful people suffer. We know the stories. We know Scripture. We know that discipleship does not guarantee safety. Yet somewhere beneath that intellectual understanding, many people still carry quieter expectations. We expect God to intervene. We expect certain tragedies to be prevented. We expect some prayers to receive obvious answers. We expect suffering to make sense eventually.

When those expectations collide with reality, the result can be deeply unsettling. The suffering itself is painful. The collapse of the assumptions surrounding the suffering can be equally painful. In many cases, theological injury begins not because God has disappeared, but because the image of God we carried can no longer bear the weight of our experience.

That distinction matters.

Many people assume that theological disruption means abandoning faith. Often it means something else entirely. It means realizing that the God we imagined may not be identical to the God who actually is.

That realization can feel frightening.

It can also feel like loss.

The loss is not merely emotional. It is theological. The believer is grieving not only what happened but also the framework through which they once understood what happened.

Psychologist and grief researcher Robert Neimeyer has spent much of his career studying how people reconstruct meaning after significant loss. His work suggests that grief often disrupts the stories people use to make sense of their lives. The challenge is not merely coping with pain. The challenge is rebuilding meaning after the old story no longer works.

Theological disruption frequently follows a similar pattern. People are not simply grieving an event. They are grieving the collapse of an explanation. The world no longer functions according to the narrative they previously trusted, and something essential must be reconsidered.

That process can feel disorienting because human beings depend upon meaning. We need frameworks that help us understand suffering, hope, prayer, justice, and divine presence. When those frameworks fracture, uncertainty follows, and for many people that uncertainty becomes one of the most difficult aspects of suffering itself.

The pain hurts.

The confusion lingers.

The questions remain.

For many believers, the deepest struggle is not simply that suffering occurred. It is that suffering occurred despite everything they believed about God. A parent prays for protection and receives a phone call in the middle of the night. A congregation prays for rain and watches a drought continue. A family prays for healing and attends a funeral instead.

The event itself is painful.

The theological implications can be equally difficult.

Questions emerge that previously felt unnecessary.

If God is loving, why did this happen?

If God is powerful, why was it not prevented?

If prayer matters, why did nothing change?

If God is present, why did God seem absent?

These are not new questions. They have accompanied believers for centuries. Yet when they emerge from personal experience rather than abstract reflection, they carry a different weight. The question is no longer theoretical. It has become personal.

One of the most influential books on this subject was written by Rabbi Harold Kushner after the death of his young son. Faced with a loss that defied explanation, Kushner wrestled openly with questions many grieving people carry. His work resonated with countless readers because he refused to offer easy answers. Instead, he acknowledged the painful reality that suffering often disrupts our assumptions about how God operates in the world.

Whether one agrees with all of Kushner's conclusions is less important than recognizing the courage of the questions he raised. He gave voice to something many people were already experiencing. The old explanations were no longer sufficient.

That experience remains remarkably common.

When tragedy strikes, people often search for explanations almost immediately. We want events to fit within a coherent framework. We want suffering to make sense. We want reasons.

Sometimes those reasons appear.

Often they do not.

Yet religious communities can feel pressure to provide explanations anyway.

"Everything happens for a reason."

"God must have needed another angel."

"This is part of God's plan."

"You'll understand someday."

Most people who offer such statements are trying to help. Yet these explanations often create additional pain. Not because they are malicious, but because they can feel disconnected from the reality of the person's experience. The grieving parent does not necessarily need an explanation. The disaster survivor does not necessarily need a theological formula. The exhausted caregiver does not necessarily need a defense of divine providence. More often, they need someone willing to sit beside them in uncertainty.

Over the years, I have noticed that people rarely remember the explanations offered during the worst moments of their lives.

They remember presence.

They remember who stayed.

They remember who listened.

They remember who allowed difficult questions to remain difficult.

In disaster response, this lesson appears repeatedly. Survivors rarely begin by asking theological questions. They talk about homes, pets, photographs, insurance claims, family members, and the practical realities of rebuilding. Yet eventually deeper questions emerge. Not always aloud. Sometimes quietly. Sometimes indirectly.

A person stands in front of a damaged home and says, "I never thought something like this would happen here."

Another says, "We've always trusted God."

Another simply shakes their head and stares at what remains.

Beneath those statements lies a deeper disruption. The world no longer behaves according to expectations. Something about reality feels different. Something about God feels different.

Theological injury often begins in precisely that space—not in the rejection of God, but in the disruption of assumptions.

One of the surprising discoveries many people make during this season is that God may be less predictable than they imagined. This realization can initially feel threatening. Predictability offers security. If we understand how God works, perhaps we can understand how life works. If we understand how life works, perhaps we can protect ourselves from uncertainty.

Suffering often exposes the limits of that hope.

Many of the assumptions we carry about God are attempts to create predictability in an unpredictable world. We want formulas. We want guarantees. We want outcomes. We want assurance that faithful living will produce understandable results.

Life rarely cooperates.

Scripture itself repeatedly challenges these assumptions. The book of Job is perhaps the clearest example. Job's friends spend much of the story defending a theological system built upon predictability. Good people are rewarded. Bad people are punished. Suffering must have an explanation.

Job's experience refuses to fit that framework.

The conflict is not merely about suffering.

It is about a worldview that can no longer explain suffering.

By the end of the story, Job receives many things.

A simple explanation is not one of them.

Instead, he encounters a God who is larger than the categories he had previously used to understand the world.

Something similar often happens during seasons of theological disruption. The old framework collapses. The questions remain. The explanations fail.

Yet occasionally, beneath the uncertainty, another possibility begins to emerge.

Perhaps God is larger than the assumptions we inherited.

Perhaps mystery is not the enemy of faith.

Perhaps faith can survive even when predictability does not.

One of the reasons this process can feel so painful is that people are often grieving losses they do not immediately recognize. The visible loss is obvious. A loved one dies. A home is destroyed. A diagnosis changes the future. A career ends. A marriage collapses. A community experiences tragedy.

Those losses are real, and they deserve to be acknowledged.

Yet another loss often accompanies them.

The loss of assumptions.

The loss of predictability.

The loss of a theological world that once felt stable and understandable.

Many people struggle to understand why their spiritual lives feel unsettled after tragedy because they focus entirely on the visible loss. What they fail to recognize is that another layer of grief may be operating beneath the surface. They are grieving the God they thought they understood.

Not God.

Their understanding of God.

That distinction became increasingly important to me over the years. Early in ministry, I sometimes assumed that theological disruption represented a failure of faith. If people were struggling with God, perhaps they simply needed better answers, stronger beliefs, or greater confidence.

Experience taught me otherwise.

Many of the people asking the hardest questions were also among the most faithful people I knew. They were not rejecting God. They were refusing explanations that no longer matched reality.

There is a difference.

Over the years, I have discovered that some of my own assumptions about God have changed as well. Certain explanations that once felt sufficient no longer do. Years of ministry, disaster response, grief, and listening to the suffering of others have left me less confident in easy answers than I once was. They have also left me more convinced that God remains present even when explanations fail.

I suspect many people who spend enough time in the company of suffering eventually arrive at a similar place.

Not a loss of faith.

A deeper awareness of mystery.

I remember a conversation after a community presentation several years ago. Most people had already left. Chairs were being folded and stacked against the wall. One woman lingered near the back of the room.

Eventually she approached and said, "I don't think I believe the same things I used to."

Then she quickly added, "That probably sounds terrible."

I told her it sounded human.

She laughed softly before describing a series of losses that had unfolded over several years. None of them would have made national headlines. None would have attracted public attention. Yet together they had quietly reshaped her understanding of life.

At one point she said something I have never forgotten.

"I still love God. I just don't understand God anymore."

That sentence captures the experience of many people this book is attempting to describe. The relationship remains, but the framework through which that relationship was previously understood no longer feels sufficient. The longing for God continues. The desire to pray continues. Yet the explanations that once seemed capable of holding everything together no longer carry the same weight.

This is why theological injury can feel so lonely. Faith communities often know how to support people through grief. They know how to bring meals, send cards, organize prayer chains, and provide practical assistance.

Those responses matter.

Yet many communities have less experience helping people navigate theological grief.

What do we do when a person's understanding of God has been disrupted?

How do we accompany someone who is no longer sure what they believe about prayer?

How do we support someone who cannot reconcile their experience with their previous assumptions?

Too often, we rush toward explanation. We try to repair uncertainty before we understand it. We attempt to answer questions that may need to be lived for a season before they can be addressed.

The people who helped me most during my own seasons of uncertainty rarely provided answers. They provided presence. They listened. They asked thoughtful questions. They allowed difficult realities to remain difficult. Most importantly, they trusted that God was capable of meeting people within uncertainty.

That trust matters because theological disruption often creates pressure to choose between certainty and faith. Many people assume those are the only available options.

Either maintain certainty.

Or lose faith.

Experience suggests otherwise.

There is a third possibility.

Faith may continue even when certainty does not. In fact, some of the most mature faith I have encountered emerged only after earlier certainties had been stripped away. Not because uncertainty is desirable. Not because suffering is good. But because disruption sometimes reveals the difference between trusting God and trusting our explanations about God.

That distinction is not always easy to recognize. For many people, the two have become deeply intertwined. When the explanation collapses, it feels as though God has collapsed as well.

Yet over time, some discover that the loss of an explanation is not necessarily the loss of God. The journey toward that realization can be long. It can involve grief, anger, disappointment, and questions that remain unanswered for years. Yet many eventually discover that while their understanding of God has changed dramatically, their relationship with God has somehow endured.

Not unchanged.

But alive.

The process rarely feels like progress while it is happening. More often it feels like wandering—like standing in unfamiliar territory without a reliable map or trying to speak a language that no longer communicates what experience has taught us. Yet this wandering may be one of the most important spiritual experiences a person ever undergoes, because sooner or later many believers discover that faith cannot mature without confronting mystery. The God we thought we knew eventually becomes too small. The assumptions we inherited eventually prove insufficient. The explanations we trusted eventually reach their limits.

When that happens, we face a choice. We can cling to explanations that no longer fit reality, or we can begin the difficult work of allowing our understanding of God to grow. That work is rarely comfortable, but it may be necessary.

One of the great paradoxes of faith is that many of the people who know God most deeply are also the people most aware of how much remains unknown. Certainty often speaks with confidence, while wisdom tends to speak with humility. Over the years, I have noticed that people who have endured profound suffering frequently become less interested in defending God and more interested in seeking God. They become less concerned with preserving explanations and more concerned with remaining in relationship.

Something about suffering strips away the illusion that life can be fully understood. Something about grief exposes the limits of certainty. Something about prolonged exposure to loss forces people to confront mystery whether they want to or not. At first this confrontation can feel threatening. Eventually, however, some discover that it can also be liberating.

If God is larger than our explanations, then the collapse of an explanation does not necessarily mean the collapse of faith. If God is larger than our assumptions, then the failure of an assumption does not necessarily mean the failure of God. If God is larger than our theological systems, then suffering may challenge those systems without destroying the relationship those systems were meant to serve.

This realization does not remove pain. It does not answer every question or explain every tragedy. What it does offer is space—space to admit uncertainty, to acknowledge grief, to tell the truth about experiences that do not fit easy formulas, and to remain faithful without pretending to understand everything.

For many people, that space becomes the beginning of healing. Their questions do not disappear, but neither do they feel compelled to deny them.

One of the most important lessons I have learned through ministry and disaster response is that people can carry enormous uncertainty and still possess genuine faith. They can wrestle with difficult questions and still pray. They can feel disappointed, confused, or even angry and still remain deeply connected to God. Scripture repeatedly bears witness to this reality. Job questioned. The psalmists lamented. Jeremiah protested. Habakkuk argued. None of them were excluded from the story of faith. Their questions became part of the story.

Perhaps ours can as well.

The goal of theological reconstruction is not to return people to the assumptions they carried before suffering occurred. In many cases, that is impossible. The old framework no longer fits, and the old explanations no longer satisfy. The goal is not the restoration of certainty but the formation of a faith capable of telling the truth, acknowledging mystery, and surviving reality.

Such faith is often quieter than the faith that preceded it. It is less triumphant, less interested in winning arguments, and more willing to accompany others through uncertainty. It becomes more compassionate, more patient, and more willing to sit beside suffering without immediately trying to explain it. It is the kind of faith I have encountered repeatedly among caregivers, survivors, responders, pastors, and ordinary believers who have walked through difficult seasons and emerged changed.

Not untouched.

Changed.

Near the end of our conversation, the widower who had spoken about "the God I thought I knew" sat quietly for several moments. The fellowship hall was nearly empty. Volunteers were cleaning tables and gathering supplies while evening shadows settled across the church parking lot.

Finally he looked up and said something that has stayed with me ever since.

"I don't think I can go back to what I believed before."

He paused before adding, "But I don't think I want to lose God either."

For a moment neither of us spoke. The grief remained. The questions remained. The future remained uncertain. Yet beneath all of it, something else remained as well: the desire to keep seeking, the willingness to continue the conversation, and the quiet conviction that unanswered questions did not necessarily signify God's absence.

As we stood to leave, volunteers folded the last of the chairs and switched off the lights in the fellowship hall. We walked toward the door together, neither of us pretending that the questions had been resolved. Some questions would remain. Some mysteries would remain. Some losses would remain. But so would the possibility that faith could continue after the collapse of assumptions—not as it had been before, but as something humbler, more honest, and perhaps even deeper.

The God we thought we knew may not be the God who ultimately meets us. That realization, painful as it can be, may become the beginning of a different kind of faith: one capable of surviving the realities of a broken world, one capable of living with mystery, and one capable of continuing the conversation even when the answers no longer answer.

The lights clicked off behind us as we stepped into the evening air. The parking lot lay quiet beneath the fading sky. Neither of us had found the explanation we wanted, but neither of us had walked away from the conversation.

Sometimes that is where faith begins again.

## *Chapter 6*

# Too Much Suffering

The responder did not say it dramatically. In fact, he almost seemed embarrassed by the admission.

We were sitting together after a long day of disaster work. The operational period had ended. Most people had returned to their hotels. Our conversation drifted from deployments to family, from family to ministry, and eventually to the quieter realities that people do not always discuss openly.

At one point he stared into his coffee and said something I have never forgotten.

"The destruction doesn't shock me anymore."

He paused before quietly adding, "That's what worries me."

For a moment neither of us spoke.

I knew exactly what he meant.

He was not describing a loss of compassion. He was describing adaptation. After years of deployments, disasters that once felt overwhelming had become familiar. Flooded neighborhoods. Tornado damage. Wildfire destruction. Families standing beside what remained of their homes. Stories of grief and loss repeated in different communities under different names.

The suffering had not become less real.

It had become less surprising.

That realization disturbed him.

In some ways, it disturbed me as well.

Most people assume that theological disruption emerges from a single catastrophic event. Sometimes it does. A devastating diagnosis, the death of a child, or a disaster that alters life forever can reshape a person's understanding of God almost immediately. Certain experiences arrive with enough force to change how people see the world in a matter of moments.

Not all theological injury develops that way.

Sometimes it emerges through accumulation rather than catastrophe. It is born not from one tragedy but from many tragedies, not from one loss but from repeated exposure to loss, not from one unanswered question but from years of unanswered questions. Over time something begins to change.

The change is often subtle at first. A story that once would have lingered for days now lingers for hours. A loss that once felt overwhelming now feels familiar. A tragedy that once seemed unimaginable begins to feel expected.

The person continues functioning. They continue helping. They continue caring.

Yet beneath the surface, something is happening.

The soul is adapting to suffering.

In many professions, that adaptation is necessary. Emergency managers cannot become immobilized every time disaster strikes. Healthcare workers cannot collapse emotionally during every difficult case. Pastors cannot become overwhelmed during every funeral. Responders cannot function effectively if every deployment affects them exactly as the first one did.

Adaptation allows people to continue serving. Without it, many helping professions would become impossible.

The challenge is that adaptation often comes with costs.

Some of those costs are emotional.

Others are moral.

Still others are theological.

The person begins asking questions they never expected to ask. Why does suffering seem endless? Why do the same tragedies repeat themselves? Why does injustice persist? Why does God seem so difficult to find amid so much pain?

These questions rarely emerge after a single difficult day. They emerge after years of repetition, after accumulated losses, and after witnessing more suffering than the human heart was ever designed to carry alone.

One of the hidden realities of caregiving, ministry, healthcare, chaplaincy, disaster response, and emergency management is that exposure accumulates. Individual experiences matter, but cumulative experiences matter even more. A responder remembers one deployment, then another, then another. A pastor remembers one funeral, then twenty, then two hundred. A nurse remembers one difficult patient, then hundreds. A caregiver remembers one difficult season, then years of responsibility.

Eventually, the question is no longer simply what happened.

The question becomes what repeated exposure is doing to the person experiencing it.

That question lies at the heart of this chapter because theological injury is not always born from catastrophe. Sometimes it is born from accumulation. Sometimes it emerges when a person discovers that the world contains far more suffering than they ever imagined, and that discovery quietly changes everything.

One of the most common misconceptions about suffering is that people become wounded only by what happens directly to them. Certainly personal loss matters. A diagnosis changes a life. A death alters a family. A disaster disrupts a community. Yet many people are affected not only by their own suffering but also by repeated exposure to the suffering of others.

Caregivers know this.

Pastors know this.

Healthcare workers know this.

Teachers, social workers, chaplains, counselors, emergency managers, and responders know this as well.

The burden they carry is often cumulative. One story alone may not overwhelm them. Neither may the next, or the next. But stories accumulate. Faces accumulate. Memories accumulate. Years accumulate. Over time, people begin carrying a collection of losses that are not entirely their own.

A pastor remembers the funeral of a child decades after the service ended. A nurse remembers a patient whose family sat vigil for weeks. A responder remembers a neighborhood reduced to debris. A caregiver remembers the slow decline of someone they loved.

The individual experiences begin to blur together.

Yet they never completely disappear.

One of the reasons cumulative suffering is so difficult to recognize is that it rarely announces itself dramatically. There is seldom a single moment when a person can point to a particular day and say, "That is when everything changed." Instead, the transformation unfolds gradually. A person becomes a little more tired, a little more guarded, a little less surprised, and a little more familiar with grief. Eventually, they realize they are carrying far more than they once did.

Researchers who study helping professions have long recognized this reality. Terms such as compassion fatigue, secondary traumatic stress, and vicarious trauma attempt to describe the effects of prolonged exposure to suffering. While these concepts differ in important ways, they all acknowledge a similar truth: human beings are affected by what they repeatedly witness. We do not observe suffering from a safe distance. We absorb it—not completely, not equally, but significantly.

Among the most influential voices in this field is Charles Figley, whose pioneering work on compassion fatigue helped explain what many caregivers, counselors, responders, and healthcare professionals had already experienced. Figley observed that people who spend years caring for those who suffer often absorb part of that suffering themselves. The cost is not simply physical exhaustion or emotional depletion. Repeated exposure gradually affects how people see the world, how they understand themselves, and how they make sense of human suffering. Compassion remains essential to helping professions, but compassion itself becomes costly when carried for long periods without adequate support, rest, or opportunities to process grief.

This insight helps explain why some theological questions emerge only after years of service. A person may begin ministry with confidence and optimism. A responder may begin disaster work with a strong sense of purpose. A healthcare worker may enter the profession believing they can make a meaningful difference.

None of those convictions are wrong.

Most remain partially true.

The challenge arises when repeated exposure begins complicating the picture. The pastor discovers that not every prayer receives the hoped-for answer. The responder discovers that disasters never entirely stop. The nurse discovers that some patients cannot be saved. The caregiver discovers that love does not always produce healing.

Over time these realities accumulate.

And with them come questions.

Not necessarily questions about whether God exists.

More often, questions about how God relates to a world marked by so much suffering.

I have encountered these questions repeatedly among disaster responders. At first, many deployments feel extraordinary. The destruction is shocking. The grief is palpable. The needs seem overwhelming.

Then another deployment occurs.

And another.

And another.

Eventually, a responder may find themselves standing in yet another damaged neighborhood, listening to yet another family's story of loss, and wondering why the cycle seems endless. The question is no longer merely operational.

It has become spiritual.

What do we do with a world in which suffering appears to renew itself generation after generation? How do we understand God amid such relentless repetition?

These questions rarely emerge because a person lacks faith. More often, they emerge because a person has spent years paying attention.

The same dynamic appears in ministry. When I first entered pastoral work, every funeral felt unique. In many ways, they were. Every family carried a different story. Every loss had its own texture. Every grief was deeply personal.

Yet after decades of ministry, another reality became apparent.

The losses never stopped.

One funeral led to another.

One hospital visit led to another.

One family crisis led to another.

The names changed.

The grief remained.

That realization can be difficult, not because compassion disappears but because compassion keeps encountering the same realities over and over again. Eventually, many caregivers begin asking a question that feels uncomfortable to admit.

How much suffering can a person witness before something inside begins to change?

The answer, of course, is that something always changes. The real question is what kind of change is taking place. Some changes deepen wisdom. Some deepen compassion. Some deepen humility. Others leave people exhausted, cynical, discouraged, or spiritually disoriented.

Often those changes occur simultaneously. A person becomes both wiser and more tired, more compassionate and more burdened, more understanding and more aware of mystery.

Theological injury frequently develops in precisely that space—not because people stop caring, but because they continue caring for so long. The burden is not indifference.

The burden is accumulation.

And eventually, accumulation demands attention.

One of the reasons cumulative suffering can be difficult to recognize is that it rarely looks dramatic. The person continues functioning. They continue working. They continue showing up. From the outside, very little appears different. Internally, however, subtle changes begin occurring.

A caregiver discovers there is less emotional energy than there once was. A pastor finds it harder to enter fully into another story of grief. A responder notices that scenes which once would have been shocking now feel routine. A healthcare worker catches themselves moving too quickly past suffering they once would have lingered beside.

These changes often create guilt because people assume that a diminished emotional response means diminished compassion.

Sometimes it does.

Often it does not.

More frequently, it reflects the reality that human beings have limits. The heart was never designed to carry unlimited sorrow. The mind was never intended to absorb endless tragedy. The soul was never meant to bear suffering indefinitely without consequence.

One common symptom of cumulative exposure is emotional numbing. This experience can be frightening because people often interpret it as evidence that they no longer care. The responder notices that devastation no longer evokes the same emotional response. The pastor feels strangely detached during a funeral. The caregiver realizes they are simply going through the motions. The healthcare worker discovers that another difficult case affects them less than it once would have.

These moments often produce shame because people wonder what has happened to them.

In reality, emotional numbing is frequently less about the absence of compassion than the exhaustion of emotional capacity. The human system begins protecting itself—not always effectively, not always healthily, but understandably. Charles Figley argued that one of the great paradoxes of caregiving is that the very capacity allowing people to care deeply also makes them vulnerable to cumulative strain. The problem is rarely that helpers stop caring. More often, they have cared for so long and carried so much that their emotional reserves begin showing unmistakable signs of fatigue.

Another symptom is what I have come to think of as theological fatigue. People become tired of explanations, tired of formulas, and tired of easy answers. They grow weary of hearing the same responses to questions that no longer seem capable of carrying the weight of experience. Years earlier, certain explanations may have felt reassuring. Over time, they begin sounding incomplete—not necessarily false, but insufficient.

Gradually, people find themselves less interested in defending theological systems and more interested in discovering how to live faithfully within mystery. This shift can be deeply disorienting, particularly for those whose faith communities place a high value on certainty. Individuals may wonder whether something is wrong with them when, in many cases, they are simply encountering the limits of explanations that were never designed to address the cumulative weight of suffering.

I have seen this repeatedly among disaster responders. Early in a person's disaster response journey, questions often focus on immediate events. Why did this tornado happen? Why did this family lose their home? Why did this community experience such devastation?

After years of deployments, however, the questions become broader.

Why does suffering repeat itself so relentlessly?

Why do vulnerable people seem to suffer disproportionately?

Why does recovery take so long?

Why do some wounds never fully heal?

The scope changes.

The questions deepen.

Theological disruption frequently follows—not because faith has disappeared, but because experience has expanded. The person now knows things they did not know before. They have seen things they cannot unsee. They have listened to stories they cannot forget. That knowledge becomes part of them.

Looking back, I can recognize seasons in my own ministry and disaster response work when some of these changes were occurring long before I had language for them. There were times when another deployment felt heavier than it should have. There were seasons when suffering seemed more familiar than surprising and when I found myself carrying stories home that I could not easily set aside.

At first, I assumed this was simply part of the work.

In some ways, it was.

What I understand more clearly now is that I was not becoming less compassionate. I was carrying more than I realized. The cumulative weight of grief, loss, unanswered questions, and repeated exposure to suffering had quietly become part of my own spiritual landscape.

I suspect many caregivers, responders, clergy, and healthcare professionals eventually discover the same thing. The challenge is not whether suffering affects us.

The challenge is recognizing that it already has.

Another symptom of cumulative exposure is what might be called spiritual weariness. Prayer becomes harder—not impossible, but harder. Scripture remains familiar, although it may no longer offer comfort in quite the same way. Worship continues to matter, yet it can begin to feel strangely distant from lived reality. The person continues practicing faith, but with far less confidence in easy explanations than before.

I have encountered this reality among clergy, chaplains, healthcare workers, and disaster responders alike. Many continue serving faithfully. Many continue believing. Yet they quietly wonder why their spiritual practices feel different than they once did. Often the answer is simpler than they imagine. They have simply been carrying too much for too long.

One of the mistakes helping professions sometimes make is assuming that competence eliminates vulnerability.

It does not.

Experience does not remove the effects of suffering. In many cases, experience actually increases exposure to suffering. The seasoned caregiver has usually witnessed more loss than the beginner. The experienced responder has seen more devastation than the newcomer. The veteran pastor has walked through more grief than the recent seminary graduate.

The accumulation grows.

So do its effects.

This reality does not mean that long-term service is harmful. Far from it. Many people become wiser, more compassionate, and more resilient through years of caregiving and service. Yet wisdom often comes with awareness, awareness comes with burden, and burden eventually raises spiritual questions—questions about God, suffering, hope, and how much sorrow a human being can carry before something inside begins asking for help.

Those questions deserve attention, not because they signify weakness, but because they signify humanity. Recognizing our humanity may be one of the first steps toward healing.

Scripture offers surprisingly honest companionship for people carrying the cumulative weight of suffering. Many biblical figures were not wounded by a single event. They were worn down by repetition. Jeremiah is perhaps one of the clearest examples. When many people think about prophets, they imagine courage, conviction, and spiritual strength. Jeremiah possessed all of those qualities, but he also carried something else.

Exhaustion.

For years he witnessed violence, injustice, suffering, and national decline. He delivered warnings that often went ignored. He watched people make destructive decisions. He carried burdens he could not resolve and responsibilities he could not escape. At times, his words sound remarkably familiar to modern caregivers and responders. He is frustrated, weary, disappointed, and occasionally angry with God.

What makes Jeremiah so important is that Scripture does not hide those reactions. It preserves them. The Bible allows us to see a faithful person struggling beneath the cumulative weight of what he has witnessed.

The same dynamic appears throughout the Psalms. Many lament psalms are not responses to a single moment of suffering. They emerge from prolonged exposure to hardship. When the psalmist cries, "How long, O Lord?" the question itself reveals repetition. It is no longer asking, "Why today?" but "How much longer? How many more losses? How many more disappointments?" The language of lament emerges when suffering stops feeling temporary.

That is why lament is so important for people experiencing theological injury. Lament tells the truth. It refuses denial, rejects shallow optimism, and resists explanations that arrive too quickly. At the same time, it continues speaking to God. That final detail matters because lament is not the absence of faith.

Lament is faith refusing to remain silent.

Over the years, I have become increasingly convinced that many caregivers, responders, clergy, and helping professionals need permission to lament. Not because they lack resilience, but because resilience alone cannot carry everything. Eventually, the accumulated weight of suffering requires expression. The grief must be named. The frustration must be acknowledged. The questions must be spoken. Otherwise, they remain buried beneath the surface, where they continue shaping the soul without ever receiving attention.

One of the most important discoveries people make during this process is that acknowledging limits is not failure.

It is wisdom.

The responder who admits exhaustion is not weak. The caregiver who acknowledges burden is not inadequate. The pastor who recognizes spiritual fatigue is not necessarily losing faith. More often, they are simply telling the truth.

And truth is often where healing begins.

For years I assumed that maturity meant carrying more.

Now I am not so sure.

Increasingly, I suspect maturity involves recognizing how much we were never intended to carry alone. The people I most admire in ministry and disaster response are rarely the ones who pretend to be unaffected. More often, they are the ones who understand their limits. They know when to rest. They know when to ask for help. They know when to grieve. They know when to lament. Most importantly, they know that acknowledging the weight of suffering is not the same thing as surrendering to it.

That distinction matters because cumulative suffering often whispers a dangerous lie. It tells us that because suffering continues, hope is naïve; because tragedy repeats, compassion is pointless; because losses accumulate, faith is futile. Many people never speak those conclusions aloud, yet they begin living as though they are true.

Theological injury frequently grows in precisely that soil—not through dramatic rejection of God, but through slow erosion. One disappointment at a time. One loss at a time. One unanswered question at a time.

The challenge is not merely to keep believing.

The challenge is to remain human.

To remain compassionate.

To remain capable of grief.

To remain open to hope.

Even after years of witnessing suffering.

That work is difficult.

It is also sacred.

Near the end of one deployment, I stood with a responder as families loaded the last of their belongings into vehicles and prepared to leave a temporary shelter. For weeks volunteers had listened to stories, distributed supplies, offered comfort, and helped people begin the long process of recovery. By that point everyone was tired. The residents were tired. The volunteers were tired. The staff were tired.

The responder beside me watched quietly as one family carried boxes through the shelter doors. After several moments he said, "I think what gets to me isn't any one disaster."

He paused before quietly adding, "It's how many there are."

We stood together in silence. Outside, the parking lot was beginning to empty. Volunteers folded tables and stacked chairs. The shelter that had been filled with activity only days before was slowly becoming quiet.

His words stayed with me because they reflected something profoundly true. The burden was not a single tragedy.

The burden was accumulation.

It was the realization that suffering keeps appearing in different places, wearing different faces, and telling different stories.

Yet as I watched families leave that shelter, another reality became visible as well. Compassion kept appearing too. Volunteers kept showing up. Neighbors kept helping. People kept caring.

The suffering was real.

The exhaustion was real.

The questions were real.

But they were not the only realities present.

The shelter lights dimmed one row at a time as the evening drew to a close. Conversations became quieter. The last carts were rolled away. Eventually only a few people remained. The work was not finished. It never is. Another disaster would come. Another deployment would follow. Another community would need help.

Yet even amid that certainty, another truth remained.

The presence of suffering was not the only thing that accumulated.

So did acts of compassion.

So did moments of courage.

So did quiet reminders that people were not carrying these burdens alone.

The last volunteer pushed a cart toward the storage room as the final bank of lights darkened above us. For a moment the shelter stood almost silent. The suffering that had brought people there was not over. Recovery would continue for months, perhaps years.

Yet neither was compassion finished.

People would keep showing up.

They always do.

And sometimes remembering that truth is enough to help us take the next step.

## *Chapter 7*

# Learning to Lament

Several years ago, after a disaster response training, a participant approached me during a break. She waited until most of the room had emptied before speaking, lingering quietly until the conversations had faded and only a few people remained. When she finally stepped forward, she said something that caught me off guard.

"I don't think I know how to lament."

Her honesty stayed with me long after the conversation ended. Not because her experience was unusual, but because so few people express it so directly. Most people do not say they do not know how to lament. Instead, they say things like, "I should have more faith," "I need to stay positive," "I don't want to complain," or "I know other people have it worse." Beneath those familiar statements often lies the same hidden reality. Many faithful people have never been taught what to do with grief, disappointment, anger, confusion, or unanswered questions before God. They know how to offer gratitude. They know how to offer praise. They know how to ask for help. What they often do not know is how to tell God the truth when life stops making sense.

That is unfortunate because Scripture contains an entire vocabulary for precisely those moments.

The language is called lament.

For many people, lament feels unfamiliar. Some assume it is simply another word for grief. Others associate it with despair or believe it reflects weak faith. Scripture presents it quite differently. Lament is the language faithful people use when faith collides with suffering. It is what happens when belief remains but certainty does not. It is what happens when prayer continues even though answers seem absent. It is the language of those who refuse both denial and abandonment, choosing instead to remain in relationship with God while acknowledging that the relationship has become painful, confusing, or difficult to understand.

That distinction makes lament especially important for understanding theological injury. One of the central challenges of theological injury is that people often feel trapped between silence and certainty. The explanations that once sustained them no longer work. The assumptions that once organized their faith no longer fit the realities they are living. Yet many do not know what to do next. Some stop talking about their questions altogether. Others force themselves to repeat answers they no longer find convincing, hoping certainty will somehow return if they simply say the right words often enough. Neither response brings much relief because neither allows experience and faith to remain connected.

Lament offers another path.

It allows people to tell the truth about suffering without abandoning the relationship.

This may be one of Scripture's greatest gifts. The Bible does not merely preserve stories of triumphant faith. It also preserves the voices of people whose faith was struggling—people who were confused, disappointed, angry, exhausted, and deeply uncertain, yet who continued speaking to God. That final detail is easy to overlook. The defining characteristic of lament is not sadness but direction. The lament is addressed to God. The psalmist does not simply describe suffering but deliberately brings suffering into conversation with God.

That may sound simple, yet in practice it is profoundly important.

When people experience theological injury, one of the first casualties is often honest prayer. Prayer becomes cautious, carefully managed, and emotionally restrained. People become afraid of their own questions, afraid of their anger, afraid of disappointing God, and afraid that speaking honestly somehow represents a failure of faith. Rather than risk saying too much, they often say very little.

The Bible repeatedly suggests otherwise.

The Psalms contain some of the most emotionally honest prayers ever written. They ask, "How long, O Lord?" They cry, "Why do you hide your face?" They wonder, "Why have you forgotten me?" They even dare to pray, "My God, my God, why have you forsaken me?" These are not the prayers of people who have abandoned God. They are the prayers of people struggling to understand God while refusing to let go of the relationship.

That distinction matters more than we often recognize. Many Christians have inherited the impression that mature faith means becoming increasingly certain. The Psalms suggest another possibility. Perhaps mature faith means becoming increasingly honest—honest about grief, fear, disappointment, confusion, and the reality that some experiences resist every attempt at explanation.

I know that kind of honesty once felt uncomfortable to me.

Early in ministry I often assumed that prayer should move people toward resolution. Someone brought a concern before God, received comfort, gained perspective, and moved forward. Sometimes that happens. Often it does not. Years of ministry, disaster response, and spiritual care have gradually convinced me that some prayers are not attempts to solve a problem.

They are attempts to survive one.

The person praying is not seeking an explanation nearly as much as companionship. They are trying to remain connected to God while carrying realities they cannot fully understand. Lament creates space for that kind of prayer. It allows a grieving parent to ask questions that have no immediate answers. It allows a disaster survivor to express anger without pretending otherwise. It allows a caregiver to admit exhaustion. It allows a pastor to acknowledge uncertainty. It allows a responder to name the cumulative weight of what has been witnessed. Most importantly, it allows all of those realities to be spoken honestly in God's presence.

That is why lament occupies such an important place in Scripture. Without lament, faith can easily become performative. People begin saying what they think faithful people are supposed to say. They learn the approved vocabulary, repeat familiar phrases, and suppress whatever does not fit the expected narrative. Eventually the distance between public faith and private experience becomes difficult to sustain.

Lament closes that gap.

It gives people permission to tell the truth.

For those living with theological injury, truth is often where healing begins.

One of the reasons lament feels unfamiliar to many modern believers is that much of contemporary Christian life has become far more comfortable with celebration than with sorrow. We know how to sing songs of praise. We know how to offer prayers of thanksgiving. We know how to speak about victory, hope, and blessing. These themes are deeply important and deserve their central place within the life of faith. The difficulty arises when suffering enters the picture and people discover that they possess an extensive vocabulary for joy but very little vocabulary for grief.

Many congregations unintentionally communicate that faithful people should move through pain quickly. We encourage trust, emphasize hope, and remind one another of God's promises. None of these responses are wrong. Indeed, they are essential to Christian faith. The problem is that they can sometimes arrive too soon. A grieving person may need lament before reassurance. A wounded person may need honesty before explanation. Someone struggling with theological injury may need permission to ask difficult questions before being offered carefully constructed answers.

Scripture appears to understand this reality remarkably well. The book of Psalms contains songs of praise, but it also contains an astonishing number of laments. Scholars generally estimate that roughly one-third of the Psalms contain significant elements of lament. That fact alone should cause us to pause. If lament occupies so much space within the Bible's prayer book, perhaps it should occupy more space within our own spiritual lives.

Old Testament scholar Walter Brueggemann has argued that lament performs an essential theological function because it gives voice to experiences that resist easy explanation and creates space for honest engagement with God. When lament disappears, he suggests, faith can become detached from lived experience, drifting toward abstraction rather than remaining rooted in the realities of human life. The presence of lament throughout Scripture reminds us that God welcomes not only our praise but also our questions, grief, protest, disappointment, and confusion.

Consider Psalm 13. It begins with a question that countless believers have whispered in hospital rooms, disaster shelters, funeral homes, and lonely nights: "How long, O Lord?" The psalmist repeats those words four times in rapid succession.

How long will you forget me?

How long will you hide your face?

How long must I wrestle with my thoughts?

How long will my enemy triumph over me?

Notice what the psalmist is doing. There is no attempt to soften the experience or pretend that everything is acceptable. Fear is named. Confusion is named. Loneliness is named. Delay is named. The prayer does not begin with certainty. It begins with honesty.

That pattern appears repeatedly throughout Scripture. People often assume that lament is primarily about expressing emotion. It certainly includes emotion, but lament accomplishes something even more profound. It refuses to separate faith from experience. It insists that suffering belongs within the conversation with God rather than outside it.

This insistence is especially important because theological injury often creates pressure to do precisely the opposite. People begin compartmentalizing their lives. They maintain religious language on one side while placing their actual experiences somewhere else. Publicly they continue saying the expected words. Privately they struggle with questions they no longer feel safe expressing. The distance between faith and lived experience gradually widens until prayer itself begins feeling artificial.

Lament closes that distance.

Rather than protecting God from our questions, lament brings those questions directly into God's presence. Rather than hiding confusion, lament names it. Rather than pretending certainty, lament allows uncertainty to become part of faithful prayer. In doing so, it preserves something that theological injury often threatens most—the relationship itself.

The same pattern appears in Psalm 22. Many readers recognize its opening line because Jesus himself speaks it from the cross: "My God, my God, why have you forsaken me?" These words remain startling, not because they are unfamiliar, but because they are preserved within Scripture at all. The Bible could easily have portrayed faith as unwavering confidence.

Instead, it preserves prayers that sound like abandonment, bewilderment, and protest.

That preservation matters enormously.

It suggests that God is not threatened by honesty. God does not require emotional editing before prayer. The psalmist tells the truth. Jesus tells the truth. Their words become sacred Scripture.

For people living with theological injury, this realization can be profoundly liberating. Many have spent months or even years trying to protect God from their disappointment, trying to protect faith from their questions, and trying to protect prayer from their anger. The Psalms suggest that such protection may be unnecessary. The writers do not hide their confusion. They carry it directly into conversation with God.

Perhaps the most remarkable example is Psalm 88. Unlike many biblical laments, this psalm never arrives at a triumphant conclusion. There is no dramatic breakthrough, no reassuring explanation, and no sudden resolution. The psalm simply ends in darkness. For generations readers have wondered why such a prayer was included in Scripture.

Perhaps the answer is simpler than we imagine.

Some experiences end that way.

Some seasons of life remain unresolved far longer than we expected. Some questions continue without answers. Some wounds require years rather than days. Psalm 88 reminds us that Scripture is willing to remain present even in those places where resolution has not yet arrived. The Bible refuses to abandon people whose stories are still unfinished.

Philosopher Nicholas Wolterstorff explored this reality with remarkable honesty after the death of his son. Reflecting on his own grief, he observed that suffering often creates a longing not for explanations but for presence. Those who grieve are not necessarily searching for answers. More often, they are longing for companionship in the midst of unanswered questions. That insight resonates deeply with the practice of lament.

Perhaps this is one of lament's greatest gifts.

It creates room for unfinished stories.

People experiencing theological injury often feel pressure to arrive at conclusions before they are ready. Friends ask how they are doing.

Congregations hope for encouraging testimonies. Families long for reassurance that healing has begun. Meanwhile, the individual is still grieving, still questioning, still waiting, and still struggling to make sense of what has happened.

Lament gives them permission to remain where they are.

Not forever, but honestly.

The goal of lament is never to become trapped in suffering. Neither is it to celebrate suffering. Rather, lament refuses dishonesty about suffering. It acknowledges pain without surrendering to despair. It brings wounded hope into God's presence instead of pretending hope has disappeared altogether.

That distinction is crucial.

Lament is not despair.

Despair concludes that nothing matters.

Lament continues the conversation.

Despair turns away.

Lament turns toward God.

Despair closes the relationship.

Lament refuses to let the relationship die.

The difference may appear subtle, yet spiritually it is enormous. As long as lament continues, relationship continues. And relationship is often the very thing theological injury threatens most deeply.

If lament occupies such an important place in Scripture, why does it feel so unfamiliar in many faith communities? Part of the answer may be cultural. Most societies reward confidence more readily than uncertainty. We admire people who appear strong, composed, and resilient. We celebrate those who overcome adversity and emerge victorious. Stories of triumph inspire us, while stories of unresolved struggle often make us uncomfortable because they remind us that some questions remain unanswered.

The church is not immune to these cultural tendencies. Congregations generally know how to celebrate healing better than waiting, recovery better than uncertainty, and answered prayer better than unanswered prayer. As a result, many believers receive the subtle impression that faithful people should move quickly from grief to gratitude, from suffering to hope, and from questions to answers.

Life rarely unfolds so neatly.

The caregivers, responders, clergy, healthcare workers, and survivors I have known over the years often inhabit a far messier reality. They continue believing, yet they also continue questioning. They continue praying while simultaneously struggling to understand prayer. They continue showing up for worship, ministry, and service even after certainty has largely disappeared. Their lives testify that faith and unresolved questions are not mutually exclusive.

The problem is not that these experiences are rare.

The problem is that they are often hidden.

Many people learn early which emotions seem acceptable within religious settings and which do not. Gratitude is welcomed. Joy is welcomed. Confidence is welcomed. Anger, however, feels more complicated. Confusion feels more complicated. Disappointment feels more complicated. Questions themselves can begin to feel risky.

Over time, some people begin censoring themselves—not because they are dishonest, but because they are trying to belong. They learn which parts of their experience seem safe to share and which parts appear better left unspoken. Gradually, a gap develops between public faith and private experience. People continue attending worship, participating in Bible studies, serving on committees, teaching classes, and caring for others while quietly carrying theological wounds that few people ever see.

The result is that many carry theological injury in silence.

They sit through sermons while privately wrestling with questions they no longer feel safe asking. They participate in Bible studies while wondering whether anyone else has experienced the same disruption of faith. They continue leading ministries while privately wondering whether they themselves still understand God the way they once did.

One of the unexpected gifts of disaster response has been witnessing what happens when those protective filters temporarily disappear.

Disasters have a way of stripping away pretense.

People who would normally speak cautiously often become remarkably honest. A survivor standing in front of a destroyed home rarely worries about sounding theologically correct. A grieving parent sitting beside the ruins of a familiar life is seldom concerned with appearing spiritually impressive. A responder exhausted after weeks of service often speaks with greater honesty than they have allowed themselves for months.

In those moments, lament emerges naturally.

People ask difficult questions.

They express frustration.

They name losses.

They admit fear.

Most importantly, they tell the truth.

Again and again I have watched people discover that once honesty becomes possible, healing often becomes possible as well. Not because every question is answered, but because the exhausting effort required to maintain appearances begins to fade.

I have increasingly come to believe that many faith communities would benefit from becoming places where such honesty is not merely tolerated but welcomed. Not because honesty solves suffering—it does not. Not because lament removes grief—it cannot. But because healing rarely begins with pretending. Healing begins when reality is acknowledged for what it actually is.

Henri Nouwen frequently reminded caregivers and ministers that healing begins not with strength but with honesty. The willingness to acknowledge one's own wounds often becomes the doorway through which deeper compassion emerges. In that sense, lament is not merely a response to suffering. It is an act of truthful presence before God. Rather than concealing brokenness, lament allows wounded people to bring their whole selves into God's presence.

One of the reasons theological injury becomes so painful is that people often feel pressure to recover spiritually before they have been allowed to grieve spiritually.

We understand emotional grief. We recognize the need to mourn the death of a loved one, the loss of a home, or the ending of a vocation.

Theological grief is far less familiar. Yet when assumptions collapse, when prayer changes, when certainty disappears, and when faith begins feeling unfamiliar, another kind of grief often emerges beneath the surface.

Something has been lost.

A way of understanding God.

A sense of predictability.

A theological framework that once provided stability.

People cannot move beyond those losses until they first acknowledge that the losses are real. Lament creates space for precisely that acknowledgment. It allows people to pray words they may have been afraid to speak aloud:

"This hurts."

"I do not understand."

"I am disappointed."

"I am angry."

"I am confused."

"I am tired."

Those statements may not sound especially spiritual to some ears. Scripture suggests otherwise. Many of the most faithful voices in the Bible speak in exactly those terms. Job speaks that way. Jeremiah speaks that way. The psalmists speak that way. Even Jesus speaks that way.

The common thread is not emotional tone.

It is honesty before God.

That honesty can feel frightening. Some people worry that speaking openly will weaken their faith or somehow dishonor God. My experience has increasingly suggested the opposite. What weakens faith is not honest lament but the exhausting effort required to maintain a version of faith disconnected from lived reality. Eventually that strain becomes impossible to sustain.

Lament relieves that pressure.

It allows faith and experience to occupy the same space.

It allows people to bring their actual lives—not idealized versions of their lives—into conversation with God.

For caregivers, clergy, responders, and helping professionals, this may be especially important. Many spend years focusing almost exclusively on the needs of others. They become skilled listeners, thoughtful encouragers, and dependable companions during difficult moments. Those are beautiful gifts, yet they can also become subtle obstacles.

People who spend years caring for others sometimes forget how to acknowledge their own grief. They become accustomed to being the helper rather than the helped, the listener rather than the speaker, the caregiver rather than the recipient of care. Over time, unspoken burdens accumulate. Losses accumulate. Questions accumulate. Disappointments accumulate.

Eventually, the weight becomes difficult to ignore.

Lament offers a place to begin setting some of that burden down.

Not permanently.

Not completely.

But honestly.

And honesty, simple as it sounds, may be one of the most important spiritual disciplines available to those living with theological injury.

One of the misconceptions people sometimes carry about lament is that it represents the opposite of hope. In reality, lament may be one of hope's most honest expressions. People do not lament what they have completely abandoned. They lament what still matters. A person who cries out to God is still turning toward God. A person who asks difficult questions is still engaged in the relationship. A person who wrestles with disappointment continues wrestling precisely because something precious remains at stake.

That is why lament differs so profoundly from resignation. Resignation quietly concludes that nothing can be done. Lament insists that this is not the way things are meant to be. Resignation withdraws from the relationship. Lament continues engaging it. Resignation closes the conversation. Lament refuses to let the conversation end.

This distinction becomes especially important for people experiencing theological injury. Many have lost confidence in explanations. Some have lost confidence in certainty. Others have lost confidence in religious formulas that once seemed capable of carrying the weight of their experience. What they have not necessarily lost is their longing for God.

Lament gives that longing somewhere to go.

It creates space for faith that no longer knows exactly what to say, yet refuses to stop speaking.

Over the years I have become increasingly convinced that one of the greatest gifts the church can offer wounded people is permission to lament. Not permission to remain trapped in despair, but permission to tell the truth. Permission to speak honestly about suffering. Permission to acknowledge confusion. Permission to admit anger. Permission to grieve losses that have not yet healed.

In many ways, this permission has always been present within Scripture.

The challenge is remembering it.

Again and again the Bible refuses to ask wounded people to skip over lament on their way to hope. Instead, it invites them into lament as an essential part of the journey of faith. The psalmists teach this. Jeremiah teaches this. Job teaches this. Even Jesus teaches this. Faithful people have always struggled. Faithful people have always questioned. Faithful people have always lamented.

Theological injury does not place someone outside that tradition.

It places them within it.

That realization can be profoundly comforting because one of the loneliest aspects of theological injury is the feeling that no one else has ever stood where we are standing. Lament reminds us otherwise. Others have walked this road before us. Others have asked these questions. Others have carried these burdens. Scripture preserves their voices so that we do not have to imagine ourselves alone.

This does not mean lament resolves every question.

Many questions remain.

Some wounds remain.

Some mysteries remain.

Lament is not a technique for obtaining answers. It is a practice of remaining present—present to God, present to suffering, present to reality, and present to ourselves. That kind of presence may not appear dramatic, yet it often becomes the foundation upon which healing quietly begins.

Not healing through explanation.

Healing through honesty.

Not healing through certainty.

Healing through relationship.

Near the end of one disaster deployment, I spent time with a volunteer who had been listening to survivors for several weeks. Every day brought new stories of loss: homes destroyed, families displaced, futures suddenly altered, cherished possessions reduced to debris, and lives divided into before and after. By the time operations began winding down, she looked exhausted in a way that sleep alone could not repair.

One evening we sat together after a particularly long day. For a while neither of us spoke very much. Eventually she broke the silence.

"I think I've spent weeks hearing other people cry."

She paused, looked down at the ground for a moment, and then added quietly, "And I don't think I've cried at all."

The realization seemed to surprise her. It was not that she lacked compassion. Quite the opposite. She had cared so deeply for so many people that somewhere along the way she had forgotten to acknowledge her own sorrow.

A few minutes later she began talking—not about the survivors, but about her own grief. Some of it had nothing to do with the deployment. Some of it reached back years. Some of it involved losses she had carried so long that she no longer realized how heavy they had become.

The words came slowly at first.

Then more freely.

There were tears.

There was silence.

There were no explanations.

There was simply truth.

When the conversation ended, nothing about the disaster itself had changed. Homes still needed rebuilding. Families still faced months, perhaps years, of recovery. Questions remained unanswered. Yet something had shifted within her. A burden that had been carried alone had finally been spoken aloud.

I have often returned to that evening when reflecting on the practice of lament.

Lament does not erase suffering.

It does not repair every wound.

It does not eliminate uncertainty.

What it does is refuse isolation.

It invites people to bring their grief into the presence of God and, whenever possible, into the presence of trusted companions. In doing so, it reminds us that suffering was never intended to be carried alone.

As we walked toward the parking lot that evening, the air had grown cool. Around us, volunteers gathered supplies and prepared for another day of work. A few quiet conversations drifted through the darkness before gradually fading away. The suffering that had brought us there remained. The questions remained. The losses remained.

But silence no longer carried them alone.

I have come to believe that this is often where healing truly begins. Not with answers that explain away pain. Not with certainty restored. Not even with immediate relief. Healing begins with the courage to tell the truth before God, trusting that God is not driven away by honesty but welcomes it.

The path beyond theological injury rarely begins with explanation.

More often, it begins with lament.

And perhaps that is why Scripture gives lament such a prominent place. Before faith can speak confidently again, it must first learn to speak truthfully. Before hope can become authentic, grief must be given permission to find its voice. Before theology can be reconstructed, wounded hearts must be allowed to pray without pretending.

In the end, lament is not the opposite of faith.

It is one of faith's deepest expressions.

It is the prayer that continues when certainty has ended, the conversation that survives when explanations fail, and the quiet refusal to walk away from the God who still receives every honest word we have left to say.

## *Chapter 8*

# Faith After Certainty

Several years ago, a pastor approached me after a workshop and waited until most of the room had emptied before speaking.

"I think my faith is changing," he said.

The statement itself was not unusual. What came next was.

"I don't know whether that's a good thing or a bad thing."

For a moment, neither of us spoke. Then he continued.

"I still believe. I still pray. I still preach. I still trust God. But I don't believe the same way I used to."

His words captured something I have heard repeatedly from clergy, caregivers, responders, disaster survivors, and people who have endured significant loss. They have not abandoned faith, yet they can no longer inhabit faith exactly as they once did. The assumptions have changed. The questions have changed. The language has changed. Sometimes even the image of God has changed. What remains can be difficult to describe.

Many people assume that faith follows a simple trajectory. We begin with uncertainty, acquire knowledge, strengthen our convictions, and gradually become more confident. Life often proves more complicated. For many people, faith does not move from doubt to certainty. It moves from certainty to depth.

That distinction matters. Early faith often depends upon clarity. We want answers, coherence, and explanations that help us understand suffering, prayer, loss, providence, and the presence of God. There is nothing wrong with that desire. In many ways, it is a natural part of spiritual development. The difficulty arises when life presents realities that our existing explanations cannot adequately address.

A child dies. A marriage ends. A disaster destroys a community. A prayer goes unanswered. A trusted institution fails. A caregiver reaches the limits of endurance. A responder witnesses suffering that refuses to fit familiar theological categories. In those moments, people often experience what feels like the collapse of faith.

Sometimes something else is happening.

Sometimes certainty is collapsing, not faith.

Those two realities are not identical. For years, I assumed they were. Many churches assume they are as well. When someone begins questioning long-held assumptions, we often become concerned that belief itself is disappearing. Sometimes belief is disappearing. More often, belief is changing. The old framework no longer works, and the person begins searching for another.

This process can feel frightening because certainty provides security. It tells us where we stand, how the world works, and how to interpret experience. It helps us predict outcomes and organize meaning. When certainty weakens, people often feel exposed. The questions become larger. The answers become fewer. The mysteries become more visible.

Yet something interesting often happens during this period. People begin paying closer attention. They listen differently, pray differently, and read Scripture differently. They become less interested in defending answers and more interested in seeking wisdom.

The faith that emerges may feel smaller at first—less confident, less settled, and less sure of itself. Yet over time it sometimes becomes stronger in unexpected ways. Not because it possesses more answers, but because it has learned to live with questions.

One of the most influential observations in developmental psychology came from James Fowler, whose work on faith development suggested that mature faith often involves moving beyond simplistic certainty toward greater complexity, humility, and openness. While not everyone follows the same path, Fowler recognized something many believers eventually discover for themselves: spiritual growth frequently requires letting go of understandings that can no longer bear the weight of lived experience.

Spiritual writer Richard Rohr has similarly observed that much of spiritual growth occurs through what he calls necessary loss. Experiences of disappointment, failure, suffering, and disruption often dismantle assumptions that once seemed secure. While such experiences rarely feel welcome, they can create space for deeper and more mature faith to emerge.

The process rarely feels like growth. It often feels like loss.

That is one reason theological injury can be so confusing. People assume they are losing faith when they may actually be losing an inadequate framework for faith. The experience is still painful, and loss remains loss. Yet recognizing the distinction can change how people interpret what is happening.

Biblical scholar Peter Enns has written extensively about the difference between losing certainty and losing faith. He argues that many believers eventually discover that spiritual maturity involves learning to trust God without requiring complete intellectual resolution. Questions do not necessarily undermine faith. Sometimes they become part of faith's growth.

A person who believes they are abandoning God often experiences fear. A person who realizes they are rethinking assumptions may begin experiencing curiosity instead. The questions remain. The struggle remains. But the story changes. The journey becomes less about failure and more about transformation.

This transformation rarely occurs in a straight line. People experience progress and setbacks, renewed questions and unexpected moments of grief, along with seasons when old certainties seem attractive once again. Reconstruction is seldom a destination that one reaches and permanently inhabits. More often, it is an ongoing journey of trust, questioning, discovery, and return.

Scripture contains many examples of this process. Abraham leaves familiar certainties and follows a promise he cannot fully understand. Jacob wrestles through the night and emerges changed. Job loses confidence in the theological system he once inhabited. The disciples repeatedly discover that Jesus is not who they expected him to be. Again and again, faith grows not through the confirmation of assumptions but through their disruption. The people of Scripture rarely encounter God in ways that leave them unchanged. More often, they encounter God in ways that force them to reconsider everything they thought they knew.

Perhaps that should not surprise us. If God is truly God, then every human understanding of God remains partial. Every theological framework remains incomplete. Every explanation eventually reaches its limits. Theological injury often begins when those limits become impossible to ignore. Faith after certainty begins when people discover that relationship with God may continue even after certainty has collapsed.

That discovery does not arrive quickly, nor can it be forced. It usually begins with a simple realization. The questions have not disappeared, yet neither has God.

Recognizing that God may remain even when certainty does not is often the beginning of a new stage in faith. It is rarely a comfortable stage. Many people would gladly return to the clarity they once possessed. They miss the confidence of earlier years, the straightforward answers, and the reassuring feeling that the world made sense. What they eventually discover, however, is that they cannot go back. The old framework no longer fits. The questions they now carry cannot be unasked. The experiences they have endured cannot be undone. The person who emerges from theological injury is not the same person who entered it.

This reality can feel deeply discouraging at first. Eventually, however, it can become surprisingly liberating. One of the hidden burdens of certainty is the pressure to defend it. When people believe they must possess answers for every question, uncertainty becomes threatening, ambiguity becomes dangerous, and mystery becomes something to overcome rather than something to inhabit.

Theological injury often dismantles that expectation gradually. A person begins recognizing how much remains beyond explanation. They discover that some questions have multiple faithful answers while others appear to have no answer at all. Rather than weakening faith, this realization sometimes deepens it. The person becomes less interested in certainty and more interested in trust, less interested in explanations and more interested in presence, less interested in winning arguments and more interested in wisdom.

This shift is subtle but profound because trust and certainty are not the same thing. Certainty depends upon confidence in what we know. Trust depends upon confidence in whom we know. A person can lose certainty while retaining trust.

In fact, many of the most faithful people I have known describe precisely that experience. They no longer claim to understand everything. They no longer speak with the same confidence they once possessed. They no longer feel compelled to explain every tragedy or justify every unanswered prayer. Yet they continue praying, worshiping, serving, and trusting—not because every question has been answered, but because the relationship itself remains.

I have encountered this repeatedly among disaster survivors. In the immediate aftermath of catastrophe, people naturally search for explanations. Why did this happen? Why us? Why now? Where was God? These questions deserve to be asked, and they often dominate the earliest stages of recovery.

Over time, however, many survivors discover that explanations carry them only so far. The need for meaning remains. The need for companionship remains. The need for hope remains. Eventually, many stop asking for a complete explanation and begin asking a different question: How do I live now?

That question marks an important transition. The focus shifts from understanding everything to living faithfully within what cannot be understood.

The same movement appears throughout Scripture. Much of the book of Job centers on attempts to explain suffering. Job's friends repeatedly offer answers. They defend theological systems and insist upon explanations that preserve their understanding of how God governs the world. Job refuses those explanations because they no longer correspond to reality as he has experienced it.

When God finally speaks, readers often expect a comprehensive explanation. Instead, they encounter something altogether different: a larger vision, a wider horizon, and a reminder that reality contains depths beyond human comprehension. Job receives many things by the end of the story, but a complete explanation is not one of them. What he does receive is a deeper encounter with God, and that encounter changes him even though many of his questions remain unresolved.

The transformation does not emerge through certainty. It emerges through relationship. That distinction is profoundly important because theological injury often leaves people searching for explanations, while faith after certainty frequently grows through encounter with the living God. The difference may appear subtle, yet it changes everything. One path seeks mastery while the other seeks companionship. One seeks closure while the other seeks presence. One hopes to eliminate mystery while the other learns to live faithfully within it.

This perspective can be difficult for people raised in faith communities where certainty is highly valued. Some worry that embracing mystery means abandoning conviction, while others fear that acknowledging uncertainty will inevitably lead to unbelief. Rachel Held Evans frequently challenged that assumption throughout her writing. She described faith as a journey marked by questions, doubt, curiosity, and continued trust. For many readers, her work offered reassurance that questioning inherited assumptions does not necessarily lead away from God. Sometimes it becomes part of discovering a faith capable of surviving adulthood.

In my experience, the opposite of certainty is not doubt. More often, it is humility. People who acknowledge uncertainty honestly frequently develop a more resilient faith than those who spend years pretending to possess certainty they no longer feel. The resilient believer is not the person who never questions but the person who continues seeking God amid unanswered questions. That kind of faith is less fragile because it depends less upon having the right answers and more upon remaining within the relationship.

Theological injury often exposes the limits of certainty. Faith after certainty begins discovering the possibilities of trust.

What does faith look like after certainty? There is no single answer because every person's journey is different. Some reconstruct faith quickly, while others require years. Some eventually return to convictions remarkably similar to those they once held, while others discover that significant portions of their theological framework have changed. What matters is not uniformity but honesty.

One of the mistakes people sometimes make is assuming that reconstruction means replacing old certainties with new certainties. In reality, reconstruction is often less about acquiring answers than about developing wisdom. Wisdom differs from certainty in important ways. Certainty seeks conclusions, while wisdom learns discernment. Certainty seeks control, while wisdom learns humility. Certainty longs for final answers, while wisdom recognizes that some questions remain open.

This shift can be difficult to appreciate because certainty feels stronger than humility. It sounds stronger and often appears stronger. Yet humility frequently proves more durable. A faith built entirely upon certainty can be shaken when certainty fails. A faith built upon humility already expects limitations. It recognizes that human understanding is partial and that God is always greater than our explanations.

This is one reason reconstructed faith often feels quieter than the faith that preceded it. People become less interested in making grand claims, defending every theological position, or proving themselves right. Instead, they become more interested in listening, more interested in compassion, and more interested in accompanying others through suffering. The questions have not disappeared. They simply no longer occupy the same place they once did.

I have observed this pattern repeatedly among people who have endured significant loss. Someone who once spoke confidently about suffering becomes more cautious after experiencing it personally. A pastor who once offered quick answers begins leaving more room for mystery. A caregiver who has walked through years of grief develops greater patience with the struggles of others. The change is not merely intellectual. It is deeply relational.

Suffering often enlarges a person's capacity for compassion. Not automatically, and certainly not in every case, but often enough to recognize the pattern. One reason is that theological injury creates empathy. People who have wrestled with difficult questions become less alarmed by the questions of others. Those who have experienced uncertainty become less threatened by uncertainty. Those who have lived through spiritual disruption become more capable of accompanying others through similar experiences.

This may be one of the hidden gifts of wounded faith. The person no longer feels compelled to fix every struggle. Instead, they become more willing to remain present within it.

In many ways, this reflects the ministry of Jesus. The Gospels portray him answering some questions while refusing to answer others. He teaches, challenges, comforts, and heals, yet much of his ministry consists simply of presence. He sits with people, listens to them, notices what others overlook, and accompanies them through suffering rather than explaining it away.

For years I assumed that spiritual maturity meant becoming increasingly certain. Now I suspect it may involve becoming increasingly present—present to God, present to others, present to reality, and present to the complexities of life that resist easy explanation.

This kind of presence requires courage because certainty often provides distance. Presence requires engagement. Certainty can remain abstract, but presence always becomes personal. Theological injury frequently pushes people toward this realization. The collapse of old assumptions leaves them with fewer explanations and a greater awareness of human vulnerability. At first this feels like loss. Over time it often becomes a source of wisdom.

The reconstructed believer gradually discovers that faith is less about possessing certainty than practicing trust. It becomes less about understanding everything and more about remaining faithful amid uncertainty, less about defending God and more about learning to recognize God's presence in unexpected places.

None of this means that all beliefs become equally valid. Reconstruction is not theological relativism. People continue holding convictions. They continue reading Scripture, worshiping, praying, and discerning truth. What changes is the posture with which those convictions are held. There is more humility, more curiosity, more patience, and a deeper awareness of mystery. Perhaps most importantly, there is greater compassion toward those whose journeys differ from their own.

Theological injury often dismantles simplistic judgments. People who have struggled become less eager to condemn struggle. People who have wrestled with doubt become less fearful of doubt. People who have experienced God's presence amid uncertainty become less dependent upon certainty as the foundation of faith.

What does faith look like after certainty? There is no single answer because the journey is different for every person. Some reconstruct faith relatively quickly, while others require years. Some eventually return to convictions remarkably similar to those they once held. Others discover that significant portions of their theological framework have changed. What matters is not uniformity but honesty.

One of the mistakes people sometimes make is assuming that reconstruction means replacing old certainties with new certainties. In reality, reconstruction is often less about acquiring answers than about developing wisdom. Wisdom differs from certainty in important ways. Certainty seeks conclusions, while wisdom learns discernment. Certainty seeks control, while wisdom learns humility. Certainty longs for final answers, while wisdom recognizes that some questions remain open.

This shift can be difficult to appreciate because certainty feels stronger than humility. It sounds stronger and often appears stronger. Yet humility frequently proves far more durable. A faith built entirely upon certainty can be shaken when certainty fails. A faith built upon humility already expects limitations. It already recognizes that human understanding is partial and that God is always larger than our explanations.

This is one reason reconstructed faith often feels quieter than the faith that preceded it. People become less interested in making grand claims, less interested in defending every theological position, and less interested in proving themselves right. Instead, they become more interested in listening, more interested in compassion, and more interested in accompanying others through suffering. The questions have not disappeared; they simply no longer occupy the same place they once did.

I have observed this pattern repeatedly among people who have endured significant loss. A person who once spoke confidently about suffering becomes more cautious after experiencing it personally. A pastor who once offered quick answers begins leaving more room for mystery. A caregiver who has walked through years of grief develops greater patience with the struggles of others. The change is not merely intellectual. It is profoundly relational.

Suffering often enlarges a person's capacity for compassion. Not automatically, and certainly not in every case, but often enough to notice. One reason is that theological injury creates empathy. People who have wrestled with difficult questions become less alarmed by the questions of others. Those who have experienced uncertainty become less threatened by uncertainty. Those who have lived through spiritual disruption become more capable of accompanying others through similar experiences.

This may be one of the hidden gifts of wounded faith. The person no longer feels compelled to fix every struggle. Instead, they become more willing to remain present within it.

In many ways, this reflects the ministry of Jesus. The Gospels portray him answering some questions while refusing to answer others. He teaches, challenges, comforts, and heals, yet much of his ministry consists simply of presence. He sits with people, listens to them, notices what others overlook, and accompanies them through suffering rather than explaining it away.

For years I assumed that spiritual maturity meant becoming increasingly certain. Now I suspect it may involve becoming increasingly present—present to God, present to other people, present to reality, and present to the complexities of life that resist easy explanation.

This kind of presence requires courage because certainty often provides distance. Presence requires engagement. Certainty can remain abstract, but presence always becomes personal. Theological injury frequently pushes people toward this realization. The collapse of old assumptions leaves them with fewer explanations and a greater awareness of human vulnerability. At first this feels like loss. Over time it often becomes a source of wisdom.

The reconstructed believer gradually discovers that faith is less about possessing certainty than practicing trust. It becomes less about understanding everything and more about remaining faithful amid uncertainty, less about defending God and more about learning to recognize God's presence in unexpected places.

None of this means that all beliefs become equally valid. Reconstruction is not theological relativism. People continue holding convictions. They continue reading Scripture, worshiping, praying, and discerning truth. What changes is the posture with which those convictions are held. There is more humility, more curiosity, more patience, and a deeper awareness of mystery. Perhaps most importantly, there is greater compassion toward those whose journeys differ from their own.

Theological injury often dismantles simplistic judgments. People who have struggled become less eager to condemn struggle. People who have wrestled with doubt become less fearful of doubt. People who have experienced God's presence amid uncertainty become less dependent upon certainty as the foundation of faith.

This reconstructed faith rarely emerges all at once. People move forward and backward. New experiences raise new questions. Old assumptions occasionally resurface. Periods of clarity are followed by renewed uncertainty. The process is seldom linear. Yet over time many people discover that their faith has become less fragile—not because every question has been answered, but because unanswered questions no longer determine whether faith survives.

The result is not weaker faith. More often it is deeper faith: a faith tempered by experience, tested by suffering, refined through unanswered questions, and enlarged by both lament and hope. Such faith may appear less impressive from a distance, but it is often far more resilient up close. The person no longer trusts because life makes perfect sense. They trust because they have discovered that God remains present even when life does not. That discovery rarely arrives through theory. It emerges through experience, and once experienced, it changes faith forever.

The transition from certainty to trust is rarely dramatic. Most people do not wake up one morning and discover that their faith has been reconstructed. The change usually occurs gradually, one prayer at a time, one disappointment at a time, and one act of quiet faithfulness at a time. They continue showing up. They continue praying, even when prayer feels different. They continue worshiping, even when certainty has diminished. They continue seeking God, even while many questions remain unanswered. Looking back, they eventually realize that something important has changed. They no longer believe because everything makes sense. They believe because they have learned to trust amid what does not make sense.

This may be one of the most significant developments in spiritual maturity. Children often trust because trusted adults provide answers. Adults eventually discover that some questions exceed every available explanation. The challenge then becomes learning how to remain faithful within that reality.

Many people assume that unanswered questions represent a threat to faith. In my experience, unanswered questions often become the environment in which faith learns to breathe. Not because uncertainty is pleasant or suffering desirable, but because life itself contains mystery. Faith that requires complete explanation cannot survive long in such a world. Faith that learns trust can.

Years ago, after a disaster deployment, I spoke with a woman whose community had experienced devastating loss. During the earliest days of recovery she had asked the questions one would expect. Why had this happened? Why had so many lives been disrupted? Why had God allowed it? Months later, when I saw her again, I asked how she was doing.

She thought quietly for a moment before answering.

"I still don't have answers," she said with a slight smile. "But I don't think that's what I'm looking for anymore."

When I asked what she meant, she looked toward a group of volunteers helping a family recover what little remained of their belongings.

"I think I spent a long time trying to understand why God allowed this to happen," she said. "Now I'm paying attention to how God is helping people get through it."

Her words have stayed with me because they captured a profound shift in perspective. They did not solve the problem of suffering or answer every theological question. Instead, they reflected a movement from explanation to presence, from certainty to trust, and from answers to relationship.

That movement lies at the heart of reconstructed faith. Theological injury often begins when old certainties collapse. Faith after certainty begins when people discover that God's presence may remain even when those certainties do not. The questions continue. Mystery remains. Suffering does not disappear. Yet something new becomes possible—a faith that no longer depends upon complete understanding, a faith capable of both lament and hope, a faith willing to live with unanswered questions because it has learned that trust rests not upon certainty but upon the God who remains faithful even when certainty fails.

Perhaps that is why reconstructed faith often feels both humbler and stronger than the faith that preceded it. It no longer depends upon possessing the right answer for every question. Instead, it rests upon the quiet confidence that God remains present even when answers are unavailable. If theological injury teaches us anything, it is that certainty was never the deepest foundation of faith. Trust was. And it is that trust, tested by suffering and refined through mystery, that prepares us for the journey still ahead.

## *Chapter 9*

# The God Who Remains

One of the most painful questions raised by theological injury is also one of the oldest: Where is God? It is a question that emerges in hospital rooms, disaster shelters, funeral homes, burned neighborhoods, flooded communities, emergency operations centers, and quiet bedrooms long after everyone else has gone to sleep. It arises whenever suffering becomes large enough to challenge our assumptions about how God works in the world.

For many people, theological injury begins with questions about suffering. Eventually, however, the questions become more personal. They are no longer simply asking, Why did this happen? They are asking, Where was God when it happened? That distinction matters because questions about suffering seek explanations, while questions about God seek relationship. When people experience theological injury, they often discover that many of the answers they once relied upon no longer provide comfort. Explanations that once seemed reassuring begin to feel hollow, and familiar theological formulas lose much of their power. At first, this can be deeply unsettling. If the old answers no longer work, what remains?

For some people, the answer appears to be very little. For others, however, a different discovery slowly begins to emerge. The explanations may have failed, but the relationship has not. That realization rarely arrives through argument or theological debate. More often it develops through experience, through the quiet recognition that even when understanding has disappeared, something—or rather Someone—has remained.

I remember sitting with a disaster survivor several years ago after a major response. The immediate crisis had passed, but recovery was still unfolding. She had lost far more than a house. Family photographs collected over decades had vanished. Heirlooms that connected generations had disappeared beneath debris. Familiar routines that once gave shape to ordinary life had been swept away in a matter of hours.

As we talked, she described the many things people had said in an effort to comfort her. Some assured her that God had a plan. Others insisted that everything happened for a reason. Still others promised that one day she would understand why this tragedy had occurred. She listened graciously to every one of those conversations, but eventually she looked at me and said something I have never forgotten.

"The people who helped me most weren't the ones who explained where God was."

She paused for a moment before continuing.

"They were the ones who stayed."

Over the years, I have returned to that statement again and again, not because it answered every theological question, but because it revealed something essential about suffering. When pain becomes overwhelming, presence often matters more than explanation. People may remember very little of what was said during the darkest days of their lives, but they almost always remember who remained beside them, who listened without trying to fix them, who sat quietly when words were inadequate, and who refused to leave simply because the conversation had become uncomfortable.

The longer I have served in ministry and disaster response, the more convinced I have become that this is not merely a pastoral observation. It is a profoundly theological one. Many of us learn to think about God primarily in terms of action. We ask what God is doing, why God allows certain events, or how God intervenes in human affairs. These are important questions, and Scripture itself wrestles with them repeatedly. Yet alongside those questions, the biblical story consistently presents another image of God that is just as significant.

It is the image of the God who remains.

Throughout the biblical narrative, God's presence becomes as important as God's power. The Exodus story certainly emphasizes divine action.

God delivers Israel from slavery, guides the people through the wilderness, and provides what they need for the journey. Yet one of the most significant promises is not about miraculous intervention at all. It is the promise, "I will be with you." Again and again throughout Scripture, God's presence becomes the foundation upon which hope is built.

The same pattern appears in the Psalms. Certainly the psalmists pray for deliverance, healing, justice, and rescue, but beneath all of those requests lies a deeper longing. They seek the nearness of God. "The Lord is near to the brokenhearted." "You are with me." "Do not be far from me." These prayers reveal something essential about faith. Human beings do not merely long for solutions. They long for companionship. They long to know that they have not been abandoned.

That longing becomes especially visible during seasons of suffering. Theologian Karl Rahner once suggested that the Christian of the future would be someone who had experienced God rather than merely accumulated information about God. While Rahner used the language of mysticism in a particular theological sense, his insight remains remarkably relevant. Faith ultimately depends upon encounter and relationship, not simply upon possessing correct ideas. Theological injury often exposes that reality with unusual clarity. When suffering becomes personal, information may prove inadequate. Explanations may fail. Arguments may lose much of their persuasive power. What many people discover they need most is not a better theory about God. They need God. They need relationship. They need the assurance of divine presence.

As theological injury unfolds, many people's image of God begins to change. They often become less certain about how providence operates, less confident in explanations that once seemed straightforward, and more cautious about speaking with certainty where mystery remains. Yet at the very same time, many become more aware than ever of the importance of God's presence. The God they encounter after theological injury is often less predictable than before, less easily explained, yet strangely closer. Not because every question has finally been answered, but because relationship has become more important than explanation.

This movement appears repeatedly throughout Scripture. Moses encounters God in the wilderness and discovers that the Holy One who calls him is not merely issuing instructions but promising companionship for an impossible task. Elijah, exhausted after years of conflict and ministry, finds that God is not revealed through the dramatic displays of wind, earthquake, and fire he may have expected, but through what Scripture describes as the sound of sheer silence—a gentle presence that restores rather than overwhelms. Job receives encounter before he receives understanding, and the disciples repeatedly discover that Jesus is not primarily an idea to be mastered but a companion who walks with them through confusion, disappointment, and fear. Again and again, the biblical story points toward a God who is known relationally before being understood intellectually.

This emphasis does not eliminate mystery. In many ways, it deepens it. The God who remains is not a God we fully comprehend or control. Rather, the God who remains is a God who refuses to abandon. For people living with theological injury, that distinction can become life-giving because the central question gradually begins to change. Instead of asking, "Can I explain everything God is doing?" they begin asking, "Can I trust that God remains present even when I cannot explain what God is doing?" That question does not solve suffering, remove grief, or eliminate uncertainty, but it creates space for faith to continue. Sometimes that is enough. Sometimes that is where healing quietly begins.

If the central question of theological injury is often, "Where is God?" Scripture responds in a surprising way. It does not begin with a philosophical argument or a comprehensive explanation. Instead, it tells stories of divine presence. Again and again, the Bible portrays God drawing near to people precisely when their understanding has failed.

Consider Elijah. After his dramatic victory on Mount Carmel, he flees into the wilderness exhausted, frightened, and deeply discouraged. The prophet who had stood boldly before kings now sits alone beneath a broom tree, overwhelmed by despair and convinced that he cannot continue. He even prays that his life might end. The great prophet is no longer triumphant or fearless. He is simply exhausted.

Many readers expect God's response to arrive through another spectacular demonstration of power. Instead, the story unfolds very differently. There is wind powerful enough to shatter rocks. There is an earthquake. There is fire. Yet the text repeatedly tells us that the Lord is not found in any of these displays. Finally comes the quietness, the gentle whisper, the still small voice through which Elijah encounters God. The story suggests something profound. God's presence is not always experienced through dramatic intervention. Sometimes it is encountered through quiet companionship. Sometimes it is discovered in the gentle assurance that we are not alone.

For people living with theological injury, that distinction matters deeply. Many continue waiting for certainty while God may instead be offering presence. Many continue hoping for explanations while God quietly invites them into relationship. The longing for answers is understandable, but Scripture repeatedly reminds us that God's first response to suffering is often not explanation but nearness.

The same pattern appears in the story of Job. No biblical figure wrestles more intensely with suffering than he does. Job loses his children, his wealth, his health, and the theological framework through which he once understood the world. Throughout much of the book, his friends attempt to explain his suffering. They defend a carefully ordered theological system in which suffering must always correspond to guilt and prosperity must always correspond to righteousness. Their explanations preserve their worldview, but they fail to honor Job's experience.

Anyone who has experienced theological injury understands that tension. An explanation may be internally consistent, yet no longer feel true because it no longer corresponds to reality as it has been lived. Theories that once seemed reassuring begin sounding strangely hollow when measured against actual grief.

What is remarkable is the way the book eventually reaches its turning point. When God finally speaks, readers often expect a comprehensive explanation of why Job suffered. Instead, they receive something entirely different. God does not answer every question or provide a detailed account of the reasons behind Job's losses. Rather than offering explanations, God offers encounter. The relationship is restored before the mystery is resolved.

Job's circumstances matter, and his questions matter, but the deepest transformation occurs not because he finally understands suffering but because he encounters the living God. His world remains marked by mystery, yet he is no longer alone within that mystery.

Years ago, after a particularly difficult disaster deployment, I found myself sitting alone in a hotel room late one evening. The day had been filled with stories of loss—families displaced from their homes, communities struggling to imagine recovery, and lives permanently altered by events no one could have prevented. As often happens in disaster work, the suffering felt larger than anything I could meaningfully address.

I remember praying that evening, though not eloquently or confidently. I was not searching for a brilliant theological insight or even for an explanation of suffering. I simply wanted reassurance that God had not disappeared. Nothing dramatic happened. No revelation arrived. No sudden clarity emerged. Yet as I sat quietly in that room, I became aware of something disaster survivors have taught me repeatedly over the years. It was not certainty that settled over me. It was presence.

The questions remained exactly as they had been before. The suffering I had witnessed did not become easier to understand. Yet I no longer felt alone with those questions. That experience did not solve the problem of suffering, but it profoundly reshaped my understanding of faith. Faith is not always confidence that we understand God. Sometimes faith is confidence that God remains present even when understanding fails.

This theme reaches its fullest expression in the New Testament. The Gospel writers introduce Jesus with a name that captures the heart of Christian faith: Emmanuel—God with us. The significance of that title is easy to overlook precisely because it has become so familiar. Yet within those simple words lies one of Christianity's most profound claims. God's response to human suffering is not distance but presence. It is not merely instruction, guidance, or explanation. It is God entering the human story.

That truth becomes especially important when we consider the cross. Christians have interpreted the meaning of the cross in many different ways throughout history, and those conversations continue today. Yet whatever else the cross reveals, it unmistakably portrays a God who chooses to enter human suffering rather than remain detached from it. Jesus experiences grief, betrayal, abandonment, physical pain, and death itself. The God revealed in Christ is not insulated from the brokenness of the world. The God revealed in Christ willingly participates in it.

This realization shaped much of the work of theologian Jürgen Moltmann, whose reflections on the crucifixion emphasized that Christian faith cannot portray God as distant from human pain. In the crucified Christ, Moltmann argued, we encounter a God who suffers with humanity rather than observing suffering from afar. While that insight does not answer every question raised by tragedy, it does transform the character of the God we encounter. Instead of imagining a detached deity watching events unfold from a safe distance, we meet a God who has entered the very depths of human sorrow.

For people experiencing theological injury, this can become a deeply healing discovery. Many carry an image of God as remote, uninvolved, or emotionally untouched by human suffering. When catastrophe occurs, that image often collapses under the weight of experience. What sometimes emerges in its place is a different understanding—not a God who stands outside suffering, but a God who enters it; not a God who merely observes grief, but a God who shares it; not a God who explains every tragedy, but a God who refuses to abandon those who endure tragedy.

The mystery remains, of course. The questions do not disappear, and the pain is not erased simply because God is present within it. Yet the character of God begins to look different. The focus gradually shifts from divine control to divine companionship, from explanation to presence, and from certainty to relationship. That shift does not resolve every theological question, but it offers a different place from which to ask those questions. Instead of asking them in isolation, people begin asking them in the presence of a God who remains. For many, that changes everything—not because suffering suddenly makes sense, but because suffering no longer has the final word. The final word belongs to a God who continues drawing near to wounded people even when their understanding has failed, and it is often within that nearness that faith quietly begins to heal.

One of the unexpected discoveries many people make after theological injury is that God's presence often becomes visible through other people. This realization can feel surprising because, when suffering first strikes, many individuals search for unmistakable signs of divine intervention. They hope for dramatic answers, miraculous outcomes, or clear explanations. Sometimes those things appear. More often, however, what they discover is something quieter. God's presence becomes visible through companionship, kindness, acts of care, and people who simply refuse to leave.

Over the years I have heard countless disaster survivors describe the moments that sustained them most deeply. Rarely do they begin by talking about theological explanations. They seldom remember detailed arguments about providence, suffering, or divine purpose. What they remember are people. They remember the volunteer who helped them sift through debris, the neighbor who quietly brought a meal, the shelter worker who listened without hurrying the conversation, the friend who called again and again, and the stranger who kept showing up long after the television cameras had disappeared. Again and again the stories sound remarkably similar. Someone remained. Someone cared. Someone made it possible to believe they had not been abandoned.

One particular memory has stayed with me for years. Following a disaster, I met an older man sitting quietly outside a temporary housing site. He had lost much of what he owned and faced an uncertain future. During our conversation he spoke very little about the disaster itself. Instead, he told me about a volunteer who had visited repeatedly throughout the previous week. The volunteer had not solved any major problems, offered profound advice, or attempted to explain why the disaster had happened.

"He just kept coming back," the man told me with a gentle smile. "I think that's what saved me."

His words echoed something I had heard many times before. Presence is rarely dramatic, yet it can be profoundly transformative. In many ways, this reflects one of the central patterns of Christian theology. God's presence is frequently mediated through human presence. When the Apostle Paul describes the church as the body of Christ, one implication is especially important here. God's care for people is often expressed through the actions of other people—the hands that help, the voices that encourage, and the hearts that refuse to walk away.

The church has not always remembered this. At times Christians have become so focused on explaining suffering that we have overlooked the ministry of presence. We rush toward answers when companionship is needed. We offer explanations when listening would be the more faithful response. The impulse is understandable because most of us feel uncomfortable in the presence of pain. We want to help, to fix what has been broken, and to relieve suffering as quickly as possible. Yet many experiences cannot be fixed. They can only be accompanied.

This truth has become increasingly clear to me through years of disaster spiritual care. One of the first lessons many new caregivers learn is that presence is often more important than expertise. Survivors rarely need a theological lecture in the immediate aftermath of loss. They need someone willing to listen, someone willing to sit with uncertainty, and someone willing to acknowledge pain without rushing past it. That ministry may appear simple, but it demands remarkable courage, patience, and humility. Above all, it requires resisting the temptation to make another person's suffering about our own need for certainty.

This understanding of presence has significant implications for the way we think about God and the way we understand our own calling. If God's primary response to suffering is presence, then perhaps God's people are called to embody that same response. Not every believer can explain suffering. Not every believer can resolve difficult theological questions. Not every believer can provide satisfying answers to the mysteries that accompany loss. Every believer, however, can remain present. In that sense, presence becomes a form of witness, a testimony not merely to what we believe about God but to the way God chooses to relate to wounded people.

Henri Nouwen often wrote about the ministry of presence and the importance of accompanying others in their suffering. He reminded readers that the word compassion literally means "to suffer with." Genuine care does not stand at a safe distance offering explanations. It moves toward pain rather than away from it. That observation carries profound theological significance because the God revealed in Scripture consistently moves toward wounded people. God comes to Hagar in the wilderness, to Elijah beneath the broom tree, to Job in his anguish, to Israel during exile, to frightened disciples behind locked doors, and ultimately to humanity in Jesus Christ. Again and again, God's response to suffering is not withdrawal but nearness. The God who remains is always the God who moves toward.

Many people discover this only after theological injury has stripped away older assumptions. They may lose confidence in formulas, explanations, or theological systems that once seemed secure. Yet as those certainties fall away, they begin noticing something else. They begin recognizing a quiet but persistent presence. It is not always dramatic or easily identified. Sometimes it is experienced in prayer. Sometimes it comes through worship or Scripture. Sometimes it is encountered in silence. Very often it appears through other people—a friend who listens without judgment, a caregiver who stays beyond the end of a shift, a volunteer who returns day after day, or a congregation that quietly refuses to abandon someone in grief.

These moments rarely eliminate suffering or answer every question. What they do is testify to a deeper reality. The God who remains often becomes visible through people who remain. For those recovering from theological injury, that realization can become an important source of hope. Faith may no longer rest upon possessing every answer or maintaining complete certainty. Instead, it gradually learns to recognize presence. Sometimes that presence is enough to keep faith alive until understanding catches up—or until we discover that understanding was never the point. The deeper gift has always been relationship. The deeper gift has always been companionship. The deeper gift has always been knowing that even in our most painful moments, we are not alone.

The longer I have served in ministry and disaster response, the less convinced I have become that most wounded people need better explanations. Theology matters deeply. Our beliefs shape how we understand God, suffering, hope, prayer, and the meaning of our lives. Yet there are moments when theology reaches the limits of what it can explain. There are moments when grief is too immediate, loss is too overwhelming, and questions are simply too large. In those moments, presence often becomes more powerful than explanation. That is not a weakness of faith. It may be one of faith's deepest truths.

Theological injury frequently begins when a person's understanding of God can no longer account for lived experience. Old assumptions collapse. Familiar explanations stop working. Questions multiply. At first, this feels like losing God. Over time, many people discover something unexpected. They have not lost God. They have lost an explanation of God. The distinction is crucial because explanations can fail while relationships endure.

That realization rarely arrives all at once. Most people move through seasons of uncertainty, frustration, grief, and reconstruction. Some continue wrestling with difficult questions for years. Others discover that certain questions never fully disappear. Yet amid those questions many report a growing awareness of something they had previously overlooked. They become aware of a God who continues accompanying them through the uncertainty rather than rescuing them from it. The God who remains is often not the God they expected. This God is less predictable, less manageable, and less easily explained. Yet this God is also more compassionate, more patient, and more deeply present than they had previously imagined.

Nicholas Wolterstorff wrote after the death of his son that suffering often creates a longing not for explanation but for companionship. Gerald Sittser reached a similar conclusion after losing his wife, daughter, and mother in a tragic automobile accident. Reflecting on that experience, he observed that healing does not erase suffering. Instead, life gradually grows around suffering until the wound becomes part of a larger story rather than the whole story itself. Something similar often happens in theological injury. The questions remain. The grief remains. The mystery remains. Yet faith slowly learns how to live around them—not by denying them or explaining them away, but by discovering that God's presence remains available within them.

One evening near the end of a disaster deployment, I found myself sitting in a community center where volunteers and survivors had gathered for a simple meal. Operations were beginning to wind down, but recovery still stretched far into the future. People were tired. Some were grieving. Others were anxious about what would come next. As I watched the room, I became aware that very little of the conversation involved explanations. No one was solving the problem of suffering. No one was answering every theological question. No one was constructing elaborate theories about why the disaster had occurred. Instead, people were sharing stories, passing food across tables, laughing occasionally, checking on one another, and quietly carrying the burden together.

The scene was profoundly ordinary, and precisely because of that, it felt profoundly holy.

Years later I still think about that evening whenever someone asks me where God can be found after catastrophe. I think about the conversations around those folding tables, the volunteers who lingered after the meal had ended, and the quiet determination of people who continued caring for one another even though they had no explanations to offer. It reminded me that God's presence is often discovered not through certainty but through companionship, not through arguments but through relationship, and not through distance but through nearness.

In many ways, that evening captured the heart of what I have come to believe about faith after theological injury. Healing rarely begins when every question has been answered. More often, it begins when people discover that neither God nor community has abandoned them. Theological injury can strip away illusions, dismantle assumptions, and expose the limits of certainty. Yet it can also reveal something enduring. It can reveal the God who remains, the God who accompanies, the God who enters suffering rather than avoiding it, and the God who stays.

Christians ultimately make this claim because they believe God has already chosen not to remain distant. In Jesus Christ, God entered the human story, embraced its suffering, and refused to abandon it. The God who remains is not merely an idea or a doctrine. The God who remains is the One who has already drawn near. That conviction does not eliminate mystery, remove grief, or guarantee understanding. What it offers is something many wounded people need even more than explanations. It offers companionship. It offers presence. It offers relationship.

For some readers, that conclusion may seem surprisingly modest. For others, it may prove profoundly hopeful. If faith ultimately depends upon complete understanding, many of us will eventually find ourselves without faith. If faith rests instead upon the presence of God, then even amid unanswered questions there remains a path forward. It is not always an easy path, and it is seldom a clear one, but it remains open. The questions may continue, the suffering may continue, and the mystery may continue. Yet the final word belongs neither to suffering nor to uncertainty. The final word belongs to the God who remains.

For many people recovering from theological injury, that discovery becomes the beginning of hope. As important as God's presence is, however, another question soon emerges. How do we continue walking when answers remain incomplete? How do we live faithfully when uncertainty has become part of faith itself? And who helps us make that journey?

Those are the questions to which we now turn.

# *Chapter 10*

# When Answers Are Not Enough

Most of us spend much of our lives searching for answers. We want answers when we are young because the world feels vast and unfamiliar. We want answers when we are afraid because uncertainty unsettles us. We want answers when life becomes confusing because explanations promise stability. And when suffering enters our lives, the desire for answers becomes even more urgent. We instinctively believe that if we can understand what has happened, we will somehow be better able to endure it.

That longing is entirely understandable. Answers help us make sense of the world. They create order out of apparent chaos, reduce uncertainty, and give us the reassuring sense that life remains intelligible and manageable. In many ways, our earliest experiences of faith develop in exactly this manner. We learn doctrines, memorize Scripture, receive theological instruction, and discover language for speaking about God, prayer, salvation, providence, suffering, and hope. Faith requires content. It requires language. It requires convictions capable of sustaining belief.

The difficulty arises when life presents questions that answers alone cannot resolve. There comes a point for many people when carefully learned explanations no longer seem capable of carrying the weight of lived experience. Theological injury often emerges precisely in that space, not because faith has disappeared, but because familiar answers have become too small for the realities people now face.

I remember sitting in a disaster shelter late one evening after most of the day's activity had finally subsided. The fluorescent lights still hummed overhead, casting their familiar pale glow across rows of cots and folding tables. A handful of residents lingered quietly in conversation while volunteers completed end-of-day responsibilities. The frantic pace that characterizes the first days of disaster response had slowed, yet uncertainty remained everywhere. No one knew exactly what recovery would require. No one knew how long displacement would last. Everyone carried questions that extended well beyond the practical concerns of food, shelter, and paperwork.

A woman approached and asked whether we could talk. For nearly an hour she described everything that had happened since the disaster struck. She spoke of losing her home, sorting through damaged belongings, making impossible decisions while exhausted, and trying to comfort family members even as she struggled to comfort herself. Her story unfolded with the weary cadence that often accompanies profound loss. She was not simply recounting events. She was trying to make sense of a life that no longer resembled the one she had known only days before.

Eventually she looked at me and asked a question I had heard many times over the years.

"Why did this happen?"

I recognized the question immediately, and with it came the familiar awareness that I knew many possible answers. I could have quoted passages from Scripture. I could have spoken about living in a broken world or reflected on God's providence, human freedom, or the hope of redemption. Years of theological education and pastoral ministry had given me language for addressing such questions.

Yet as we sat together beneath those humming fluorescent lights, another realization quietly settled over me. She was not asking for a lecture. She was asking for understanding.

That distinction has grown increasingly important to me over the years. Early in ministry I often assumed people came to pastors primarily because they needed answers. Seminary had trained me to think carefully, interpret Scripture responsibly, and communicate theological truth with clarity. Those remain essential responsibilities. Good theology matters, and thoughtful teaching continues to shape healthy faith. Gradually, however, experience taught me that many people who came seeking pastoral care were looking for something different from what I initially imagined.

They were not merely asking for information. More often, they were looking for someone willing to accompany them while they carried questions that had no immediate resolution. Their deepest need was not always an explanation but a companion who could remain present while explanations proved insufficient.

This realization helps explain why theological injury can become so confusing. Many people already possess answers that are technically correct. They know that God is loving. They know that God remains present in suffering. They know that the world is broken by sin and that God can bring good even from painful circumstances. None of those convictions are false, yet knowing them does not immediately relieve grief. They do not erase confusion, remove loss, or answer every question that suffering inevitably raises.

After one extended disaster response, I found myself reflecting on dozens of conversations with survivors over several weeks. Again and again people asked remarkably similar questions. Why had their community been devastated while another nearby town had been spared? Why had one family lost everything while another escaped with relatively little damage? Where had God been when lives changed in a matter of minutes?

As I thought back over those conversations, I noticed something I had previously overlooked. Very few people were actually asking for theological instruction. Most already knew the standard answers. They had heard them in churches, Bible studies, conversations with friends, and countless sermons over the years. They were not searching for additional information.

They were searching for understanding.

The difference between those two pursuits is subtle, yet profoundly important. Explanation seeks information. Understanding seeks meaning. Explanation attempts to answer a question. Understanding attempts to help us live faithfully within a reality that may never be fully explained.

That distinction changed the way I began listening to people.

I remember one woman whose home had been destroyed during a disaster. During the weeks that followed, she listened graciously as well-meaning people tried to encourage her. Some assured her that God had a larger purpose she would one day understand. Others emphasized that blessings would eventually emerge from the tragedy. Still others spoke about lessons that suffering might teach or opportunities that hardship might create.

None of those responses were necessarily wrong. Each reflected sincere attempts to offer hope. Yet none of them seemed to address the reality she was actually living.

Finally, after listening patiently, she said quietly, "I understand what they're trying to tell me. I just don't know how to live with this yet."

Her words have remained with me because they exposed the deeper question hidden beneath so many conversations about suffering. She was not asking for additional facts. She was asking how to carry a reality that had fundamentally altered her life. Beneath the theological questions lay a far more personal one.

How do I continue living when everything I believed has been shaken?

That, I have come to believe, is often the true question raised by theological injury. People are not simply asking, "What is true?" They are asking, "How do I live with what is true?" There is a profound difference between those questions, and recognizing that difference changes the way we care for wounded people. It also changes the way we understand faith itself.

Frederick Buechner once observed that doubts are "the ants in the pants of faith." They keep faith awake, unsettled, and moving forward. His familiar image reminds us that questions do not necessarily threaten belief. Sometimes they become one of the primary ways belief matures. Faith that is never questioned often remains untested. Faith that survives honest questioning frequently emerges humbler, deeper, and more resilient than before.

The Book of Job illustrates this distinction with remarkable clarity. Throughout much of the narrative, Job's friends are never at a loss for explanations. They offer carefully reasoned arguments, defend longstanding theological assumptions, and construct logical systems intended to account for Job's suffering. Their confidence is impressive. Their compassion is not. Although they speak extensively about God, they fail to understand the man sitting before them. They never fully grasp the depth of his anguish or appreciate the collapse of the world he once inhabited. Their explanations become increasingly disconnected from the reality Job is living.

The tragedy is not that everything they say is completely false. Much of it contains elements of genuine theological truth. The tragedy is that truth, separated from understanding, becomes strangely incapable of offering comfort. Their answers are logically coherent, yet emotionally hollow. Rather than helping Job carry his suffering, they unintentionally increase his isolation by insisting that his experience must fit within a system that no longer corresponds to his reality.

Anyone who has experienced theological injury recognizes this tension. There are moments when an explanation may be intellectually satisfying while remaining spiritually inadequate. The answer itself may be true, yet it somehow fails to address the actual burden the person is carrying. The difference lies not in the accuracy of the theology but in its inability to meet a wounded human being where they actually are.

Over the years I have come to appreciate the wisdom of Henri Nouwen, who frequently reminded caregivers that some forms of suffering cannot be solved. They can only be entered, shared, and accompanied. That simple observation captures one of the most important lessons ministry and disaster response have taught me. Human beings often need presence before they need explanation. Sometimes, at least for a season, they need presence instead of explanation.

This is not because truth has somehow become unimportant. Truth remains indispensable. Healthy theology matters deeply because our understanding of God shapes the way we understand ourselves, our neighbors, and the world we inhabit. Yet there are moments when truth must be carried by compassion if it is to be heard at all. Detached correctness rarely comforts a grieving parent. A carefully constructed theological argument seldom eases the heart of someone standing in the ruins of a home. Before people can receive explanations, they often need to know that they are not carrying their suffering alone.

One of the hidden temptations within religious communities is the assumption that every difficult question deserves an immediate answer. We become uncomfortable with uncertainty and instinctively move toward explanation. When someone voices confusion, we reach for familiar passages of Scripture. When someone expresses disappointment with God, we hurry to reassure them. When someone laments unanswered prayer, we often feel compelled to defend God before we have fully listened to the wounded person speaking.

Theological injury quietly challenges that instinct. It reminds us that not every question can be answered immediately, and not every answer should be offered immediately. Some questions require patient companionship before they require careful explanation. Others require lament before reassurance. Still others require silence because any attempt to explain too quickly diminishes rather than honors the reality of another person's suffering.

There are questions that remain unresolved for years, and some that may remain unresolved for an entire lifetime. A parent may never understand the death of a child. A survivor may never fully comprehend why one neighborhood was destroyed while another remained untouched. A caregiver may never discover why years of faithful prayer seemed to receive no visible answer. Living faithfully does not guarantee that every mystery will eventually become clear.

At first, this realization can feel deeply threatening. It seems to suggest that certainty will always remain incomplete. Over time, however, many people discover that acknowledging this limitation is strangely liberating. They no longer carry the impossible burden of resolving every theological tension before they can continue living. They begin to understand that faith's survival does not depend upon possessing an answer to every question that suffering raises.

This realization naturally leads to another challenge, one that theological injury eventually forces almost every believer to confront. How do we think about mystery?

For many people, mystery initially feels like failure. If we cannot explain something, we assume we have not studied hard enough or prayed deeply enough. If uncertainty remains, we conclude that our faith must somehow be deficient. We have been taught, often without realizing it, to equate maturity with increasingly complete explanations. The presence of unanswered questions therefore feels like evidence that something has gone wrong.

Life has a way of exposing the limitations of that assumption. Suffering introduces realities that resist simple formulas. Catastrophe raises questions that cannot be settled by a single Bible verse or carefully crafted theological statement. Long seasons of caregiving, repeated exposure to tragedy, institutional betrayal, or profound personal loss gradually reveal that some realities cannot be mastered through explanation alone.

In those moments, people encounter mystery.

The word itself often makes us uneasy because we confuse it with ignorance. Yet the two are very different. Ignorance is simply the absence of knowledge. Mystery is the recognition that reality exceeds our capacity to comprehend it fully. Ignorance assumes there is something we ought to know but do not. Mystery acknowledges that even genuine knowledge has limits because God and God's world are infinitely larger than our understanding.

That distinction has become increasingly important to me over the years. I no longer think mystery represents the failure of faith. More often, I have come to see it as one of the places where mature faith begins.

I remember standing with a volunteer during one deployment as we looked across a neighborhood that had been devastated by a tornado. Entire blocks had been transformed into fields of broken lumber, twisted metal, and scattered possessions. Families moved quietly through the debris, trying to recover photographs, keepsakes, and anything that might still be salvageable. Recovery teams had only begun what everyone knew would become a long and demanding process.

For several minutes neither of us spoke. The silence seemed appropriate. There are moments when words feel too small for what lies before us, and this was one of them.

Finally, the volunteer shook his head and said, "I don't understand why some families were hit so hard while others across the street lost almost nothing."

Neither did I.

The question lingered between us for a long time before he spoke again.

"I guess there are some things I'll never understand."

At the time I heard his words as an expression of resignation, as though he had given up trying to make sense of the tragedy. Looking back, I think I misunderstood him. He was not surrendering his faith. He was acknowledging its limits. What sounded like defeat was actually humility.

There is an important difference between those two postures. Resignation gives up because it believes nothing meaningful can be known. Humility continues seeking truth while recognizing that human understanding will always remain incomplete. One abandons the search. The other simply accepts that some realities exceed our ability to master them.

The longer I have spent in ministry and disaster response, the more convinced I have become that humility is one of the most important spiritual virtues people can develop after theological injury. Humility allows us to acknowledge that God's ways are often larger than our explanations. It reminds us that every theological system, no matter how carefully constructed, remains an attempt to describe a reality that ultimately surpasses human language.

This perspective is woven throughout Scripture. Isaiah reminds us that God's thoughts are not our thoughts and God's ways are not our ways. The psalmists repeatedly marvel at the vastness of creation and the mystery of God's works. The Apostle Paul speaks of seeing "through a glass, darkly," acknowledging that our understanding remains partial until the fullness of God's kingdom is revealed.

Biblical faith, in other words, has never been built upon exhaustive knowledge. It has always held together two seemingly opposite realities: deep conviction and profound mystery. Those realities are not enemies. They belong together. The Scriptures consistently call people to trust God wholeheartedly while simultaneously recognizing that no human being fully comprehends God's purposes.

Theological injury often forces us to recover that forgotten balance.

One of the mistakes many people make after suffering is assuming they must choose between absolute certainty and complete skepticism. Either every question must have a satisfying answer or nothing can be known at all. The world appears divided into only two possibilities: perfect clarity or utter confusion.

Life rarely works that way.

Most of our lives unfold somewhere between those extremes. We know some things with deep confidence while acknowledging that other questions remain unanswered. We trust certain truths because they have been confirmed by Scripture, experience, and the witness of generations before us. At the same time, we recognize that many aspects of God's providence remain beyond our understanding.

Mature faith learns to inhabit that tension rather than trying to escape it.

Karl Rahner suggested that genuine faith ultimately involves encounter with a reality infinitely greater than ourselves. Such encounters do not eliminate mystery. They deepen it. The closer people draw to God, the more aware they often become of the vastness that still lies beyond their comprehension. What initially appears to be uncertainty gradually becomes reverence.

Spiritual director Gerald May expressed a similar conviction. He believed that authentic spiritual growth involves learning to live faithfully within uncertainty while remaining open to God's presence. The goal of the spiritual life is not perfect control or complete understanding. It is growing trust amid life's inevitable ambiguities.

This realization gradually changes the character of faith.

Instead of demanding mastery, faith begins cultivating wonder.

Wonder differs from certainty in important ways. Certainty seeks final conclusions. Wonder remains open to discovery. Certainty often closes the conversation. Wonder continues asking questions without anxiety. Certainty attempts to control mystery. Wonder receives mystery as an invitation to deeper relationship.

Theological injury has a remarkable way of stripping away the illusion that we can master God through explanation. At first this feels like devastating loss. Familiar systems collapse. Long-held assumptions no longer seem adequate. People often grieve not only what has happened but also the loss of the confidence they once possessed.

Over time, however, many discover that something unexpected has emerged from the rubble.

Freedom.

They no longer feel responsible for defending answers they do not possess. They no longer exhaust themselves trying to explain every tragedy or reconcile every unanswered prayer. Instead, they become free to acknowledge uncertainty honestly while continuing to trust faithfully. That freedom often brings a surprising sense of peace.

I have met many people who spent years carrying the impossible burden of resolving questions that simply could not be resolved. They believed faith required certainty, so every unanswered question felt like a personal failure. Every lingering doubt became evidence that something was wrong with either their faith or with themselves.

Eventually, some discovered another possibility.

Perhaps faith is not the absence of mystery.

Perhaps faith is learning to trust within mystery.

That realization does not erase grief, nor does it eliminate every difficult question. The losses remain real. The uncertainty remains real. Yet something changes in the person's relationship to those realities. They no longer experience every unanswered question as a threat to faith itself. Instead, unanswered questions become part of the landscape through which faith continues to travel.

For many people recovering from theological injury, that shift marks the beginning of genuine healing. They stop measuring the strength of their faith by the completeness of their explanations. Instead, they begin measuring it by their willingness to continue trusting God when explanations remain incomplete.

The questions do not disappear.

They simply no longer occupy the center.

God does.

The realization that faith can live within mystery naturally raises another question. How do we continue when answers remain incomplete? Most people can tolerate uncertainty for a little while. The greater challenge comes when uncertainty lingers. Days become months, months become years, and the explanation we hoped would arrive never does. Life continues moving forward while the deepest questions remain unanswered.

This is often where theological injury becomes most difficult. The problem is not simply that answers are unavailable. The problem is that life must still be lived in their absence. People must continue making decisions, caring for families, serving communities, loving neighbors, and praying to a God they do not always understand. The unanswered questions become part of the landscape through which they travel rather than obstacles that can simply be removed.

Many people assume that living with unresolved questions inevitably leads to cynicism. Certainly that can happen. Some become bitter. Others grow disillusioned. A few eventually conclude that faith itself has become impossible. Yet over the years I have watched many people move in a very different direction. Rather than becoming hardened, they have become gentler. Rather than becoming defensive, they have become more patient. Rather than insisting upon certainty, they have learned compassion for others who also struggle.

Some of the wisest people I have ever known carried unanswered questions they expected to take with them for the rest of their lives. They had buried children, endured devastating illnesses, survived disasters, or spent decades caring for loved ones whose suffering never seemed to end. They did not pretend these experiences made sense. They did not claim to possess explanations that satisfied every theological difficulty. Instead, they had learned something quieter and, I believe, more profound. They had learned how to remain faithful without requiring complete understanding.

I once visited with a retired pastor whose decades of ministry had taken him through every imaginable season of congregational life. He had officiated at countless weddings and funerals, celebrated baptisms, walked with families through tragedy, and accompanied people through questions that neither of us could fully answer. As we reflected on his years in ministry, he smiled and said, "When I was younger, I thought my job was to answer people's questions. Now I think my job was to help people carry them."

I have never forgotten those words because they describe a transformation that occurs not only in ministry but in faith itself. Spiritual maturity often involves moving from solving mysteries to helping people live faithfully within them. Looking back over my own years in pastoral ministry and disaster response, I recognize the same change taking place in me. Early on, I felt responsible for providing answers. Whenever someone came with difficult questions, I assumed my task was to explain, clarify, and resolve. There remains great value in thoughtful teaching and careful theology, and I continue to believe both are essential.

Experience, however, taught me that many burdens cannot be lifted by explanation alone. A grieving parent did not need another theological argument. A disaster survivor rarely needed a carefully reasoned theory. A caregiver overwhelmed by years of responsibility did not need a lecture on providence. More often than not, they needed someone willing to remain beside them while they carried questions that had no immediate resolution.

That realization changed not only the way I practiced ministry but also the way I understood faith itself.

The Scriptures reveal this same pattern repeatedly. The Psalms are filled with unanswered questions. The prophets often speak from places of uncertainty and disappointment. Even the disciples spend much of the Gospels misunderstanding what Jesus is doing. Yet through all of these stories, one reality remains remarkably consistent. The questions continue, but so does the relationship. The uncertainty remains, but so does God's faithfulness. The journey moves forward even when understanding does not.

Theological injury often becomes a source of wisdom because it teaches people to distinguish between what is essential and what is merely desirable. Many concerns that once seemed absolutely necessary gradually lose their urgency. The need to explain everything. The need to eliminate every tension. The need to possess certainty before acting faithfully. These ambitions slowly loosen their grip.

In their place, other priorities begin to emerge. Compassion becomes more important than winning arguments. Humility becomes more valuable than appearing certain. Patience, faithfulness, kindness, and presence gradually move toward the center of spiritual life. People begin paying greater attention to how they live than to whether they can answer every theological question.

This does not diminish the importance of theology. Theology remains indispensable because it shapes the way we understand God, ourselves, and the world. What changes is theology's purpose. Instead of functioning primarily as a system designed to eliminate uncertainty, it becomes a framework that helps people navigate uncertainty faithfully. That is a very different task. One seeks certainty. The other cultivates wisdom.

The Book of Proverbs repeatedly associates wisdom with humility because the wise recognize the boundaries of human knowledge. The foolish imagine those boundaries do not exist. Theological injury often forces people to confront those boundaries. At first the experience feels like failure because cherished assumptions have collapsed. Over time, however, it often becomes the beginning of genuine growth.

Dallas Willard frequently emphasized that spiritual formation occurs through daily practices of trust and obedience rather than through intellectual mastery alone. Faith matures not merely because we understand more but because we gradually learn to live differently. That insight becomes especially important after theological injury. People may never receive every answer they seek, but they can continue choosing faithfulness. They can continue praying. They can continue serving. They can continue practicing compassion and extending mercy.

I remember speaking with a volunteer after an especially difficult day on one disaster deployment. We had spent hours listening to stories of grief, uncertainty, and profound loss. As we prepared to leave for the evening, he quietly said, "I don't know why any of this happened. But I know these people shouldn't have to face it alone."

I have reflected on that statement many times. He acknowledged uncertainty without surrendering responsibility. He admitted what he did not know while remaining fully committed to what he could do. In many ways, that simple observation captures the healthiest response to theological injury. Not certainty. Not resignation. Faithful presence.

People recovering from theological injury may never understand everything they wish they understood. Some questions will remain unanswered. Some mysteries will never be fully resolved this side of eternity. Yet they can still choose compassion. They can still choose kindness. They can still choose faithfulness. They can still choose love. Those choices do not eliminate mystery, but they do provide a faithful way of living within it.

Over time, many discover that unanswered questions are not the greatest challenge of faith. The greater challenge is learning how to live well in their presence.

As I look back over years of ministry and disaster response, I realize I still carry questions I cannot answer. I remember names, faces, conversations, and moments when I desperately wished explanations had been available. Earlier in life I assumed faith depended upon resolving such questions. Experience has taught me something different. Faith has survived those questions. In some ways, it has grown because of them. The questions remain, but they no longer occupy the center of my spiritual life.

God does.

I think often of a woman I visited several months after a disaster response had ended. Recovery was progressing, but the future remained uncertain. Homes were still being rebuilt, financial pressures continued, and many decisions still lay ahead. When I asked how she was doing, she smiled thoughtfully and said, "I still have questions. I probably always will. But I don't wake up every morning needing answers anymore."

Driving away from that conversation, I realized she had taught me something no classroom ever could. She was not dismissing the importance of questions. She was describing what happens when life becomes larger than explanation. At some point, continuing to live faithfully becomes more important than continuing to solve every mystery.

There is remarkable wisdom in that realization. Much of life is lived one step at a time rather than one explanation at a time. Faith often grows in exactly the same way. Eugene Peterson described discipleship as "a long obedience in the same direction," and his words capture something essential about reconstructed faith. People continue walking. They continue praying. They continue loving. They continue trusting, even when answers remain incomplete.

Theological injury often strips away the illusion that faith is sustained primarily by explanation. What remains can feel frightening at first. Eventually, however, many discover something profoundly liberating. Faith was never carried by answers alone. Answers teach, guide, clarify, and illuminate, but they cannot bear the full weight of a lifetime. Only relationship can do that. Only trust can do that. Only the continuing experience of God's presence can sustain faith when explanations reach their limits.

Seen in that light, theology assumes its proper place. Theology serves relationship; relationship does not serve theology. We seek understanding because we long to know God more deeply. We do not know God merely so that we can possess understanding. That distinction transforms unanswered questions from threats into invitations—invitations to humility, to trust, and to a deeper dependence upon the God who remains faithful even when our understanding does not.

Theological injury often begins with questions. Somewhat surprisingly, the journey toward healing also ends with questions. The difference is that the questions no longer occupy the center of the story. God does. The questions remain. The relationship remains. And in the end, the relationship proves stronger.

For many people, that becomes one of the most important lessons wounded faith can teach. Not every mystery will be solved. Not every answer will arrive. Not every wound will fully heal. Yet faith can continue. Hope can continue. Love can continue.

And sometimes that is more than enough.

It is the beginning of wisdom.

It is the practice of trust.

It is the quiet, enduring faith that emerges when answers are no longer enough.

## *Chapter 11*

# The Ministry of Presence

One of the most important lessons theological injury teaches is surprisingly simple: people do not always need answers. More often than we realize, they need companions. After years of ministry and disaster response, I have become increasingly convinced that presence is one of the most underestimated forms of care available to us. We frequently assume that helping requires solving problems, providing explanations, or offering advice. Those responses certainly have their place, but many of life's deepest wounds resist repair. They cannot be solved in the ordinary sense of the word. They can only be accompanied.

This truth became clear to me through countless conversations with disaster survivors. Again and again, I found myself asking people what had helped them most during the difficult days following a tornado, flood, wildfire, or other catastrophe. Rarely did they mention a theological explanation, a carefully crafted argument, or a particular piece of advice that had changed everything. Instead, they remembered people. They remembered the volunteer who quietly listened without interrupting, the neighbor who stopped by every afternoon to check on them, the shelter worker who pulled up a chair and stayed longer than necessary, the pastor who called repeatedly over the weeks that followed, and the friend who simply refused to disappear when the initial crisis had passed.

The individual stories differed in countless details, yet the pattern remained remarkably consistent. What people remembered most clearly was not what someone had said but the fact that someone had shown up. Someone had remained. Someone had cared enough to enter their suffering rather than observing it from a comfortable distance.

In many ways, this should not surprise Christians. The ministry of presence lies at the very heart of the biblical story. Again and again, Scripture portrays God not merely as one who acts on behalf of humanity but as one who accompanies humanity through every season of life. God walks with Adam and Eve in the garden, journeys with Israel through the wilderness, remains present with exiles far from home, draws near to Elijah beneath the broom tree when exhaustion overwhelms him, and refuses to abandon Job in the midst of questions that never receive complete answers. Ultimately, the biblical story reaches its fulfillment in Jesus Christ, whose very identity is announced with the name Emmanuel—God with us.

The Christian faith is therefore not simply a story about divine intervention. It is fundamentally a story about divine presence. Before God explains, God accompanies. Before God resolves every mystery, God enters the human story and remains within it. That truth carries profound implications for those who seek to care for wounded people. If God's response to suffering so often takes the form of presence, then perhaps ours should as well.

The idea sounds beautifully simple until we attempt to practice it. Most people are deeply uncomfortable around pain. We instinctively want to help, to fix, and to make things better. When confronted with suffering, we often experience an almost irresistible urge to say something—anything—that might relieve another person's discomfort. Silence feels awkward. Uncertainty feels inadequate. Remaining present without offering solutions can feel like doing nothing at all.

Yet many wounded people do not need immediate explanations nearly as much as they need someone willing to remain beside them long enough to understand what they are experiencing. They need someone who is willing to resist the temptation to hurry the conversation toward resolution before the story has fully been told.

One of the most difficult lessons I learned as a disaster spiritual care provider was that presence often matters more than expertise. Early in my disaster-response work, I frequently felt pressure to find exactly the right words. I worried about saying the wrong thing, searched my memory for meaningful Scripture passages, and rehearsed possible responses before approaching survivors. I assumed that effective spiritual care depended largely upon knowing what to say.

Looking back, I realize I carried exactly the same assumption into parish ministry years earlier. Like many young pastors, I believed people came to clergy primarily because they were searching for answers. I worked diligently to prepare sermons, study theology, and respond thoughtfully to difficult questions because I assumed that clear explanations were among the greatest gifts I could offer. Those responsibilities remain important, and I continue to believe careful theological reflection matters deeply. Over time, however, experience taught me something seminary alone could not.

Many people who sought pastoral care were not primarily looking for explanations.

They were looking for companionship.

They needed someone willing to sit beside them while the answers remained elusive. They needed someone who did not feel compelled to rescue them from uncertainty before fully entering their experience. Gradually I began to understand that pastoral care was often less about solving theological problems and more about sharing the burden of living with them.

That realization transformed not only my understanding of ministry but also my understanding of faith itself. The longer I served, the more convinced I became that most people are less interested in having every question answered than in knowing they do not have to carry those questions alone. The ministry of presence begins precisely there. It begins not with expertise, not with certainty, but with companionship. It begins with the simple yet demanding willingness to remain.

One of the persistent misconceptions about spiritual care is the belief that effective caregivers possess extraordinary wisdom unavailable to everyone else. Pastors, chaplains, counselors, and spiritual care providers are sometimes imagined to have answers hidden from ordinary people, as though years of experience eventually produce the perfect response for every difficult situation.

My experience has been almost the opposite.

Again and again, I have discovered that the most meaningful moments of care are built from remarkably ordinary acts of attention. They emerge through an unhurried conversation, a thoughtful question, a period of shared silence, or the simple decision to remain present a little longer than convenience might suggest. Those moments rarely appear dramatic from the outside. Yet they often become the moments people remember years later.

During disaster responses I frequently watched survivors begin conversations intending to discuss only practical concerns. They would describe damage to a home, difficulties with insurance, or uncertainty about temporary housing. Gradually, however, the conversation would shift. A damaged photograph would become a story about a parent who had died years earlier. A ruined piece of furniture would become a memory of raising children. What initially appeared to concern property slowly revealed itself to concern identity, family, belonging, and love.

The visible damage had never been the whole story.

That realization has remained with me because it explains why presence matters so deeply. People often do not fully understand what they themselves are carrying until they are given the opportunity to speak about it. Listening creates that opportunity. It allows experiences to unfold naturally rather than forcing them into predetermined categories. It helps people hear their own stories in new ways, sometimes discovering griefs, fears, or hopes they had not fully recognized until they found someone willing to listen.

Years ago, I assumed good pastoral care meant saying the right thing at exactly the right moment. While thoughtful words certainly have their place, experience gradually taught me a different lesson. People rarely remember our most eloquent explanations. They remember whether they felt heard. They remember whether someone remained long enough for the truth to emerge.

Over the years I have occasionally encountered disaster survivors months or even years after a response had ended. Very few remembered specific things I had said during our conversations. Most could not have repeated a Scripture passage I shared or summarized any theological reflection we discussed. What they remembered instead was the experience of being listened to. They remembered that someone treated them with dignity rather than as another case to be processed. They remembered that someone cared enough to slow down, to stay present, and to hear their story without trying to rush them toward recovery before they were ready.

Those encounters reinforced an important lesson that has continued to shape both my ministry and my understanding of theological injury. Presence is not a preliminary step before ministry begins. Presence is the ministry. It is not merely preparation for the "real work" of caregiving. It is often the very place where healing quietly begins.

That lesson became clearer with every passing year in congregational ministry and disaster response. Spiritual care training often emphasizes active listening, a phrase so familiar that it can easily lose its meaning. At first glance the concept appears almost self-evident. Everyone assumes they know how to listen. Genuine listening, however, requires a discipline that most of us must learn slowly. It involves temporarily setting aside our own assumptions, our own agendas, and our own need to provide solutions so that another person's experience can occupy the center of our attention.

That is far more difficult than it sounds.

Most of us naturally listen with the intention of responding. Even while another person is speaking, we find ourselves preparing advice, searching for appropriate Scripture, remembering similar experiences, or planning what we hope will be a helpful reply. Caregivers must gradually learn a different way of listening. They learn to listen not primarily in order to respond but in order to understand.

The distinction may appear subtle, but it changes the entire character of a conversation. Listening in order to respond often moves us quickly toward advice. Listening in order to understand moves us toward compassion. One approach seeks solutions. The other seeks connection. For people living with theological injury, connection is frequently the deeper need.

Individuals wrestling with faith-related questions are seldom looking for a theological debate. They are rarely interested in defending or attacking particular doctrines. Much more often they are attempting to make sense of experiences that have disrupted their understanding of God, themselves, or the world they thought they knew. Before they can explore new theological possibilities, they need someone willing to honor the reality of what they have lived through.

What they need first is not correction.

What they need first is accompaniment.

I remember speaking with a responder after a particularly difficult deployment. We sat together after operations had slowed for the evening while the rest of the team gradually drifted back toward their lodging. He described scenes that continued replaying in his mind long after each day had ended and questions he found himself asking that he had never expected to ask. As he spoke, his voice eventually grew quiet. He stared at the floor for several moments, and neither of us felt compelled to interrupt the silence.

Finally he looked up and said, almost with surprise, "Thank you for not trying to fix this."

His comment caught me off guard because I had not done very much—or at least that was how it seemed to me. I had asked a few questions. I had listened. I had remained quiet when words seemed unnecessary. I left the conversation wondering whether I had offered anything of real value.

Only later did I realize that something important had happened. He had been given permission to speak honestly without immediately being redirected toward a solution. No one had tried to minimize his experience, reassure him prematurely, or move him too quickly toward resolution. For that brief time, being heard mattered more than being advised.

Experiences like that have profoundly shaped my understanding of ministry. They have convinced me that presence is anything but passive. Remaining fully attentive to another person's pain requires emotional courage, patience, humility, and discipline. It demands that we resist the temptation to become experts in another person's life. Instead of assuming responsibility for solving every problem, we become companions willing to walk beside someone through terrain neither of us can fully control.

Companions do not carry another person's journey for them. They simply refuse to let that person travel alone.

This truth appears repeatedly throughout Scripture. Again and again God declines to provide complete explanations for suffering, yet God repeatedly offers something equally important: divine presence. The wilderness journey, the years of exile, the prayers of lament, and ultimately the incarnation itself all point toward the same remarkable reality. God remains. Not every question receives an answer. Not every mystery is resolved.

Not every wound is immediately healed. Yet throughout the biblical story God refuses to abandon wounded people.

The ministry of presence becomes a living reflection of that divine pattern. We accompany because God accompanies. We remain because God remains. We sit with uncertainty because God continues meeting humanity within uncertainty. Through those quiet acts of faithfulness, people often begin discovering that healing does not always arrive through explanation. Sometimes it begins through the simple realization that they no longer have to suffer alone.

As the years passed, I noticed that the moments I remembered most vividly from ministry rarely involved profound insights or eloquent sermons. They involved attention, listening, compassion, and silence. Again and again, the experiences that stayed with me were those in which another human being entrusted me with a story that needed to be heard more than it needed to be solved.

One afternoon I spent nearly an hour sitting with a man whose home had been destroyed. He described not only the physical damage but also the countless memories attached to the things he had lost. Family photographs, children's artwork, furniture built by his father, and keepsakes gathered over decades all became part of a much larger story about identity, belonging, and love. As he spoke, I found myself wishing there were something practical I could offer that might ease the weight he was carrying.

When our conversation ended, I walked away wondering whether I had helped at all. I had offered no solutions, answered no major theological questions, and provided no strategy capable of restoring what had been taken from him. I had simply listened.

As he prepared to leave, however, he paused, turned toward me, and quietly said, "Thank you for letting me tell my story."

That brief sentence taught me something I have never forgotten.

People often carry experiences that need witnesses more than explanations.

That conversation stayed with me because it revealed something I have seen repeatedly in ministry and disaster response. Stories have a way of restoring dignity. When people experience profound loss, they often feel that control has been taken from them. Disasters, illnesses, betrayals, and unexpected tragedies can leave individuals feeling powerless, as though the narrative of their lives has been seized by forces beyond their control. The opportunity to tell their story does not erase what happened, but it allows them to reclaim ownership of their experience. They are no longer merely victims of an event. They become witnesses to their own lives.

This insight is echoed by physician and author Rachel Naomi Remen, who distinguishes between helping, fixing, and serving. Fixing assumes something is broken and needs to be repaired by someone with greater expertise. Serving, by contrast, recognizes the wholeness that remains even in the midst of suffering. Her perspective reminds caregivers that our primary calling is not always to repair another person's life but to honor the humanity that continues to exist within it. Presence often accomplishes that more effectively than problem-solving ever could.

Theological injury frequently creates exactly this kind of need. People wrestle with questions about God, prayer, justice, suffering, forgiveness, and meaning. Sometimes they voice those questions openly. More often they carry them quietly, uncertain whether anyone else could understand. Many fear their doubts will be interpreted as unbelief. Others worry that their uncertainty will disappoint family members, church leaders, or trusted friends. Some simply conclude that no one else has ever felt the way they do.

The ministry of presence quietly challenges that isolation by communicating a simple but profoundly important truth: you do not have to carry this alone.

I have watched that truth unfold countless times during disaster responses. Survivors often begin conversations cautiously. They describe insurance forms, damaged property, temporary housing, or the endless practical decisions that follow catastrophe. Gradually, however, deeper concerns begin surfacing. Questions about fear, grief, guilt, faith, regret, and hope emerge as trust develops. The visible losses become a doorway into the invisible ones.

Rarely does this happen because someone has offered the perfect theological answer.

Much more often it happens because someone has listened long enough for honesty to become possible.

Henri Nouwen wrote extensively about accompanying people through pain, suggesting that the deepest forms of care arise not from expertise but from the willingness to enter another person's experience with humility and compassion. Parker Palmer expresses a similar conviction, arguing that one of the greatest gifts we can offer another person is a respectful, non-intrusive presence that creates space for truth to emerge naturally rather than forcing it into predetermined conclusions. Both writers remind us that authentic care is less about directing another person's journey than about faithfully sharing it.

Presence, then, is anything but passive. Listening requires sustained attention. Patience demands emotional discipline. Compassion asks us to remain engaged even when another person's pain awakens our own discomfort. Few forms of ministry require greater courage than remaining beside someone whose suffering cannot be quickly resolved.

Silence is often one of the hardest disciplines for caregivers to learn. Most of us instinctively want to fill every pause with reassurance, encouragement, explanation, or advice. Sometimes those responses are appropriate. At other times they interrupt something sacred that is beginning to unfold. Silence can communicate realities that words often cannot express. It quietly says, "I am listening. I am not leaving. You do not need to protect me from your pain. You are safe enough here to tell the truth."

Learning to become comfortable with silence took me years. Early in ministry I frequently interpreted silence as failure. If conversation slowed, I assumed I needed to ask another question or offer another observation. Experience gradually taught me otherwise. Some of the most meaningful moments of care occur precisely when another person realizes that no performance is required. They discover they do not have to entertain the conversation, defend their emotions, or reach reassuring conclusions before they are ready.

The courage to tell the truth is often where healing begins.

One of the greatest gifts presence offers is permission. When people genuinely feel heard, they often become willing to acknowledge thoughts and emotions they have been carrying in isolation for months or even years. Grief that has remained hidden begins finding words. Doubts that have been carefully concealed are finally spoken aloud. Anger, disappointment, fear, and confusion no longer need to remain locked behind polite religious language.

The emotions themselves are not new.

What changes is that they no longer have to remain hidden.

This matters because theological injury thrives in isolation. Questions that are never spoken tend to grow heavier. Doubts that remain secret often become more frightening than they really are. People begin imagining they are alone in their struggles because no one around them seems willing to admit similar experiences. The silence itself deepens the wound.

The ministry of presence interrupts that cycle. It creates an environment where honesty becomes possible and where people gradually discover that questions do not automatically destroy faith. Powerful emotions do not automatically weaken belief. Struggle does not necessarily indicate spiritual failure. Sometimes struggle is simply one expression of what it means to be fully human before God.

I remember sitting beside a hospital bed with a family waiting for news everyone feared might soon arrive. Very little needed to be said. No theological explanation would have improved the moment. No carefully chosen words could have removed the uncertainty that filled the room. We prayed occasionally, but mostly we waited together in quiet companionship.

Looking back, I remember almost nothing that was spoken during those long hours.

What I remember is presence.

Years later I have become convinced that presence was precisely the ministry that family needed most. It did not erase their fear, but it reminded them that fear did not have to be carried alone.

I remember another afternoon spent in a funeral home before a memorial service. Family members sat quietly, exhausted by grief and overwhelmed by the countless practical responsibilities that accompany death. They did not need another lecture about heaven or a carefully reasoned explanation of suffering. They needed someone willing to sit with them while the weight of loss slowly settled over the room.

Presence was not a substitute for ministry.

Presence was the ministry.

Scripture repeatedly affirms this same reality. The psalmists question God with astonishing honesty. Jeremiah protests. Habakkuk argues. Job demands explanations. Even Jesus cries out from the cross. The Bible contains remarkably little pressure to pretend that faith eliminates emotional struggle. Instead, it repeatedly invites honesty before God.

That invitation can become profoundly healing for people living with theological injury.

Over the years I have noticed that healing often begins the moment people stop trying to protect God from their questions. They stop censoring their prayers. They stop filtering every emotion through what they imagine faithful people are supposed to feel. They stop performing certainty.

They begin telling the truth.

Not because the truth is easy.

Because the truth is necessary.

One of the most sacred responsibilities of a pastor, chaplain, caregiver, or trusted friend is creating the kind of space where that truth can emerge safely. Doing so requires humility because it means acknowledging that we are not responsible for controlling another person's spiritual journey. It requires patience because healing rarely unfolds according to our preferred timetable. Most of all, it requires trust—trust that people do not need to be rescued from every difficult emotion, trust that honest faith is stronger than artificial certainty, and trust that God is fully capable of receiving the questions people bring without becoming threatened by them.

I learned this lesson repeatedly during disaster responses. Survivors often apologized before expressing anger, disappointment, or doubt.

"I know I shouldn't feel this way."

"I probably shouldn't say this."

"I don't want to sound ungrateful."

Again and again I watched people visibly relax when they discovered that no one intended to judge them for telling the truth. Shoulders lowered. Voices softened. Tears finally came. Nothing about their circumstances had changed, yet something important had happened. Their questions had not been answered, but they no longer had to carry them in isolation.

Several months after one disaster, I met with a survivor whose recovery was progressing far more slowly than she had hoped. During our conversation she admitted, almost reluctantly, that she was still angry—angry about the losses, angry about the disruption of her life, and angry with God. After saying those words she looked at me nervously and asked, "Is it okay to say that?"

I smiled and answered as honestly as I could.

"The Bible contains an entire book called Psalms."

She laughed.

Then she cried.

Nothing in that conversation solved her questions or erased her grief. What it accomplished was something equally important. It created space where honesty no longer had to compete with faith. She discovered that truthful prayer and genuine trust were not enemies after all.

The philosopher Martin Buber argued that authentic human encounters occur when we meet one another as persons rather than as problems requiring solutions. That insight has profound implications for spiritual care. Presence begins when we recognize another person's full humanity instead of viewing them primarily as someone who needs to be repaired. We encounter an individual whose life carries dignity even amid confusion, sorrow, or doubt.

The ministry of presence offers many gifts, but perhaps its greatest gift is permission. It gives people permission to be honest about grief, fear, disappointment, doubt, anger, and hope. It assures them that they do not need to hide the most difficult parts of their experience in order to remain welcome before God or within the community of faith.

Again and again I have seen honesty become the doorway through which healing quietly enters.

Theological injury is rarely repaired through arguments. More often it begins healing through relationships. Someone listens. Someone remains. Someone creates enough space for truth to emerge without trying to manage it. Within that space wounded people often discover something surprising. God was never threatened by their questions. God was never frightened by their anger. God was never driven away by their doubts. The relationship endured even when certainty did not.

For many people that realization becomes a turning point in the long journey toward healing. They begin trusting again, not because every uncertainty has disappeared, but because they discover that honesty and faith can coexist. The God they encounter is not fragile. God does not require carefully edited prayers or emotionally sanitized worship. The God revealed throughout Scripture welcomes people who come with lament as well as praise, with confusion as well as confidence.

The ministry of presence does not eliminate suffering. It does not remove mystery or answer every question. What it does is remind wounded people that they are not alone. In a culture that measures effectiveness by visible results, that may sound surprisingly modest. We naturally want wounds healed, problems solved, and questions resolved. Presence can appear small by comparison.

Yet some of the most important moments in human life cannot be measured by outcomes alone.

A hand gently held beside a hospital bed.

A friend who sits quietly after a funeral.

A volunteer who patiently listens to a survivor's story.

A pastor who remains present through a season of doubt without demanding quick resolution.

None of those moments necessarily changes external circumstances.

They often transform how those circumstances are experienced.

The difference matters.

Theological injury frequently leaves people feeling abandoned—abandoned by institutions, communities, leaders, certainty, and sometimes even by God. Loneliness often becomes one of the deepest dimensions of the wound. Presence speaks directly to that loneliness, not by denying it or arguing against it, but by entering it.

This is one reason the incarnation stands at the very heart of Christian faith. In Jesus Christ, God does not respond to human suffering from a safe distance. God enters the human story completely, embracing grief, betrayal, loss, injustice, pain, and death. The Christian proclamation is not merely that God understands suffering intellectually. It is that God has chosen to participate in it.

Jürgen Moltmann emphasized this reality in his reflections on the suffering of God. The God revealed in Christ is not detached from human pain but fully present within it. That insight becomes especially important for those living with theological injury because it gradually changes the question. Instead of asking only, "Why did this happen?" people begin asking, "Where is God within this?" Scripture's answer remains remarkably consistent. God is near. Not always in the way we expect. Not always in the way we desire. But near nonetheless.

I have witnessed this repeatedly during disaster response. Near the conclusion of one deployment, volunteers and survivors gathered for a simple evening meal. Recovery was far from complete. Homes still needed repair, insurance claims remained unresolved, and families were struggling to imagine what the months ahead might hold. Yet around those tables people shared food, exchanged stories, checked on one another, and laughed occasionally despite everything they had endured.

The scene was profoundly ordinary.

It was also profoundly holy.

No one was solving the problem of suffering. No one was offering comprehensive theological explanations. Yet healing was quietly taking place because people were no longer carrying their burdens alone. Kenneth Doka has often observed that grieving people need companions more than solutions. Disaster work confirmed that lesson repeatedly. Survivors seldom remembered the exact words I spoke. They remembered that someone listened, someone prayed, and someone stayed long enough to hear their story.

When I look back over more than three decades of ministry, I rarely remember the sermons that once seemed especially successful or the meetings that felt urgent at the time. Many administrative decisions that once occupied enormous amounts of energy have long since faded from memory.

What remains are people.

I remember conversations in hospital rooms late at night. I remember families gathered quietly in funeral homes. I remember disaster shelters filled with uncertainty. I remember kitchen tables where painful truths were spoken aloud for the first time. I remember recovery centers where survivors struggled to imagine life beyond overwhelming loss.

Most of all, I remember the extraordinary privilege of being invited into those stories.

Those experiences have convinced me that presence is never a small thing. It is one of the primary ways love becomes visible. Maya Angelou once observed that people may forget what we said and forget what we did, but they will never forget how we made them feel. Although she was not writing about theological injury, her insight captures something essential about caregiving. People remember being accompanied. They remember being seen. They remember being heard.

Perhaps that is why the ministry of presence remains so powerful. It embodies the very truth it proclaims. The God who remains is reflected through people who remain. The God who accompanies is revealed through people who accompany. The God who listens becomes visible through people who genuinely listen.

In that sense, presence becomes far more than a caregiving technique. It becomes a theological practice—a lived expression of faith and a quiet witness to divine companionship. For people recovering from theological injury, that witness may be among the greatest gifts the church can offer. Not certainty. Not explanations. Not solutions. Simply the willingness to stay, to listen, and to walk beside another person when the path ahead remains uncertain.

Long after people forget our advice, they often remember something far more important.

They remember who remained.

They remember who listened.

They remember who stayed.

And in those quiet acts of faithfulness, the ministry of presence becomes more than ministry.

It becomes a living witness to the God who remains.

## *Chapter 12*

# The Slow Work of Restoration

One of the most difficult truths about healing is that it rarely happens as quickly as we would like. When people experience theological injury, they naturally hope for a moment when everything suddenly makes sense again. They imagine a breakthrough conversation, a profound spiritual experience, or a decisive insight that resolves their questions and restores the confidence they once possessed. Occasionally such moments occur, but far more often healing unfolds gradually. Restoration advances through ordinary days rather than dramatic breakthroughs and through quiet acts of faithfulness rather than unforgettable moments of revelation.

In many ways, this should not surprise us. Theological injury is seldom created overnight. More often it develops through accumulated experiences that slowly reshape a person's understanding of God and the world. Unanswered prayers, painful losses, difficult decisions, repeated exposure to suffering, disappointments within communities of faith, moral compromises forced by impossible circumstances, and the gradual erosion of assumptions that once seemed secure all leave their mark over time. If the wound itself develops slowly, it is only natural that healing should follow a similar pattern. Restoration is ordinarily less like recovering from a broken bone and more like the slow strengthening of muscles after a long illness. Progress is real, but it often becomes visible only in retrospect.

This pace can be deeply frustrating because we live in a culture that prizes speed. We want immediate results, measurable improvement, and visible evidence that things are getting better. We expect healing to feel dramatic, and when it does not, we are tempted to conclude that nothing is happening. Yet some of the most significant forms of growth occur beneath the surface, hidden from immediate observation. Roots spread quietly long before branches reach toward the sky. Trust often begins returning before confidence does. Hope frequently emerges while certainty still feels distant. The deepest transformations of the soul usually begin in places that neither we nor anyone else can readily see.

I learned this lesson repeatedly through years of disaster response. In the immediate aftermath of a catastrophe, attention naturally focuses on urgent needs. Families require shelter, food, medical care, information, and practical assistance. Volunteers clear debris, distribute supplies, establish shelters, and help communities stabilize. The damage is obvious, and the work that follows is necessarily immediate. News organizations document these early efforts, and the public watches communities begin the long road toward recovery.

The deeper work, however, begins only after the cameras have disappeared. Weeks after volunteers return home and public attention shifts elsewhere, another kind of rebuilding quietly begins. People start asking questions that cannot be answered by cleanup crews, insurance adjusters, or recovery plans. They begin wondering how to live with what has happened, how to move forward into an unfamiliar future, who they have become because of their experience, and what faith now looks like in a world that no longer feels as predictable as it once did.

Those questions belong to an entirely different kind of recovery. They cannot be resolved with a chainsaw, a cleanup bucket, or a carefully organized case management plan. They belong to the slow restoration of the heart, the mind, and the spirit.

I have experienced that same reality after difficult disaster deployments. Returning home did not automatically bring the emotional or spiritual work to an end. The operational responsibilities were finished, but the stories I had heard and the suffering I had witnessed often continued accompanying me long after I unpacked my bags. Sometimes recovery took only a few weeks. At other times it unfolded over many months. There were deployments that quietly continued shaping my theology and my understanding of ministry years after the response itself had ended.

Looking back now, I can recognize that restoration was often occurring beneath the surface even when I was completely unaware of it. While I sometimes believed I was simply carrying unanswered questions, God was patiently reshaping the way I understood those questions. The work was not dramatic enough for me to recognize in the moment. Like roots extending beneath the soil, it remained largely hidden until much later.

Years ago I spoke with a disaster survivor nearly two years after a major response. During the disaster she had lost her home along with many of the possessions that connected her to a lifetime of memories. In the months that followed, practical recovery proved exhausting, but the deeper struggle involved questions about fairness, faith, and the presence of God. During our earliest conversations those questions seemed to dominate everything else. Every discussion eventually returned to what had happened and why it had happened.

When we met again nearly two years later, I noticed something had changed. The questions had not disappeared. She still wondered about many of the same things we had discussed before, yet they no longer occupied the center of every conversation. She spoke about her grandchildren, friendships that had sustained her, plans for the future, and unexpected opportunities that had emerged during recovery. The disaster remained part of her story, but it was no longer the only story she could tell.

At one point she smiled thoughtfully and said something I have never forgotten.

"I don't think I got over it. I think I grew through it."

Her words captured something I had been observing for years but had never heard expressed so clearly. Many people imagine restoration as returning to the person they were before suffering entered their lives. Theological injury rarely allows such a return. We are changed by what we experience, and no amount of healing can erase that reality. The goal is not to become who we once were. It is to become the person God is patiently shaping us into through everything we have lived.

Gerald Sittser expresses a similar insight in his reflections on profound loss. Healing, he argues, does not remove suffering from our lives. Instead, life slowly expands around suffering. The loss remains part of our story, but it gradually ceases to define the whole story. I have found that theological injury often follows the same path. Questions remain. Memories remain. Scars remain. Yet over time they begin occupying a different place within the larger landscape of a person's life. They no longer govern every conversation, every prayer, or every thought. They become part of the story rather than the whole story.

Ministry has also taught me that people are often far more patient with others than they are with themselves. I have sat beside countless individuals who extended remarkable compassion to grieving friends while criticizing themselves for experiencing the very same emotions. They freely granted others permission to heal slowly but expected themselves to recover quickly. Learning to offer ourselves the same patience we instinctively extend to others is itself an important part of restoration.

The slow work of healing requires that kind of grace—not only grace received from God, but grace learned toward ourselves. Only then can we begin accepting that restoration is not measured by how quickly we recover but by the quiet, faithful work God continues accomplishing within us, often long before we recognize it ourselves.

One of the most discouraging aspects of healing is that it rarely moves in a straight line. Most people begin the journey of restoration expecting steady progress. They assume that if healing is truly occurring, each day will be a little easier than the one before, each month stronger than the last, and every step forward permanently secure. Experience tells a different story. Healing tends to unfold in cycles rather than in straight lines. There are seasons when hope feels close at hand and periods when faith seems quietly renewed. Then, without warning, an anniversary arrives, a familiar hymn is sung, a passage of Scripture is read, or a conversation awakens an old wound. Questions that once seemed settled suddenly return with surprising force.

These moments can be profoundly discouraging because people often interpret them as evidence that they have failed. They conclude they are back where they started and that all the work of healing has somehow been undone. In most cases, however, that is not what is happening at all. They are not returning to the beginning of the journey. They are encountering another layer of it.

I witnessed this repeatedly in both ministry and disaster response. A survivor might appear to be doing remarkably well for months, rebuilding routines and beginning to imagine a future again. Then the anniversary of the disaster would approach, and emotions that had remained quiet for some time would suddenly rise to the surface. Memories became vivid. Grief that seemed distant returned with unexpected intensity. Many people interpreted these experiences as proof that healing had never truly occurred.

What I gradually learned was something quite different. The grief had never disappeared. It had simply changed its place within their lives. Healing does not erase memory. Instead, it changes our relationship with memory. The events remain exactly as they were, but over time they lose their power to define every part of our present.

The same pattern often appears in theological injury. Questions that once felt overwhelming may return unexpectedly. A sermon may reopen an old struggle. A tragedy in the news may awaken doubts that seemed long resolved. Another painful experience may expose questions that had been quietly resting beneath the surface. When this happens, many people panic because they assume their faith has somehow regressed.

More often, the opposite is true. The return of a question does not necessarily mean healing has failed. It may simply mean that healing has continued deeply enough for another layer of the question to be explored with greater wisdom and greater honesty than before.

I have found Henri Nouwen's reflections especially helpful at this point. Nouwen observed that healing does not necessarily mean the disappearance of wounds. Sometimes healing means learning to live with our wounds in ways that no longer allow them to dominate our lives. That distinction changes expectations considerably. Many people recovering from theological injury assume that mature faith means never struggling again. Such an expectation almost guarantees disappointment.

Faithful people continue to struggle. Mature believers continue asking difficult questions. Even deeply healed people encounter seasons of uncertainty. The difference is not that the struggle disappears but that it no longer possesses the same authority over their lives.

There have been seasons in my own life when questions I believed had been settled unexpectedly resurfaced. A difficult disaster deployment, a painful pastoral conversation, or another encounter with profound suffering would reopen lines of theological reflection I thought had long been resolved. Earlier in my ministry I interpreted these moments as personal failure. I assumed that mature faith should have moved beyond such questions.

Experience has taught me something gentler. Sometimes growth requires revisiting familiar questions because we ourselves have become different people. The question may remain essentially the same, but the one asking it has gained years of experience, greater humility, and deeper compassion. What once threatened faith now becomes an invitation to continue growing.

I remember speaking with a pastor who had endured a profound crisis of faith earlier in his ministry. Years later he described himself as spiritually healthy and deeply grateful for the journey God had carried him through. Then he smiled and admitted that some of the same questions still occasionally resurfaced. His honesty surprised me because I had imagined that someone with such evident wisdom had somehow left those struggles permanently behind.

Sensing my surprise, he quietly said something I have never forgotten.

"The questions came back. They just stopped being in charge."

His words captured the very heart of restoration. Healing does not always remove the question. More often it changes the question's authority. Earlier in the journey, uncertainty occupies the center of a person's attention. Every experience is filtered through it. Every conversation circles back to it. Every prayer seems overshadowed by it.

Gradually, however, the question begins moving toward the edge of the landscape. It remains present, but it no longer governs everything else. Faith, hope, relationships, service, and joy slowly reclaim the center.

Scripture portrays this pattern repeatedly. The Israelites revisit familiar fears throughout their wilderness journey. The Psalms return again and again to lament, uncertainty, and trust. Even after profound encounters with God, biblical figures continue wrestling with weakness and doubt. Spiritual maturity never eliminates human vulnerability. Instead, it teaches people how to live faithfully within it.

One reason setbacks feel so discouraging is that many of us compare ourselves to an imaginary picture of complete healing. We imagine people who never doubt, never revisit old wounds, and never struggle with unanswered questions. Such people simply do not exist. What does exist are women and men who have learned to continue trusting God despite those realities. Their faith is not built upon the absence of struggle but upon the presence of God within it.

Richard Rohr has often described spiritual transformation as a continual rhythm of loss, disruption, and renewal. Growth, he suggests, rarely follows a straight upward path. Instead, people often revisit familiar places with new eyes and deeper understanding. That observation resonates strongly with what I have witnessed in both pastoral ministry and disaster response. Theological healing frequently follows exactly that rhythm.

A familiar question returns, but the person encountering it is no longer the same individual who first asked it. They have gained perspective through suffering, compassion through disappointment, wisdom through years of experience, and humility through recognizing the limits of their own understanding. The question itself may appear unchanged, but the soul engaging it has quietly matured.

This is one reason restoration often feels so difficult to measure. We tend to evaluate healing by asking whether our questions have disappeared. God often measures healing by asking whether we have become more capable of carrying those questions with trust, grace, and hope. Those are very different standards, and recognizing the difference can itself become an important step in the slow work of restoration.

Research on resilience reinforces this observation. Developmental psychologist Ann Masten describes resilience as "ordinary magic," emphasizing that recovery most often grows through ordinary relationships, daily routines, supportive communities, and small acts of perseverance rather than dramatic breakthroughs. That description feels remarkably consistent with what I have observed throughout decades of ministry. Most healing is surprisingly ordinary. A conversation with a trusted friend, a familiar prayer spoken again, a worship service attended despite lingering questions, a walk taken in quiet reflection, or an act of kindness offered to someone else may appear insignificant when viewed individually. Over months and years, however, these ordinary practices become the very means through which restoration quietly takes root.

Perhaps one of the most important lessons people can learn is that a difficult day does not erase years of growth. A painful memory does not cancel healing. The return of an old question does not negate faith. God continues working even when progress feels invisible, and hope remains trustworthy because the One who accompanies us through the journey is far more patient than we are with ourselves.

The slow work of restoration requires that kind of hope. It asks us to believe that healing is larger than today's discouragement, that growth continues even when it cannot yet be measured, and that God remains faithfully at work beneath the surface of our lives long before we recognize the evidence ourselves.

One of the encouraging discoveries people eventually make is that growth often becomes visible to others before it becomes visible to themselves. When we are living inside a season of struggle, our attention naturally settles on what still hurts. We notice the questions that remain unanswered, the grief that has not disappeared, and the uncertainties that continue to shadow our faith. What we often fail to notice are the quiet ways in which we have already begun to change.

This is especially true for people recovering from theological injury. Because they continue carrying difficult questions, they assume little progress has been made. Because moments of doubt still occur, they conclude their faith remains fragile. Because pain occasionally resurfaces, they imagine that healing has stalled. The reality is frequently much more hopeful than they realize.

I have watched this unfold repeatedly over the course of ministry. Someone would come into my office convinced that they were spiritually stuck. They would describe lingering uncertainty, recurring questions, and a faith that felt weaker than it once had. As they spoke, however, I often found myself noticing evidence of remarkable growth. They were more compassionate than they had been several years earlier. They listened more carefully. They judged others less quickly. They demonstrated greater patience with people whose experiences differed from their own. The questions remained, but the person asking those questions had been quietly transformed.

Years ago, I met with someone who had experienced a profound crisis of faith. During our conversation he spoke at length about the uncertainty he still carried. He described unanswered questions, lingering doubts, and frustrations that had never completely disappeared. As I listened, however, I found myself noticing something he could not yet see.

Before his crisis, he had approached faith with great confidence and very little curiosity. He tended to divide people neatly into categories. There were those who believed correctly and those who did not, those who understood God rightly and those who needed correction. His theological injury had humbled him, not in a way that diminished him but in a way that made him profoundly more human. He listened differently now. He spoke more gently. He extended grace more freely. He had become slower to judge and quicker to understand.

When I finally shared those observations with him, he grew quiet. After several moments he simply said, "I never thought about that."

Growth often hides in plain sight.

I remember experiencing something similar myself when a colleague remarked that I seemed more patient than I had been years earlier. My immediate response was disbelief. I remained fully aware of my own frustrations, limitations, and unanswered questions. Yet his observation stayed with me. It reminded me that we often live too close to our own struggles to recognize the ways grace has been quietly reshaping us.

James Fowler's work on faith development offers an important perspective on experiences like these. Fowler argued that spiritual maturity frequently involves increasing complexity rather than increasing certainty. As faith develops, people become more capable of holding ambiguity, paradox, and unanswered questions without feeling compelled to resolve everything immediately. Theological injury often accelerates that process. What initially feels like the collapse of faith may, in time, become the deepening of faith—not because questions disappear, but because faith becomes spacious enough to coexist with them.

The work of Brené Brown points toward a similar truth. Brown has argued that courage and growth emerge not from avoiding uncertainty but from learning how to live honestly within it. That observation resonates deeply with those who have experienced theological injury. They know what it means to lose easy answers. They understand the discomfort of vulnerability. Yet many also discover that authenticity creates a stronger foundation for faith than pretending certainty ever could.

Richard Rohr likewise suggests that spiritual growth frequently begins when our familiar frameworks become inadequate. Such moments rarely feel like progress. They often feel like disorientation, disappointment, or even failure. Yet the dismantling of old assumptions can create space for greater wisdom to emerge. The collapse of certainty may become the beginning of deeper trust.

I have seen this dynamic repeatedly among disaster responders. Many begin their work believing that competence, preparation, and determination can solve almost every problem. Experience gradually teaches otherwise. There are situations that cannot be fixed, losses that cannot be reversed, and questions that remain unanswered despite every effort. At first, this realization can feel discouraging. Over time, however, it often becomes a source of wisdom.

Responders gradually become less focused on controlling outcomes and more attentive to accompanying people. They become less concerned with appearing strong and more willing to acknowledge vulnerability. They develop greater patience with suffering because they have learned that not every wound can be repaired on demand. The work changes them, often in ways they recognize only after many years have passed.

The same pattern appears in ministry. Looking back over decades of pastoral work, I realize that some of the lessons I value most emerged through experiences I never would have chosen. Difficult congregational conflicts, painful pastoral situations, disappointments, unanswered prayers, and years spent walking beside grieving families all shaped my understanding of God in ways that success never could. At the time, many of those experiences felt like interruptions to ministry. In retrospect, they became some of its greatest teachers.

I would never romanticize suffering or suggest that pain is somehow desirable. There is nothing inherently good about tragedy, betrayal, or loss. Yet I have become convinced that God often works within painful experiences in ways we cannot immediately recognize. The growth usually remains hidden while it is taking place. Only later do we begin to see its fruit.

People who once demanded certainty gradually learn humility. Those who once feared questions discover curiosity. Individuals who judged others quickly become more compassionate. People who relied almost exclusively on explanations begin recognizing the profound value of presence. These changes matter because they reveal that healing is not measured solely by what has disappeared. Healing is also measured by what has emerged.

Greater patience.

Greater empathy.

Greater resilience.

Greater honesty.

Greater trust.

These qualities develop so gradually that they often escape our notice. Like roots growing beneath the surface of the earth, they remain hidden for a long time before their presence becomes visible. Then, almost unexpectedly, we notice that we respond differently than we once would have. A difficult conversation unfolds with greater grace. An old question no longer produces the same fear. A painful memory still hurts, but it no longer defines the entire day. What appears to be a small change often reflects years of quiet transformation.

Healing may continue to feel slow. Growth may remain difficult to measure. Yet the work of restoration continues beneath the surface, shaping us in ways we seldom recognize until much later.

Perhaps the clearest evidence of healing is not the disappearance of questions but the emergence of wisdom. It is found in a deeper compassion for others, a quieter confidence in God's faithfulness, and the growing realization that faith has become gentler, humbler, and more resilient than it was before. The questions may still accompany us, but they no longer occupy the center of the story. Grace does.

As people continue through the long process of healing, they often discover that restoration looks very different from what they originally imagined. Early in the journey, many hope simply to recover what they once had. They long for the certainty they remember, the confidence that existed before the injury, and the reassuring sense that life and faith once possessed. Those desires are entirely understandable. Most of us naturally long to return to what feels familiar after something precious has been lost.

Restoration, however, rarely consists of returning to an earlier version of ourselves. More often, it involves becoming someone new.

Theological injury changes people. The questions they ask change. The assumptions they carry change. Their understanding of God often changes, and their understanding of themselves changes as well. At first these developments can feel deeply unsettling because they seem to signal that something essential has been lost. Over time, however, many discover that these changes are not necessarily signs of spiritual decline. They may instead be signs of spiritual growth.

The faith that emerges after theological injury is often noticeably different from the faith that existed before it. It tends to be less certain yet more trusting, less rigid yet more compassionate, less dependent upon having answers and more dependent upon the faithfulness of God. That distinction has become increasingly important to me. Earlier in life, I unconsciously placed far more trust in explanations than I realized. I trusted my theological understanding, my ability to make sense of Scripture, and my confidence that the world ultimately fit together in ways I could comprehend. Theology remains indispensable, but experience has taught me that theology cannot bear the full weight of faith.

Theological injury exposes the limits of that assumption. Questions emerge that cannot be answered completely. Experiences arise that refuse to fit established categories. Mysteries remain even after careful study and earnest prayer. For a time this can feel like collapse. Eventually it can become liberation. Faith no longer depends upon possessing certainty. Instead, it learns to rest within relationship.

This is one reason I find myself returning again and again to the stories of Scripture. The great figures of the biblical narrative are rarely portrayed as people who understood everything. Abraham left home without knowing where the journey would lead. Moses spent decades leading a people through uncertainty while frequently struggling with his own questions. David moved repeatedly through seasons of fear, failure, lament, and renewed trust. The prophets wrestled openly with God's apparent silence. The disciples misunderstood Jesus with astonishing consistency, even while walking beside him every day.

Yet they continued.

Their faithfulness did not rest upon complete understanding but upon their willingness to continue trusting the One who had called them.

That pattern remains profoundly relevant for us today. Theological injury strips away many illusions that quietly shape our spiritual lives. It exposes the illusion that faith guarantees certainty, that prayer always produces the outcome we desire, that suffering can always be explained, and that life will unfold according to our expectations. Losing those illusions is undeniably painful, but their disappearance also creates room for something far more durable: a faith rooted in relationship rather than certainty, a faith capable of surviving disappointment, a faith willing to live with mystery because it has learned to trust the God who remains within mystery.

The psychiatrist and Holocaust survivor Viktor Frankl observed that human beings can endure extraordinary suffering when they are able to discover meaning within it. Frankl never suggested that suffering itself is good or desirable. Rather, he recognized that people can discover purpose, wisdom, and hope even in circumstances they never would have chosen. That distinction is crucial. Theological injury is not a gift in itself. Yet growth sometimes emerges through the long and often painful work of healing.

Parker Palmer offers a similar perspective when he describes the spiritual journey as a movement toward greater wholeness rather than greater perfection. That insight resonates deeply with my own experience. Earlier in ministry I often imagined that spiritual maturity meant becoming increasingly certain. Today I think differently. Wholeness matters more than certainty. Compassion matters more than appearing right. Faithfulness matters more than possessing answers.

As I have grown older, I have noticed that I admire different qualities than I once did. Earlier in my ministry I was drawn toward confidence, expertise, and theological precision. Today I find myself far more deeply moved by humility, patience, compassion, and the quiet wisdom that emerges from people who have suffered honestly. I continue to value careful theology, but I no longer view it primarily as a means of controlling uncertainty. Instead, I have come to see theology as a faithful companion that helps us continue walking with God through uncertainty.

That shift has not felt like a loss.

It has felt like grace.

I think often of the many people I have encountered through congregational ministry and disaster response whose faith became stronger after it had been wounded. Their strength did not emerge because suffering itself was somehow good. It emerged because they refused to abandon God while carrying their wounds. They lamented. They questioned. They doubted. They prayed. They struggled. Through that long and often exhausting process, their relationship with God gradually deepened.

The faith that emerged on the other side looked different from the faith they once possessed. It was not simpler. It was wiser. It was not more confident in itself. It was more dependent upon grace. It was not free from questions. It had simply learned how to carry them without allowing them to eclipse the presence of God.

I recognize that same pattern within my own life. There are questions I carry today that I never imagined carrying when I first entered ministry. Years of pastoral care, congregational leadership, disaster response, and ordinary life have confronted me with experiences that continue to resist easy explanation. Earlier in my vocation I assumed maturity would bring greater certainty. Instead, it brought greater humility. It taught me that faith is always larger than my understanding, that God remains faithful even when my explanations fail, and that trust often proves more important than certainty.

Perhaps that is one of restoration's greatest gifts.

It does not finally offer certainty.

It offers wisdom.

It does not promise invulnerability.

It cultivates compassion.

It does not produce mastery.

It teaches grace.

When I look back across decades of ministry and disaster response, I no longer see a neat progression from confidence to certainty. I see seasons of clarity and seasons of confusion. I remember questions that were answered and questions that remain. I recall moments when God seemed wonderfully near and other moments when God's presence was difficult to perceive. Yet woven through every season is another reality that has become unmistakable.

I see a God who continued walking beside me even when I struggled to recognize that companionship.

The slow work of restoration does not erase every scar. It does not answer every question. It does not return us to the people we once were. Instead, it patiently shapes us into the people we are becoming. The process often feels frustratingly slow. Progress may remain hidden for long stretches of time. The journey includes setbacks, disappointments, and days when very little seems to have changed.

Yet healing is occurring.

Growth is occurring.

God is at work.

Perhaps that is the final lesson restoration teaches. The story is not over simply because the questions remain. The scars remain, but they no longer define the whole story. Faith continues to grow, hope continues to deepen, and grace continues to reshape the soul in quiet ways that often become visible only with time.

Most importantly, God remains.

And in the end, that abiding presence is what makes restoration possible.

## *Chapter 13*

# The Wisdom of Wounded Faith

One of the surprising realities of theological injury is that it sometimes produces wisdom. This is not because suffering is inherently good. It is not. Loss wounds us. Disappointment wounds us. Betrayal wounds us. Confusion wounds us. No one should seek theological injury as a path toward spiritual growth, nor should we romanticize experiences that leave people questioning the goodness of God or the stability of their own faith. The wounds are real, and they deserve to be named honestly.

Yet there is another reality that deserves equal attention. People who have traveled through seasons of profound questioning often emerge with a perspective they did not possess before. They begin to see differently. They listen differently. They understand differently. The struggle does not simply alter what they believe; it reshapes the way they inhabit their beliefs. Earlier chapters have explored the pain of theological injury and the long, uneven process of restoration. This chapter turns toward another question altogether: What remains after healing begins? What kind of wisdom sometimes grows from wounded faith?

Many people assume that wisdom is acquired primarily through study, knowledge, or accumulated experience. Those things certainly matter, and they have always occupied an important place within the life of faith. Scripture repeatedly commends the pursuit of understanding, and the Christian tradition has long valued careful reflection, theological learning, and spiritual discipline. Yet there are forms of wisdom that seem to emerge only after cherished assumptions have been challenged by reality. Theological injury often creates exactly that kind of disruption. Questions arise that cannot be ignored. Certainties collapse beneath the weight of lived experience. Explanations that once seemed sufficient prove incapable of bearing the full weight of suffering, and the world becomes more complicated than it once appeared.

For a season, that complexity feels deeply unsettling. The loss of familiar certainty can resemble the loss of faith itself, leaving people wondering whether they have become spiritually adrift. In time, however, many discover that what first appeared to be disorientation has quietly become illumination. They begin recognizing truths that remained hidden while certainty occupied the center of their attention. Rather than weakening faith, the struggle has enlarged it. Rather than narrowing their vision, it has expanded it. They begin seeing life with greater realism, greater compassion, and greater humility than before.

Perhaps the first and most enduring form of wisdom that wounded faith produces is humility. Humility is often misunderstood. It is not self-deprecation, insecurity, or a lack of conviction. Neither is it intellectual timidity. Genuine humility is simply the recognition that our understanding has limits. It acknowledges that however carefully we have studied, however faithfully we have prayed, and however deeply we have reflected, God will always remain larger than our explanations.

Earlier in life, many of us unconsciously assume we understand more than we actually do. Our theological systems fit together neatly, difficult questions seem manageable, and we imagine that with sufficient study or experience we will eventually possess satisfying answers to most of life's mysteries. There is a confidence that naturally accompanies youth, education, and early success in ministry. It is not necessarily arrogance. Often it is simply inexperience. We have not yet encountered enough of life's complexity to recognize how much remains beyond our grasp.

Then life begins asking questions that cannot be answered so easily. A child dies despite fervent prayers. A marriage ends despite years of faithfulness. A trusted institution betrays those it was meant to protect. A disaster devastates an entire community without regard for character, goodness, or prayer. A devoted believer experiences years of silence from heaven. Suddenly, the carefully ordered theological framework that once explained the world begins showing signs of strain.

At first, this feels like loss, and in many ways it is. Certainty begins giving way to uncertainty, and confidence yields to questions that cannot be quickly resolved. Yet what initially feels like spiritual failure sometimes becomes the beginning of genuine wisdom. The person who once believed every mystery could eventually be solved gradually learns that some realities are simply too deep for complete explanation. Rather than producing despair, this realization often produces reverence. It becomes possible to acknowledge mystery without abandoning trust.

I have witnessed this transformation repeatedly in both ministry and disaster response. People who have suffered deeply often become less interested in winning theological arguments and more interested in understanding the people standing before them. They become slower to judge and quicker to listen. They speak with greater gentleness because they know how easily confidence can be shaken by experiences no one chooses. Their compassion grows in direct proportion to their awareness of life's complexity. Having discovered the limits of their own understanding, they become more patient with the uncertainty of others.

I have also watched this change unfold within my own life. When I first entered ministry, I assumed maturity would naturally bring greater certainty. I imagined that additional education, years of pastoral experience, and continued theological study would gradually answer many of the questions that troubled me. Seminary had given me valuable tools for thinking carefully about Scripture and doctrine, and I expected those tools to become increasingly effective with time. Some questions were answered exactly as I had hoped. Many others were not.

What experience eventually taught me was something I had not anticipated. Certain questions do not become smaller with time; they become deeper. Years spent accompanying grieving families, disaster survivors, exhausted caregivers, and congregations navigating painful transitions did not eliminate mystery. Instead, they revealed just how much mystery had always been present. My task was never to master every question. It was to learn how to remain faithful while living alongside questions that refused to disappear.

That realization quietly transformed both my ministry and my faith. I gradually became less confident in my explanations and more confident in God's faithfulness. I became less interested in defending certainty and more interested in cultivating trust. The distinction proved far more significant than I first realized. Conviction and humility need not compete with one another. Mature faith often holds them together, affirming what can be known while honestly acknowledging what cannot.

Scripture itself reflects this balance. The Bible contains some of the strongest affirmations of faith ever written, yet it also preserves some of humanity's deepest questions. The psalmists praise God with joyful confidence and, in the next breath, cry out in bewilderment. The prophets proclaim God's justice while lamenting the suffering they witness. Job refuses to surrender his relationship with God even as he demands answers that never fully arrive. These voices are not contradictions within Scripture. They are companions. They remind us that faith and uncertainty have always occupied the same sacred pages.

Karl Rahner observed that mature faith involves learning to live with mystery rather than eliminating it. Nicholas Wolterstorff's reflections following the death of his son likewise remind us that grief does not erase trust, even when it leaves many questions unanswered. Their insights resonate because they emerge not from detached speculation but from lives shaped by profound loss. Mystery is no longer merely a theological category. It becomes the environment in which faith learns to breathe. Questions remain, yet life continues. Faith continues. God remains.

That discovery often gives rise to another form of wisdom that wounded faith quietly cultivates: compassion. People who have struggled personally tend to recognize the struggles of others more readily. They understand what it feels like to pray without immediate answers, to worship while carrying doubt, and to search for God amid confusion. Because they know that landscape from within, they become safer companions for those who find themselves walking through similar valleys.

One of the unexpected gifts of wounded faith is that it often makes people gentler. Gentleness born of inexperience can disappear quickly when challenged. Gentleness refined through suffering possesses a different quality altogether. It has been tested. It understands something about the hidden burdens every person carries. It knows how quickly certainty can give way to grief and how easily appearances can conceal profound pain.

During years of disaster response, I have repeatedly noticed that some of the most effective caregivers are not necessarily those with the greatest theological knowledge or the most impressive credentials. They are the people whose compassion allows them to recognize suffering before anyone has found words to describe it. They notice hesitation in a survivor's voice. They recognize exhaustion behind practiced smiles. They understand that many wounds remain invisible until someone creates enough safety for them to be spoken aloud. Their effectiveness grows not merely from expertise but from empathy shaped through their own encounters with brokenness.

Theological injury often deepens precisely that capacity. People who have wrestled with difficult questions become more willing to remain present with the questions of others. People who have experienced disappointment become less threatened by disappointment. People who have known seasons of spiritual loneliness learn to recognize loneliness when they encounter it in someone else. The wound itself is not the wisdom. Rather, wisdom emerges from the patient work of healing, and that wisdom becomes part of the gift they carry forward into the lives of others.

Before moving into the next section, it is worth pausing to recognize that theological injury changes more than a person's beliefs. It changes the way a person sees. The shift is often so gradual that it escapes notice until much later. People may continue attending church, praying, reading Scripture, and participating in familiar patterns of worship. Outwardly, very little appears different. Inwardly, however, something fundamental has been altered. The lens through which they interpret life has become more complex, more spacious, and often more compassionate.

Questions that once seemed straightforward no longer feel simple. Assumptions that once appeared obvious now reveal unexpected layers. Situations that once invited quick judgments now evoke careful listening instead. People who once seemed easy to categorize become individuals whose stories deserve to be heard before conclusions are drawn. Theological injury frequently produces this deeper awareness of complexity, and although the transition can feel unsettling at first, it often becomes one of the most enduring marks of spiritual maturity.

Earlier in life, many of us unconsciously divide the world into neat categories. We distinguish between faithful and unfaithful people, between those who are right and those who are wrong, between certainty and doubt, strength and weakness, blessing and failure. Such categories provide a reassuring sense of order. They make the world feel understandable and predictable. Life, however, has a remarkable way of challenging those tidy divisions, and theological injury often accelerates that process.

We discover that deeply faithful people sometimes struggle to believe. We encounter generous, compassionate individuals whose lives are marked by profound tragedy. We witness earnest prayers that seem to receive no answer and devoted servants whose suffering cannot be explained by any familiar theological formula. Communities we trusted fail us. Leaders disappoint us. Circumstances arise that refuse to fit the categories we once relied upon.

The world does not become less true.

It becomes more complicated.

At first, this loss of simplicity can feel like disorientation. The certainty that once provided security begins to dissolve, leaving behind a landscape filled with ambiguity. Yet over time, many people discover that this complexity is not an enemy of faith but one of its greatest teachers. Wisdom often begins where simplistic certainty ends. Rather than weakening conviction, complexity invites a deeper dependence upon grace and a greater willingness to acknowledge the limitations of our own perspective.

I remember standing outside a heavily damaged home after one disaster, listening as a survivor described what had been lost. At first glance the conversation appeared to concern a house, but as she continued speaking it became clear that she was grieving something far more profound. She spoke about family photographs that could never be replaced, holiday traditions connected to particular rooms, birthday celebrations, children's height marks penciled onto a doorway, and quiet evenings gathered around a familiar kitchen table. The building itself mattered, but what truly grieved her was everything the building had contained.

That conversation changed the way I thought about recovery. It reminded me that people rarely mourn physical structures alone. They mourn the meanings attached to those structures. They grieve memories, relationships, identities, and stories that cannot be measured in financial terms. Ever since that day, I have found myself looking beyond the visible damage to ask what invisible losses people might also be carrying.

The same lesson has shaped my understanding of people more generally. Sitting across from disaster survivors, grieving families, exhausted caregivers, and wounded congregations has steadily stripped away the temptation toward superficial judgment. In the presence of genuine suffering, many theological debates begin to recede into the background while human dignity comes sharply into focus. Questions that once seemed central gradually give way to different concerns. Instead of asking who is correct, we begin asking who is hurting. Instead of concentrating first on explanations, we become more attentive to care. Instead of defending certainty, we practice compassion.

That shift is not merely emotional. It reflects a transformed way of seeing both the world and the people who inhabit it.

Over the years I have noticed this same transformation among clergy, chaplains, responders, physicians, counselors, and volunteers who have spent years accompanying people through profound suffering. Many of them become noticeably slower to draw quick conclusions. They ask more questions. They listen longer. They become increasingly aware that every life contains details hidden from public view and that every person's story includes chapters few others will ever fully understand.

Theological injury often teaches this lesson with unusual clarity. People who have themselves been wounded become less inclined to assume they know what another person is experiencing. They recognize how much of every struggle remains invisible. That awareness creates humility, and humility opens the door to genuine compassion. Rather than approaching people as problems to solve, they begin approaching them as fellow travelers whose lives deserve careful attention and respectful curiosity.

James Fowler's work on faith development suggests that mature faith involves an increasing capacity to live with tension, paradox, and complexity. Rather than reducing every experience to simple categories, mature believers gradually develop the ability to hold competing realities together without feeling compelled to eliminate one in favor of the other. Theological injury frequently becomes one of the experiences that pushes people toward precisely this kind of maturity. Not because they sought complexity, but because life itself required it.

The world simply proved more intricate than they had imagined.

One of the changes I have noticed in my own life is a growing reluctance to speak with absolute certainty about matters involving profound human suffering. Earlier in ministry, I often felt responsible for providing explanations whenever difficult questions arose. People came seeking guidance, and I assumed my role was to supply answers. Experience has reshaped that instinct. Today I find myself beginning with listening rather than explanation, not because truth matters less than it once did, but because people matter more than my ability to explain their circumstances.

Years of walking alongside grief have convinced me that explanations are rarely the first thing wounded people need. Before they need theology, they need compassion. Before they need analysis, they need presence. Before they need answers, they need to know they have been heard.

Theological injury has a way of reordering those priorities.

Another form of wisdom emerges as people begin seeing God differently. Earlier in life, many imagine God primarily as the one who prevents suffering, explains events, controls outcomes, or intervenes visibly in human affairs. While each of those convictions contains important theological dimensions, theological injury often exposes their limitations. Tragedies occur that seem inexplicable. Prayers appear unanswered. Intervention never arrives in the form we expected. People begin searching for God somewhere beyond the categories they previously inhabited.

Many eventually discover God not primarily in explanation but in accompaniment. They encounter God less as the source of complete certainty and more as the faithful companion who remains present within uncertainty. They begin recognizing divine faithfulness not because every mystery has been solved, but because God's presence has quietly endured through experiences that once seemed capable of destroying faith altogether.

This shift can be profoundly liberating. The God who once seemed distant or silent gradually becomes unexpectedly near. Suffering itself has not disappeared. Questions have not vanished. Yet people begin recognizing that God has been accompanying them through the very experiences that first caused them to doubt.

Scripture repeatedly bears witness to this pattern. God meets Hagar in the wilderness when she believes herself abandoned. God accompanies Israel through exile rather than sparing them from it. Elijah encounters God not in the dramatic displays of wind, earthquake, and fire but in the gentle whisper that follows them. Jesus stands beside grieving sisters outside the tomb of Lazarus before speaking words of resurrection. Again and again, the biblical story points not first toward explanation but toward presence.

That realization gradually reshapes faith itself. Faith becomes less concerned with possessing every answer and more committed to sustaining relationship. It depends less upon certainty and more upon trust. It becomes less preoccupied with control and more attentive to companionship. Richard Rohr has written that spiritual maturity often involves relinquishing the need to be certain about everything in order to trust God more deeply within mystery. Theological injury frequently becomes one of the painful experiences through which that lesson is learned.

The people who emerge from such a journey often possess a different kind of faith. It is not weaker than before but deeper. It is not less committed but more realistic. It is not free from questions but more capable of carrying them without allowing them to dominate the relationship with God.

This transformation inevitably affects the way they relate to others. They become slower to judge, more willing to listen, more patient with uncertainty, and more compassionate toward struggle. The wound itself is never the wisdom. Rather, the wisdom emerges through the long work of healing, and that wisdom becomes one of the most valuable gifts they carry into the lives of others.

One of the surprising outcomes of theological injury is that people often become remarkably safe companions for those who are struggling. They know firsthand what it means to wrestle with doubt, to feel abandoned, to question long-held assumptions, and to search for God in confusing circumstances. Because they know that landscape personally, they become guides not because they possess all the answers, but because they recognize the terrain. They have walked it themselves, and that shared humanity often becomes one of the greatest gifts wounded faith has to offer.

One of the deepest paradoxes of theological injury is that the experiences that wound us sometimes become the experiences that prepare us to care for others. This does not mean suffering is desirable, nor does it suggest that pain is somehow necessary for spiritual growth. No one should seek heartbreak as a path to wisdom. Yet history, Scripture, and ordinary human experience all testify to the same surprising reality. Many people eventually discover that the places where they were once most deeply wounded become the places from which they are able to offer the greatest compassion.

Henri Nouwen captured this reality through his familiar image of the wounded healer. His point was never that wounded people automatically become wise or compassionate. Unhealed wounds can just as easily produce bitterness, defensiveness, cynicism, or emotional withdrawal. Pain by itself does not transform anyone. Healing does. When people acknowledge their wounds honestly, allow grace to work within them, and gradually move toward restoration, they often develop an unusual ability to recognize suffering in others. They understand the terrain because they have walked it themselves.

Theological injury frequently cultivates exactly this kind of awareness. People who have wrestled with difficult questions become remarkably patient with the questions of others. Those who have experienced disappointment often become less threatened by disappointment when they encounter it in someone else's life. Those who have known spiritual loneliness learn to recognize it quickly in another person's voice, even when that loneliness remains unspoken. Their own journey has expanded their capacity for empathy in ways no amount of theoretical knowledge could accomplish.

Over the years, I began noticing this pattern among disaster responders. Some of the most gifted spiritual care providers were not necessarily the most eloquent speakers, the most experienced volunteers, or the individuals with the longest résumés. Something else distinguished them. They listened differently. They paid closer attention. They seemed able to recognize pain before it was fully expressed. Their questions were gentler, their patience deeper, and their presence steadier.

As I came to know many of them better, I discovered that these qualities rarely appeared by accident. Many had experienced significant losses of their own. Some had buried loved ones. Others had endured illness, divorce, professional disappointment, or seasons of profound uncertainty. They had learned what it felt like to live without easy answers, and those experiences had quietly reshaped the way they cared for others. Their suffering had not made them compassionate by itself. Rather, the work of healing had transformed their suffering into understanding.

I have witnessed the same pattern repeatedly throughout congregational ministry. The pastors whose compassion has impressed me most have rarely been those whose lives unfolded without hardship. More often, they have been women and men who experienced disappointment, failure, grief, illness, conflict, or seasons when their own faith was deeply tested. Those experiences enlarged their capacity to recognize the struggles of others. They no longer approached people primarily as problems to solve but as fellow travelers deserving patience and respect.

Theological injury often works in exactly this way. People who have walked through seasons of doubt frequently become safer places for others to bring their doubts. Those who have struggled with prayer become less likely to judge someone who confesses that prayer now feels difficult. Those who have questioned God themselves become far less alarmed when someone else admits similar questions. They understand that uncertainty is not always the enemy of faith. Sometimes it is one of the places where faith quietly grows.

The experience may not provide satisfying explanations, but it often produces understanding. That distinction is important because understanding frequently accomplishes things that explanations cannot. People may forget the precise words of an argument or the details of a theological explanation, but they rarely forget the experience of feeling understood. To be genuinely understood is to discover that another human being has entered your experience without attempting to dismiss, minimize, or quickly resolve it.

This is one reason the ministry of presence becomes so central after theological injury. People who have experienced the limits of explanation often become deeply convinced of the power of accompaniment. They know firsthand that some wounds begin healing not because someone finally solved the mystery, but because someone remained beside them long enough that they no longer carried the mystery alone.

I know this realization changed me.

Earlier in ministry I often felt an almost instinctive responsibility to provide answers whenever people were hurting. If someone brought a difficult question, I searched for a satisfying explanation. If someone struggled with doubt, I assumed my task was to help them arrive at greater certainty. I cared deeply, but I often believed that effective ministry depended upon resolving uncertainty.

Experience gradually altered that instinct.

Years spent in congregational ministry and disaster response taught me that many of life's most important questions resist easy answers. Some losses cannot be explained. Some suffering cannot be justified. Some mysteries remain mysteries despite our best efforts to understand them.

Yet people still need care. They still need companionship. They still need someone willing to remain beside them while they search for meaning.

That realization quietly transformed my understanding of ministry. My goal gradually shifted from solving to accompanying, from fixing to remaining, from defending certainty to cultivating compassion. I became less concerned about saying the perfect thing and more concerned about being faithfully present. I discovered that people rarely expected me to remove their pain. What they longed for was the assurance that they would not have to endure it alone.

One of the most significant changes theological injury often produces is increased patience. People who have wrestled with difficult questions understand that genuine growth cannot be hurried. Healing unfolds at its own pace. Faith matures slowly. As a result, they become less inclined to rush others through experiences that simply cannot be rushed.

This is particularly important within Christian communities. Churches sometimes communicate, even unintentionally, that grief should be brief, doubts should be resolved quickly, and spiritual maturity should proceed in predictable stages. Real life rarely follows such orderly timetables. People recovering from theological injury understand this because they know firsthand what it feels like to need more time than others expected. They remember the frustration of wanting certainty before certainty returned. Because they remember, they become more generous toward the journeys of others.

That generosity is itself a form of wisdom. It reflects the recognition that people are not projects to complete but fellow pilgrims walking difficult roads. Every person carries a story still unfolding. Every life contains chapters not yet written. Rather than measuring progress by the speed with which questions disappear, wounded faith begins measuring growth by the increasing capacity to love well in the midst of uncertainty.

Theological injury often teaches this lesson through experience rather than theory. It is an expensive education, but one whose fruits can be profoundly life-giving. Over time, wounded faith frequently produces a deeper appreciation for grace. People who once measured faith primarily by certainty begin measuring it by faithfulness. Those who once concentrated on being correct become more concerned with being compassionate. Those who once worried about possessing the right answers become increasingly attentive to whether they are loving people well.

The shift may appear subtle from the outside, but in practice it can transform entire ministries. I have watched congregations become healthier because their leaders learned this lesson. I have seen disaster response teams become stronger because experienced responders modeled this kind of compassion. I have known individuals whose quiet presence became a source of hope simply because they had discovered that gentleness often accomplishes more than certainty.

The wisdom of wounded faith is therefore never merely intellectual. It is profoundly relational. It changes how people listen, how they serve, how they lead, and how they love. It shapes their conversations, their prayers, their expectations, and their willingness to remain present when answers are unavailable. The wound itself is never the gift. The gift is the compassion that sometimes emerges through the patient work of healing, and for many people that compassion becomes one of the most valuable things they carry forward from their journey.

As people continue along the path of restoration, they often discover something they never expected when the struggle first began. The story is no longer defined only by what was lost. It also becomes a story of what remains and, perhaps even more surprisingly, a story of what has been gained. The gains are rarely the ones anyone would have chosen. No one asks for heartbreak, uncertainty, disappointment, or theological disruption. Yet many discover that these difficult experiences leave behind unexpected gifts: humility, patience, compassion, wisdom, and a deeper dependence upon grace.

Those gifts do not erase the pain that came before them.

They simply ensure that pain does not have the final word.

As people continue the long journey through theological injury and restoration, many eventually discover that the story is not defined only by what has been lost. It is also shaped by what has endured, and sometimes even by what has quietly emerged along the way. No one would willingly choose heartbreak, disappointment, betrayal, or prolonged uncertainty. No one would ask for the experiences that give rise to theological injury. Yet many who have walked this difficult road eventually recognize that healing leaves behind gifts they did not possess before. Humility deepens.

Compassion expands. Patience grows. Wisdom matures. Grace becomes more than a theological concept; it becomes a lived reality.

These qualities never erase the pain that preceded them. The wounds remain part of the story. The memories do not disappear. The unanswered questions do not suddenly resolve themselves. Yet those questions no longer occupy the center of a person's life. Something else has taken their place. Theological injury often teaches that faith is far more resilient than we first imagined. Earlier in life many of us assume that faith depends upon certainty. We believe that if enough questions arise, belief will eventually collapse. If enough disappointments accumulate, trust will become impossible. If enough suffering enters our lives, hope will inevitably disappear.

Experience often tells a different story.

People discover that faith can survive uncertainty. It can survive disappointment, unanswered prayer, prolonged grief, and mysteries that remain unresolved for decades. Not because those realities are unimportant, but because faith ultimately rests upon something deeper than explanation. It rests upon relationship. Throughout this book I have returned repeatedly to the distinction between certainty and trust because that distinction has become increasingly significant to me over the years. Theological injury frequently weakens certainty and, in many cases, dismantles it altogether. What often emerges in its place is trust—a quieter faith, a humbler faith, and ultimately a more resilient faith.

The difference between certainty and trust is subtle enough that it can easily be overlooked, yet it changes everything. Certainty depends upon understanding. Trust depends upon relationship. Certainty asks whether we possess enough knowledge to explain what has happened. Trust asks whether God remains faithful even when we cannot explain it. Theological injury often moves people from one question to the other, and in that movement many discover a deeper foundation for their faith than they knew existed.

I have witnessed this repeatedly among disaster survivors, responders, clergy, caregivers, and ordinary believers whose lives have been marked by profound hardship. Some of the most faithful people I know are also people who continue carrying unanswered questions. That observation surprised me when I was younger because I assumed certainty and maturity naturally belonged together. Years of ministry have convinced me otherwise. Faithfulness and uncertainty are not opposites. More often than not, they travel together.

Some of the people whose faith I admire most have buried children, survived disasters, endured serious illness, experienced institutional betrayal, carried decades of disappointment, or lived with questions that never received satisfying answers. Yet they continue praying. They continue serving. They continue loving. They continue hoping. Their perseverance does not arise because life finally began making sense. It arises because they have learned to trust God amid what does not make sense. That quiet trust has become one of the deepest forms of wisdom I have encountered.

Paul Tillich described faith as the state of being ultimately concerned. While theological injury may reshape many aspects of a person's beliefs, it often leaves that deeper orientation intact. People continue searching for God. They continue hoping, questioning, reaching, and praying even when certainty has become elusive. Something within them refuses to let go. That persistence reveals a faith that has been tested by reality rather than protected from it. It is no longer merely theoretical faith. It has become lived faith, formed in hospital rooms, funeral homes, disaster shelters, recovery centers, quiet sanctuaries, and long nights of prayer when no immediate answers arrived.

Several years ago, near the conclusion of a disaster deployment, I found myself talking with another responder who had spent enough years in this work to recognize its cumulative weight. We reflected on how disaster response had changed us over time. After a thoughtful silence he smiled and said, "When I started, I thought this work was about helping people."

He paused before continuing.

"I still believe that. But now I think it's also about learning how to be human."

His words have remained with me because they captured something I had gradually been discovering myself. Earlier in his career he had focused primarily on tasks, outcomes, and solutions. He was an excellent responder, committed to serving others well. Yet years of accompanying people through profound suffering had reshaped him. He had become more patient, more compassionate, less interested in appearing strong, and more willing to acknowledge uncertainty. The work had wounded him in certain ways. It had also made him wiser, not because suffering itself was a good teacher, but because he had allowed healing to teach him what suffering alone never could.

As I reflect on decades of ministry, caregiving, and disaster response, I find myself increasingly grateful for people whose faith has been wounded and restored. They are often among the wisest individuals I know, not because they possess extraordinary theological knowledge but because they possess extraordinary compassion. They know what it means to struggle. They know what it means to question, to wait, to grieve, and to rebuild. They know what it means to continue trusting God when certainty has faded. Because they know those realities personally, they become gifts to everyone around them.

Their presence reassures people who are afraid. Their honesty gives others permission to tell the truth about their own struggles. Their compassion creates space where healing can begin. Their wisdom helps others continue moving forward when they are tempted to give up. In many ways they become living reminders that theological injury is never the end of the story. Healing remains possible. Growth remains possible. Faith remains possible.

Writers such as Viktor Frankl, Parker Palmer, and Jürgen Moltmann approach suffering from different perspectives, yet all point toward a similar truth. Meaning can emerge even amid profound pain. Human beings can continue moving toward wholeness even after devastating loss. Hope survives not because suffering disappears but because God remains present within it. Together their work reminds us that the journey remains difficult, the questions remain real, and the scars remain visible. Yet life continues. God continues. Hope continues.

Perhaps that is the deepest wisdom wounded faith has to offer. It is not the wisdom of certainty, nor the wisdom of possessing flawless explanations or escaping suffering altogether. It is the wisdom of hope—the kind of hope that has survived disappointment, endured uncertainty, and discovered that God's faithfulness is never dependent upon our complete understanding.

Such hope becomes a gift to congregations, families, communities, responders, caregivers, and to anyone struggling to believe that healing is still possible. The wisdom of wounded faith is not the wisdom of people who have escaped suffering. It is the wisdom of people who have walked through suffering and discovered that God was still there.

As I have grown older, I have noticed that the people I admire most are rarely those who appear most certain. Far more often they are people who have remained kind after disappointment, compassionate after suffering, and faithful after loss. They possess a quiet wisdom that cannot be acquired from books alone. It has been shaped by experience, refined through struggle, and sustained by grace.

When I look back across my own journey, I do not see a faith that became stronger because every question was answered. I see a faith that became deeper because it learned to live with unanswered questions. I do not see a faith that mastered mystery. I see a faith that gradually learned to trust within mystery.

Looking back across decades of ministry, disaster response, and pastoral care, I cannot honestly say that I am grateful for every painful experience. Some losses still grieve me. Some questions remain unanswered. Some memories continue to ache. What I find myself grateful for instead is the quiet faithfulness of God throughout those experiences. The wounds did not become wisdom overnight. Over time, however, they taught me humility. They taught me compassion. They taught me patience. Most of all, they taught me that God's faithfulness often becomes clearer in retrospect than it is in the moment itself.

That lesson continues to shape me. The journey continues. The growth continues. And so does God.

Perhaps that is where wisdom ultimately leads—not to certainty, but to trust; not to mastery, but to grace; not to possessing all the answers, but to discovering that even when our answers fail, God remains. In the end, that may be wisdom enough.

## *Chapter 14*

# The Gift of Hope

One of the most remarkable qualities of the human spirit is its capacity for hope. Again and again, I have watched people endure experiences that, from the outside, seemed certain to leave them defeated. They have suffered losses they never imagined possible, faced disappointments they never anticipated, and carried grief that altered the course of their lives. They have encountered betrayal, illness, disaster, uncertainty, and heartbreak. Yet somehow many continue moving forward. They continue loving the people around them. They continue serving others even while carrying burdens of their own. They continue believing that tomorrow is worth entering. They continue hoping.

This quiet resilience has fascinated me throughout more than three decades of ministry and years of disaster response. I have stood beside people looking at homes reduced to little more than concrete foundations and listened as they began talking, almost immediately, about rebuilding. I have watched grieving families make funeral arrangements while simultaneously comforting one another with remarkable tenderness. I have sat with disaster survivors who described devastating losses and then, almost in the same breath, spoke about grandchildren, gardens they hoped to plant again, or plans they still wanted to pursue. Again and again I have witnessed something that refuses to disappear.

Hope persists.

Rarely does it arrive with dramatic speeches or triumphant declarations. More often it appears quietly, almost unnoticed. It reveals itself in ordinary conversations, small decisions, and simple acts of perseverance.

Sometimes it is barely visible beneath layers of grief and exhaustion, yet it remains present all the same. It continues to draw people toward tomorrow even when yesterday has left them deeply wounded.

One of the places where I have observed this most clearly is late at night in disaster shelters. During the busiest hours of a response, attention naturally centers on immediate needs. Volunteers distribute meals, families register for assistance, children search for familiar routines, and responders work through long lists of practical concerns. As evening settles over the shelter, however, the pace changes. The news cameras leave. The activity quiets. Conversations become more personal.

It is during those late hours that people often begin telling their stories. They speak about what they have lost, what they fear, and what they cannot yet imagine. They describe the homes they left behind, the neighborhoods that no longer exist, the possessions that carried decades of memories, and the uncertainty that now stretches before them. Those conversations are filled with grief, but I have noticed something remarkable about them over the years.

Eventually, they almost always turn toward the future.

Not because the future suddenly becomes certain. It does not. Rather, people continue searching for reasons to move toward it. They begin wondering where they will live, how they will rebuild, what their children will need, and who has offered help. Even while surrounded by uncertainty, something within them continues reaching forward. Hope quietly begins doing its work long before circumstances justify it.

Theological injury places that hope under enormous strain. When deeply held assumptions collapse, when prayers appear unanswered, and when familiar explanations no longer seem adequate, people naturally begin asking whether hope itself remains reasonable. If God did not prevent this tragedy, why should we continue hoping? If sincere prayers were met with silence, what confidence remains? If life has unfolded so differently than expected, what reason is there to believe the future will be any different?

These are not questions of weak faith. They are questions of wounded faith.

There is an important difference.

Weak faith often turns away from the struggle. Wounded faith enters the struggle honestly. It asks difficult questions because it still longs for relationship. Beneath every question about suffering lies a deeper question about whether hope remains possible. People experiencing theological injury are not simply trying to understand what happened. They are trying to discover whether trust can survive what happened.

Walter Brueggemann has observed that much of biblical faith is forged not during seasons of comfort and certainty but during seasons of exile, disruption, and loss. Scripture consistently portrays hope emerging in circumstances where optimism alone would seem impossible. Israel sings songs of hope while living in captivity. The prophets proclaim God's future while surrounded by national collapse. The psalmists continue praying even when they feel abandoned. Again and again, biblical hope appears precisely where ordinary optimism would have failed.

This distinction between optimism and hope becomes increasingly important after theological injury. Many people unconsciously assume the two are interchangeable, yet they are profoundly different. Optimism depends largely upon circumstances. It assumes that things will probably improve because the evidence points in that direction. Hope rests on a different foundation altogether.

Hope can survive circumstances that destroy optimism.

Optimism predicts favorable outcomes. Hope trusts that life remains meaningful even when favorable outcomes cannot be guaranteed. Optimism looks primarily at probabilities. Hope looks beyond probabilities toward faithfulness. Optimism asks whether events are likely to improve. Hope asks whether God remains trustworthy regardless of how events unfold.

That distinction gradually reshaped my own understanding of faith. Earlier in life I often found myself placing hope in outcomes without fully realizing it. I hoped prayers would be answered in particular ways. I hoped suffering would eventually make sense. I hoped faithful living would produce predictable results. Sometimes those expectations were fulfilled, and I naturally interpreted those moments as evidence that hope had been justified.

Other times they were not.

Those disappointments became invitations to ask a more important question. Was my hope rooted primarily in outcomes, or was it rooted in God? The difference did not seem significant until life forced me to confront it. As long as circumstances unfolded according to expectation, the distinction remained largely invisible. It became unmistakably clear only when expectations collapsed.

I remember speaking with a disaster survivor several months after a devastating flood had reshaped nearly every aspect of her life. During the earliest days of the response she had been overwhelmed by grief. Her home had sustained extensive damage. Possessions collected over decades were gone. Family photographs, keepsakes, handwritten letters, and ordinary objects that carried extraordinary memories had disappeared beneath muddy water. When I met her again months later, I expected our conversation to revolve around insurance claims, rebuilding plans, and the slow work of recovery.

Instead, she talked about gratitude.

Not because everything had been restored. It had not. Not because life had become easy. It certainly had not. She spoke instead about neighbors who arrived with cleanup supplies before anyone asked, family members who rearranged their lives to help, strangers who appeared carrying meals, and volunteers who treated her with remarkable kindness.

At one point she paused and smiled.

"I still don't know how everything is going to work out," she said. "But I don't feel alone anymore."

Her words have stayed with me ever since because they captured something essential about hope. Hope is not always confidence about the future. Sometimes it is confidence that we will not face the future alone. Theological injury often strips away lesser forms of hope—hope rooted in certainty, predictability, or control. What sometimes emerges in their place is a deeper hope grounded not in explanations but in presence, not in guarantees but in relationship, and not in certainty but in trust.

That kind of hope rarely draws attention to itself. It is quieter than the optimism that preceded it, yet it is also far more resilient. It has survived disappointment. It has endured uncertainty. It has learned that faithfulness does not depend upon understanding everything. Because it has already passed through suffering, it no longer fears suffering in quite the same way.

The biblical story repeatedly points toward this deeper kind of hope. Abraham begins his journey without knowing where it will lead. Israel wanders through the wilderness with no clear map of the future. The psalmists cry out from places of confusion and grief. The prophets continue proclaiming God's promises during seasons when national collapse seems inevitable. Again and again, hope appears in circumstances where optimism would seem unreasonable because biblical hope has never rested primarily upon circumstances.

It has always rested upon God.

One of the most surprising discoveries people make after theological injury is that hope can survive disappointment. At first, this seems unlikely because disappointment and hope appear to move in opposite directions. Disappointment arises when expectations collapse. Hope looks toward the future with some measure of confidence and longing. Yet some of the most hopeful people I have known were also people who had experienced profound disappointment. They had buried loved ones, survived disasters, endured illness, faced betrayal, watched dreams unravel, and carried unanswered questions for years. Still, they hoped.

They did not hope because life had spared them pain. They hoped because pain had taught them something about where hope must finally rest.

Hope is often misunderstood. Many people assume it means expecting favorable outcomes. If circumstances improve, hope appears justified. If circumstances deteriorate, hope seems naïve. Real life rarely operates so neatly. Anyone who has spent time in ministry, healthcare, caregiving, or disaster response eventually discovers that some situations do not improve in the ways we wish they would. Some losses cannot be reversed. Some illnesses cannot be cured. Some relationships cannot be repaired. Some questions remain unanswered.

If hope depends entirely upon outcomes, it becomes fragile.

Theological injury frequently exposes that fragility. A person prays fervently for healing, and the healing does not come. Someone asks God to prevent a tragedy, and the tragedy occurs. A faithful individual expects life to unfold in a particular way, and instead everything changes. The disappointment can be profound. For a time, it may feel as though hope itself has been wounded.

I have sat with people in those moments, and I have experienced some of them myself. There have been seasons when I believed I knew how a situation should unfold. I prayed, trusted, hoped, and waited. Then the outcome I expected never arrived. Looking back, I can see that some of my deepest disappointments were also moments when my understanding of hope began to change. Hope became less about receiving the answer I wanted and more about trusting God when the answer remained unclear.

One of the difficult lessons ministry taught me is that sincere faith does not guarantee predictable outcomes. Earlier in life, I often assumed that if people prayed faithfully, trusted deeply, and remained committed, life would generally make sense. Experience taught me otherwise. Good people suffer. Faithful people grieve. Prayers sometimes appear unanswered. Life is often more complicated than our explanations allow.

At first, these realities can feel threatening to hope. Eventually, however, they can deepen it. The difference lies in where hope is placed. When hope depends entirely upon outcomes, disappointment can destroy it. When hope depends upon God's presence, disappointment can coexist with it. That distinction may sound subtle, but it changes everything.

I remember speaking with a man whose wife had died after a long illness. During our conversation he spoke honestly about grief, frustration, and unanswered prayers. He did not minimize his pain, pretend everything happened for a reason, or reach for easy explanations. Yet he remained remarkably hopeful. At one point I asked what sustained him.

His answer surprised me.

"I stopped asking whether everything would turn out the way I wanted," he said. "I started asking whether God would still be with me if it didn't."

That shift transformed his understanding of hope. The outcome he desired had not occurred. The prayer he had prayed had not been answered in the way he longed for. Yet the relationship remained, and that relationship became a source of strength.

Nicholas Wolterstorff's reflections after the death of his son offer a similar witness. Grief and hope are not opposites. Deep sorrow can coexist with enduring faith. One does not cancel the other. The wounded heart may still hope, not because grief has vanished, but because love remains and God remains.

I have encountered similar wisdom among disaster survivors. Some lose homes they never fully rebuild. Others experience financial losses that linger for years. Many continue carrying emotional and spiritual scars long after the disaster ends. Yet some of these same individuals become remarkably hopeful, not because the damage disappeared but because they discovered that recovery involves more than restoring what was lost. It also involves recognizing what remains.

Family remains. Community remains. Love remains. Faith remains. God remains. Hope often grows in that soil.

The apostle Paul describes hope as something that endures alongside faith and love. That observation feels increasingly important to me. Hope is not simply a feeling, because feelings rise and fall. Hope is not merely optimism, because optimism fluctuates with circumstances. Hope is a way of seeing, a way of living, and a decision to continue believing that loss does not have the final word.

Theological injury frequently strips away illusions, and one of those illusions is the belief that hope requires certainty. It does not. Some of the deepest hope emerges precisely where certainty is absent. The psalmist in Psalm 42 cries out from despair while continuing to place hope in God. The writer of Lamentations finds hope not by denying suffering but by remembering God's steadfast love in the midst of it. They do not hope because circumstances guarantee success. They hope because God's faithfulness remains greater than their circumstances.

Viktor Frankl observed that people can endure extraordinary suffering when they retain a sense of meaning and purpose. Richard Rohr likewise suggests that spiritual maturity often emerges through experiences that dismantle our illusions. Theological injury frequently becomes one of those experiences. The hopes that depended upon certainty, control, or predictability gradually fall away. What remains may feel smaller at first, quieter and less dramatic than what preceded it, yet it is often far more durable.

It is hope that has survived disappointment. It is hope that has endured uncertainty. It is hope that no longer depends upon getting everything right. It is hope that rests in God's faithfulness rather than human understanding.

That hope is not easily shaken because it has already been tested. People recovering from theological injury sometimes worry that the loss of certainty means the loss of hope. Often the opposite is true. The loss of certainty can create space for a deeper hope than they previously imagined, a hope rooted not in explanations but in trust, not in outcomes but in presence, not in guarantees but in God.

One of the most important truths about hope is that we do not carry it alone. Many people imagine hope as an individual possession, something a person either has or lacks depending upon personality, circumstances, or strength of character. In reality, hope is often sustained through relationships. There are seasons when our own hope feels strong, seasons when it feels fragile, and seasons when we find ourselves relying on the hope of others until we are able to carry our own again.

I have witnessed this repeatedly throughout years of ministry and disaster response. In the immediate aftermath of a disaster, survivors are often overwhelmed. The damage is extensive, the future is uncertain, and decisions must be made quickly despite limited information and emotional exhaustion. Hope can be difficult to find in those moments because the losses are immediate while recovery remains almost impossible to imagine.

Yet something remarkable often begins to happen.

Neighbors arrive with tools and supplies. Volunteers show up to help clear debris. Meals are delivered. Phone calls are made. Churches open their doors. Communities gather in school gyms, fellowship halls, and recovery centers. The practical assistance matters immensely, but the relationships matter just as much. Little by little, people begin discovering that they are not facing the future alone, and that realization itself becomes a source of hope.

I have seen similar dynamics unfold in hospitals, congregations, recovery groups, funeral homes, and family living rooms. People facing profound challenges often draw strength from the presence of others, not because those individuals possess perfect answers but because they provide faithful companionship. Hope frequently grows in the soil of companionship.

Henri Nouwen often emphasized that healing occurs not only through solutions but through presence. His insight resonates deeply with what I have witnessed over the years. People rarely remember every word that was spoken during the most difficult seasons of their lives. They remember who stayed.

One of the reasons the ministry of presence matters so deeply is that presence itself communicates hope. When people choose to remain alongside those who are suffering, they proclaim something powerful without ever speaking the words. They communicate that another person's life still matters, that suffering has not made them invisible, and that they will not have to face tomorrow alone. Those messages are rarely spoken directly, yet they are often heard with remarkable clarity.

I remember sitting with a family following a particularly difficult loss. The room was quiet because there was very little that could honestly be said. The grief was fresh, the future uncertain, and no theological explanation could have lessened the weight everyone was carrying.

After several minutes, one member of the family looked around the room at the people who had gathered and began to cry. When she finally spoke, she said quietly, "I don't know how we're going to get through this."

She paused and looked around the room again.

"But I think we'll get through it together."

That simple statement has remained with me for years because it captures something essential about hope. Hope is not always confidence in the outcome. Sometimes it is confidence in companionship.

Theological injury often creates seasons when people struggle to sustain hope by themselves. Questions linger. Faith feels uncertain. Familiar assumptions no longer provide the reassurance they once offered. During those seasons, community becomes especially important because other people often carry hope for us until we are able to carry it ourselves.

This is one of the hidden gifts of healthy faith communities. At their best, congregations become places where hope is shared rather than individually generated. One person struggles while another encourages. One person doubts while another remains steady. One person grieves while another stays present. Over time, hope circulates throughout the community—not equally, not perfectly, but faithfully.

I have experienced this personally. There were seasons in ministry when I carried hope for others. There were other seasons when others carried hope for me. One of the gifts of serving within communities of faith is discovering that no one is expected to remain strong all the time. Eventually every caregiver becomes someone who needs care. Every encourager needs encouragement. Every person who carries hope for others eventually reaches a season when someone else must help carry hope for them.

There have been moments following difficult deployments, painful pastoral situations, and personal losses when certainty was unavailable and answers felt distant. During those times I often found strength in the faithfulness of other people. A colleague checked in with a phone call. A friend listened without trying to solve the problem. A congregation prayed faithfully. A fellow responder quietly offered encouragement after a difficult day. None of those moments erased the pain, yet together they reminded me that I was not carrying it alone. Sometimes that reminder was enough to take another step.

The New Testament repeatedly emphasizes the communal nature of faith. Believers are described as members of one body who bear one another's burdens and encourage one another through seasons of difficulty. Paul's invitation in Galatians to carry one another's burdens and the wisdom of Ecclesiastes that two are better than one because they help each other when one falls both remind us that human beings were never intended to carry every burden in isolation.

Hope often flourishes within relationships because relationships remind us of realities we temporarily forget. When suffering narrows our vision, other people help us see beyond the immediate moment. When grief convinces us that the future is empty, others help us imagine possibilities we cannot yet envision. In this way, hope becomes contagious—not in a superficial or sentimental sense, but in a deeply human one. One person's courage strengthens another. One person's perseverance encourages another. One person's faithfulness quietly inspires another. The effect multiplies in ways that are often impossible to measure.

Desmond Tutu frequently spoke about the interconnectedness of human beings and the ways communities help people survive suffering. His observations ring true in both ministry and disaster response. I have watched experienced responders remain calm during difficult operations, and their steadiness gave confidence to everyone around them. I have watched volunteers continue serving despite exhaustion, and their perseverance encouraged others to keep going. I have watched survivors demonstrate remarkable resilience, and entire communities drew strength simply from witnessing their determination.

Hope spread quietly through those relationships.

Theological injury can tempt people toward isolation because questions may feel embarrassing and doubts may seem threatening. Individuals sometimes withdraw because they fear misunderstanding or judgment. Unfortunately, isolation almost always weakens hope, while healthy community strengthens it.

That does not mean every community responds well to struggle. Some communities react poorly to questions and unintentionally communicate that uncertainty is unwelcome. Healthy communities do something different. They create space for honesty, space for lament, space for unanswered questions, and space for healing. Within that environment, hope begins to grow again, not because every question receives an answer but because every person receives companionship.

One of the most hopeful discoveries many people make after theological injury is that faith does not have to be carried alone. Others have traveled similar roads. Others have wrestled with similar questions. Others have experienced similar disappointments. Many of them continue moving forward, and their lives become quiet testimony that healing remains possible.

Sometimes we carry hope ourselves. Sometimes others carry it for us. Eventually, if we continue walking the journey, we discover that we are able to carry hope for someone else in return. Perhaps that is one of God's most practical gifts to the church—not simply hope itself, but a community of people who help one another hold onto it until each person is strong enough to believe again.

As people move through the long journey of theological injury, restoration, and renewed faith, they often discover that hope looks different than it once did. Earlier in life, hope may have been closely connected to expectations. We hoped for particular outcomes, specific answers, desired resolutions, or predictable results. When those expectations were fulfilled, hope seemed justified. When they were not, hope felt threatened. Theological injury often changes that relationship. It teaches us that hope cannot ultimately depend upon outcomes because outcomes change, circumstances change, people change, and life itself changes. Hope that depends entirely upon those things remains vulnerable. The deeper hope that emerges after theological injury rests elsewhere. It rests in the faithfulness of God.

This is not a simplistic claim, nor is it an attempt to avoid difficult questions or deny the reality of suffering. Rather, it is an observation that has emerged repeatedly throughout years of ministry and disaster response. I have watched people endure circumstances that would have seemed impossible to survive. I have watched families bury loved ones, communities rebuild after devastating disasters, responders continue serving after witnessing extraordinary suffering, and caregivers keep loving after years of emotional exhaustion. Again and again I have found myself asking the same question: What sustains them?

The answer is rarely certainty.

More often, it is hope.

Not hope that everything will unfold exactly as they desire, but hope that life remains meaningful, that love remains worthwhile, that God remains present, and that the future remains worth entering even when it cannot be fully understood. That kind of hope is remarkably resilient because it has already encountered disappointment, uncertainty, and loss. It survives theological injury because it has learned that faith is larger than explanation.

One of the people who taught me the most about hope never described herself as particularly hopeful. She was a disaster survivor who had endured a series of painful losses over several years. During one conversation she spoke honestly about grief, frustration, and exhaustion. Nothing about her story suggested easy optimism. Yet something about her presence communicated hope in a way I found difficult to explain.

Eventually I realized why.

She had stopped measuring God's faithfulness by whether life unfolded according to her plans. Instead, she measured God's faithfulness by God's continued presence throughout the journey. That quiet shift changed everything. Her circumstances remained difficult, many of her questions remained unanswered, and the future was still uncertain. Yet hope continued to live because her confidence no longer rested in the outcome. It rested in the One who had remained with her through every disappointment.

The theologian Jürgen Moltmann wrote extensively about hope as one of the defining characteristics of Christian faith. For Moltmann, hope was never wishful thinking or naïve optimism. It was confidence that God's future remained larger than present circumstances. That perspective becomes especially important after theological injury. People may no longer possess certainty. They may no longer possess simple explanations or the assumptions they once carried. Yet they may still possess hope. In some cases, they possess it more deeply than before.

Theological injury often removes superficial hope, the hope that depends upon guarantees, control, or predictability. What sometimes remains is hope refined by experience, hope that has endured disappointment, survived grief, and learned to trust God even when understanding remains incomplete. That hope tends to be quieter than the hope that preceded it. It is less dramatic, less confident in itself, and more confident in God.

As I have grown older, I have become less impressed by certainty and more impressed by endurance. The people who inspire me most are rarely those who possess the strongest opinions or the most persuasive arguments. They are the people who continue loving, serving, forgiving, and trusting despite everything they have experienced. Their hope is quieter than it may once have been, but it is also deeper. There is wisdom in that kind of endurance. There is courage as well—not the courage of people who possess all the answers, but the courage of people who continue walking forward without them.

I think of disaster responders who deploy repeatedly despite knowing they will encounter heartbreaking situations. I think of caregivers who continue showing up for people in pain, pastors who continue serving despite disappointment, and survivors who continue rebuilding despite devastating loss. Hope often looks like that. It is not dramatic certainty but faithful persistence. It takes one step, then another, and then another.

Over the years I have occasionally heard responders wonder whether hope is realistic after witnessing so much suffering. They have seen homes destroyed, lives disrupted, communities overwhelmed, and tragedies that resist explanation. Yet many of them continue answering the phone when the next deployment begins. They enter shelters, listen to survivors, comfort grieving families, and help communities recover. Whether they realize it or not, that willingness to keep serving is itself a profound expression of hope. It is a declaration that suffering matters, people matter, and the future remains worth investing in.

Over time I have come to believe that hope is one of God's greatest gifts, not because it eliminates suffering but because it enables people to move through suffering without surrendering to it. Hope does not erase grief. It teaches us how to carry grief. Hope does not eliminate uncertainty. It teaches us how to live faithfully within uncertainty. Hope does not answer every question. It gives us the courage to continue asking questions without abandoning faith.

Perhaps that is one of the most important lessons theological injury can teach. The goal is not returning to certainty. The goal is learning to trust God in the absence of certainty. The goal is not eliminating every question. The goal is discovering that questions and faith can coexist. The goal is not controlling the future. The goal is trusting the One who already holds the future.

Paul writes in Romans 8 that hope concerns what is not yet fully seen, and Miroslav Volf similarly reminds us that Christian hope is grounded not merely in present realities but in God's continuing work of redemption and reconciliation. Hope looks forward because God is still at work, even when we cannot yet see the full shape of that work.

When I look back across decades of ministry, disaster response, and caregiving, I do not see a life free from disappointment. I see unanswered prayers, painful deployments, difficult losses, and questions that remain unresolved. I also see something else. I see evidence of God's faithfulness, not always in the ways I expected or in the timing I preferred, but present nonetheless. Again and again I have encountered that faithfulness in relationships, in communities, in unexpected acts of kindness, in moments of grace, and in people who simply refused to give up on one another.

Those experiences have not eliminated every question. They have strengthened hope—not hope in outcomes, but hope in God.

When I think back over the years, I realize I do not remember every sermon I preached or every deployment I completed. What I remember most are the people. I remember those who kept going after devastating loss, who rebuilt after disasters, who continued loving after heartbreak, and who continued trusting God when certainty was no longer available. Those men and women became some of my greatest teachers.

They taught me that hope is not the absence of struggle.

Hope is the quiet conviction that struggle will not have the final word.

Theological injury may wound faith. It may challenge assumptions and dismantle certainty. Yet it does not have to destroy hope. Sometimes it deepens hope. Sometimes it purifies hope. Sometimes it reveals a hope that was present all along—a hope rooted not in circumstances, explanations, or guarantees, but in the enduring faithfulness of God.

That hope remains.

Because hope remains, faith remains.

Because faith remains, love remains.

Paul reminds us in 1 Corinthians 13 that faith, hope, and love endure, and the closing vision of Scripture portrays a God who is still bringing creation toward healing and restoration. The story is never over. God is still at work. Healing is still possible. The future remains open because God remains faithful.

For those who have experienced theological injury, this may be the final and most enduring gift. The journey does not conclude with certainty restored or every question answered. It concludes with a quieter confidence born of experience—a confidence that God has been present all along and will continue to be present whatever lies ahead. Wounded hope becomes enduring hope, and enduring hope becomes the steady companion of a faith that has learned, at last, to trust more deeply than it understands.

## *Chapter 15*

# Faith After the Rupture

One of the assumptions many people carry into seasons of theological injury is that faith will eventually return to what it once was. The questions will be answered, the doubts will disappear, certainty will return, the wounds will heal, and life will make sense again. Sometimes healing does bring greater clarity. More often, however, it does not. Many people eventually discover that faith after theological injury is not a return to a previous version of faith but the emergence of something new. The faith that survives the rupture is rarely identical to the faith that existed before it. It has been tested, questioned, challenged, refined, and, in some cases, broken apart and slowly rebuilt. The experience changes faith because it changes the person who believes.

This realization can be deeply unsettling. Many people spend months or even years trying to recover the faith they once possessed. They remember a time when belief seemed uncomplicated, prayer felt more natural, certainty came more easily, and life's questions appeared manageable. They long to return to that earlier confidence because it represents a season when the world felt more coherent and God seemed easier to understand.

I understand that longing. There have been seasons in my own life when I wished everything would make sense again. I wanted clear explanations. I wanted confidence that the world operated according to principles I could understand and predict. I wanted to believe that if I remained faithful enough, prayed sincerely enough, and trusted deeply enough, life would ultimately fit together in ways I could comprehend.

Theological injury gradually taught me that faithfulness and certainty are not the same thing. One can diminish while the other quietly grows. That discovery altered my understanding of spiritual maturity far more than I realized at the time.

Earlier in life I imagined mature faith as increasingly confident faith. I assumed that additional years of ministry, theological study, and practical experience would gradually answer the questions that troubled me. Some questions did become clearer. Others became deeper. Certain mysteries found satisfying resolution, while others remained stubbornly beyond my understanding. Looking back, I realize that what changed most was not the number of answers I possessed but my relationship to the questions that remained.

Faith after the rupture often involves learning how to live with questions that may never be fully resolved. This is not because the questions lack importance. Many of them remain profoundly significant. Rather, life continues even when understanding remains incomplete. People continue loving, serving, praying, grieving, forgiving, and hoping while carrying questions they may never fully answer.

I have noticed this change in my own prayer life. Earlier in ministry I often prayed for clarity, solutions, and explanations. I wanted to know what God was doing and why events were unfolding as they were. Those prayers have not disappeared entirely, but they have become less central. More often now I find myself praying for faithfulness. I ask for the strength to keep showing up, to keep loving people well, to continue trusting God, and to remain present even when understanding remains beyond my reach.

That shift has taught me something important about the nature of faith itself. Faith has become less about possessing certainty and more about cultivating perseverance. It has become less concerned with explaining God's ways and more concerned with remaining in relationship with the God whose ways often exceed my understanding.

This movement appears repeatedly throughout Scripture. Abraham leaves his homeland without knowing his destination, trusting the One who calls him rather than the map that lies ahead. Jacob emerges from his mysterious encounter with God carrying both a blessing and a limp, forever changed by an experience he cannot fully explain. Job never receives the comprehensive explanation he longs for, yet he encounters the living God in ways that transform his understanding. The psalmists repeatedly ask questions that echo through generations without receiving tidy answers, and even after the resurrection the disciples continue struggling to understand what God is doing among them.

These stories remind us that faith has always included uncertainty. Theological injury does not introduce uncertainty into faith so much as expose a reality that has always been there. It removes the illusion that mature believers eventually outgrow mystery and instead reveals that genuine faith has always required trust alongside unanswered questions.

One of the most significant changes that often occurs after theological injury is a movement away from explanation and toward trust. Earlier in life many people place enormous confidence in what they know about God. Their faith rests largely upon a theological framework that seems coherent and reliable. After theological injury, that confidence often shifts. Instead of trusting primarily in what they know about God, they begin trusting God despite what they do not know. The distinction may appear subtle, but it is profound because it changes the foundation upon which faith rests.

Paul Tillich described faith not as certainty but as ultimate concern, an orientation of one's entire life toward God even when certainty remains elusive. Thomas Merton expressed a similar insight when he wrote of learning to trust God without always knowing where the journey would lead. Those reflections resonate deeply with people whose faith has been wounded because they describe a relationship that does not depend upon exhaustive understanding.

Faith after the rupture becomes less concerned with possessing complete explanations and more concerned with remaining in relationship. The relationship gradually becomes central while the explanations assume their proper, secondary place. This does not diminish the importance of theology. Good theology continues to matter because it shapes the way we understand God and ourselves. What changes is the expectation we place upon theology. It is no longer expected to eliminate every mystery or answer every question.

Karl Rahner frequently emphasized that God ultimately remains mystery. Human beings can know God truly, but never exhaustively. Theological injury often forces people to confront that reality in ways they might otherwise avoid. Initially, this confrontation feels like loss because familiar certainties begin to crumble. Over time, however, it can become an unexpected source of freedom. There is freedom in no longer pretending to understand everything, freedom in releasing explanations that no longer satisfy, and freedom in discovering that faith does not depend upon possessing certainty.

Faith after the rupture often begins when people discover they can continue trusting God even when they cannot explain everything about God. That realization marks one of the most significant turning points in the spiritual journey. The goal is no longer recovering the faith that existed before the injury. The goal becomes learning to live faithfully with the faith that remains. More often than not, that remaining faith proves stronger, deeper, and more resilient than the faith that came before because it has survived the rupture and discovered that God remained faithful throughout it all.

One of the surprising discoveries many people make after theological injury is that mature faith often looks very different than they once expected. Earlier in life, many of us imagine spiritual maturity as a steady progression toward greater certainty. We assume that questions will gradually diminish, doubts will disappear, understanding will increase, and confidence will naturally grow with experience. It is an appealing picture of faith because it suggests that time and devotion eventually remove ambiguity from the spiritual life. Experience, however, often paints a different picture.

Some people certainly become more confident as they mature spiritually. Yet many faithful women and men discover that maturity is marked less by certainty than by humility, patience, compassion, trust, and an increasing capacity to live with mystery. Mature faith is often distinguished not by the absence of questions but by the willingness to remain faithful when those questions refuse to disappear. These qualities rarely receive the admiration that certainty commands, yet they may lie much closer to the heart of biblical faith.

Over the years I have known people whose faith appeared unshakable because they seemed to possess an answer for every question. I have also known people whose faith appeared unshakable because they continued trusting God while carrying questions that never found satisfactory answers. As I have grown older, it is the second group that increasingly impresses me. This is not because answers have become unimportant.

Theology still matters deeply, and careful reflection remains an essential part of discipleship. What has changed is my recognition that faithfulness often matters more than certainty.

I find myself paying less attention to whether people can explain every aspect of Christian belief and more attention to how they embody those beliefs in daily life. The people I admire most are often those who continue loving, serving, forgiving, and trusting despite disappointment, suffering, and uncertainty. Their faith is not merely something they profess. It has been tested in hospital rooms, funeral homes, disaster shelters, difficult congregational meetings, broken relationships, and seasons of unanswered prayer. It has survived contact with reality, and that gives it a depth that theoretical certainty alone cannot provide.

Theological injury often strips away idealized versions of faith. Assumptions that once felt secure no longer hold. Expectations collapse. Simplistic explanations prove inadequate. At first, this experience feels devastating because so much of what once seemed reliable begins to unravel. Eventually, however, it can become clarifying. People begin distinguishing between what is essential and what is merely familiar. Some beliefs remain firmly rooted. Others quietly fall away. Certain practices become more precious than ever, while others lose the importance they once held.

The process is rarely comfortable, but it often leads toward a more honest faith. James Fowler's work on faith development suggests that spiritual maturity frequently involves an increasing capacity to live with complexity. Mature faith does not eliminate tension; it learns to inhabit tension without being destroyed by it. That insight resonates deeply with what I have observed throughout years of ministry. People whose faith has been tested often become more comfortable acknowledging ambiguity because they know life itself is complex. They know suffering rarely follows predictable patterns. They know sincere believers sometimes reach different conclusions about difficult questions. Rather than threatening faith, this awareness often deepens it.

Faith gradually becomes less rigid, less defensive, and less dependent upon certainty. In many cases, it also becomes more compassionate. I remember standing beside disaster survivors who were no longer interested in theological debates they might once have considered important. After enduring profound loss, they found themselves asking different questions altogether. They wanted to know who had shown up, who had cared, who had remained beside them, and who had helped them carry the burden. Their priorities had changed because suffering had clarified what mattered most.

In many ways, theological injury produces the same transformation. People become less concerned with appearing correct and more concerned with remaining faithful. They become less interested in winning arguments and more interested in loving well. Instead of asking how every event can be explained, they begin asking how they can embody the compassion of Christ within circumstances they cannot fully understand. This shift often reflects genuine spiritual growth because it moves the center of faith away from intellectual mastery and toward faithful presence.

Henri Nouwen observed that maturity frequently involves moving from illusion to reality. Theological injury often accelerates that movement by exposing assumptions that were never as secure as we imagined. Illusions about ourselves, about the world, and sometimes even about faith itself gradually collapse. What remains is reality. God remains. Faith remains. The resulting faith is often quieter than what preceded it, yet it is also more durable because it no longer depends upon maintaining illusions that life itself cannot sustain.

I remember sitting alone late one evening during a disaster deployment after spending an entire day listening to stories of devastating loss. As the shelter grew quiet and volunteers finished their work, I realized that many of the theological explanations I had once considered indispensable no longer seemed nearly as important. What mattered that evening was not whether I could answer every question about suffering. What mattered was whether I could remain present with people whose lives had been shattered. That realization has stayed with me ever since because it fundamentally altered my understanding of ministry. Mature faith increasingly asks not, "Can I explain this?" but rather, "Can I remain faithful within it?"

One of the most important lessons ministry and disaster response have taught me is that faith does not have to be flawless to be genuine. Many people assume that doubt disqualifies faith, that unanswered questions reveal spiritual weakness, or that struggle somehow proves belief has failed. Scripture consistently suggests otherwise. The Bible is filled with women and men who questioned, struggled, argued, lamented, doubted, and wrestled with God, yet they remained in relationship. Again and again, the relationship proved more important than the certainty.

The desperate father's prayer in Mark 9 may be one of the most honest expressions of faith recorded in Scripture: "I believe; help my unbelief." Those few words capture something profoundly important about faith after the rupture. They remind us that God is not frightened by our questions, threatened by our uncertainty, or surprised by our struggle. Many people spend years trying to hide these realities because they assume authentic faith requires confidence they no longer possess. Theological injury often makes such concealment impossible. Although that can be painful, it can also become profoundly liberating because people finally stop pretending and begin telling the truth.

They speak honestly about their fears, disappointments, questions, hopes, and uncertainties. They no longer feel compelled to perform certainty for the benefit of others. In that honesty something remarkable begins to happen. Faith becomes more authentic, not because uncertainty disappears, but because authenticity replaces performance. Richard Rohr frequently writes about the transformation that occurs when people move beyond the need to appear certain, while Frederick Buechner reminds us that faith and doubt often travel together. Theological injury frequently becomes one of the experiences that ushers people into this deeper way of believing.

People stop trying to prove their faith and begin simply living it. That shift changes everything. Mature faith after theological injury rarely looks triumphant. Instead, it quietly continues praying even when prayer feels difficult, loving when love requires sacrifice, trusting when certainty remains unavailable, and hoping when circumstances offer little encouragement. Such faith may appear fragile from the outside. In reality, it is often remarkably strong because it has already survived disappointment, uncertainty, and doubt. Having endured those experiences, it possesses a resilience that uncomplicated faith never needed to develop.

Faith after the rupture is not perfect faith. It is tested faith, honest faith, humble faith. It is the kind of faith that has discovered it can live without every answer because it has learned that God remains present even when answers do not.

One of the questions people often ask after theological injury is whether faith can ever feel natural again. The answer depends partly upon what they mean by natural. If they mean effortless, the answer may well be no. Once faith has passed through profound disappointment or sustained uncertainty, it rarely returns to the innocence that existed before. If, however, they mean honest, then the answer is often yes. Faith after the rupture may no longer feel simple, but it can become deeply authentic. It grows into something that is chosen rather than assumed, embraced rather than inherited, and practiced rather than merely professed.

Earlier in life, many of us inherit assumptions about God, prayer, suffering, and the spiritual life without realizing how little those assumptions have been tested. Some of them are deeply true and continue to sustain us throughout our lives. Others remain largely unexamined until life becomes difficult. Then the testing begins. A diagnosis arrives unexpectedly. A marriage ends. A child suffers. A disaster destroys a community. A trusted leader disappoints us. A prayer remains unanswered despite our deepest longing. The assumptions that once seemed immovable suddenly feel fragile. Theological injury often emerges within the painful space between what we believed would happen and what actually happened.

For a time, that gap can seem impossible to bridge. The distance between expectation and reality feels so great that faith itself appears to be unraveling. Yet many people eventually discover that the goal is not to eliminate the gap but to learn how to live faithfully within it. The questions remain, but they no longer prevent life from moving forward. Instead, they become part of the landscape through which faith continues its journey.

One of the most significant changes that occurs after theological injury is that faith becomes increasingly intentional. Earlier in life, many people rely primarily upon inherited beliefs and familiar habits. Prayer comes naturally because it has always been part of life. Worship is familiar because it has always been practiced. Trust feels almost instinctive because the world has not yet challenged it in profound ways. After the rupture, those same practices often become conscious choices rather than automatic responses.

People choose to pray even when prayer feels difficult. They choose worship when certainty has disappeared. They choose community despite disappointment. They choose trust when understanding remains incomplete. These decisions are not signs of weaker faith. They are often evidence of a deeper faith, one that has learned perseverance through experience rather than assumption.

I have witnessed this repeatedly in both congregational ministry and disaster response. Some of the most faithful people I know are not individuals whose lives unfolded smoothly or whose questions were all resolved. They are people who experienced profound disruption and nevertheless continued choosing faithfulness day after day. Their faith became a decision long before it became a feeling again, and that distinction has increasingly shaped my own understanding of spiritual maturity.

Modern culture often treats feelings as the primary measure of authenticity. If something feels true, we assume it is true. If it feels difficult, we assume something has gone wrong. Faith rarely conforms to that pattern. There are seasons when trust comes easily and prayer flows naturally. There are other seasons when every act of faith becomes a deliberate expression of courage. Theological injury frequently introduces people to that second kind of faith—a faith sustained not by certainty but by commitment, not by emotional reassurance but by quiet perseverance.

Far from making faith less authentic, this often makes it more authentic. The decision to trust God when certainty has disappeared carries a depth that effortless belief rarely requires. Such faith has counted the cost. It has faced disappointment honestly. It has acknowledged uncertainty without allowing uncertainty to become the final word.

I often think of Jacob wrestling through the night beside the river. By morning he emerged carrying both a blessing and a limp. The encounter transformed him permanently. He was not restored to the person he had been before the struggle. Instead, he became someone new. That image has always resonated with me because it reflects the experience of so many people who have passed through theological injury.

Many of us want the blessing without the limp. We hope healing will erase every reminder of what happened and return us to the person we once were. Life rarely works that way. The experiences that deepen us often leave visible marks. Theological injury is no exception. Questions may remain. Certain losses remain. Memories remain. The limp remains. Yet so does the blessing. The relationship with God continues. Trust continues. Faith continues, even though it now bears the marks of the struggle that shaped it.

Earlier in ministry, I sometimes assumed that healing meant returning to a previous state. Restoration, I believed, involved recovering what had once existed. Years of pastoral ministry and disaster response gradually challenged that assumption. Many forms of healing do not involve returning at all. They involve becoming. A community recovering from disaster does not become exactly what it was before the event. A grieving family does not return to life as it existed before loss. A person who has experienced theological injury does not simply erase the experience and resume life unchanged.

Instead, something new emerges. The future is inevitably shaped by what has happened, and so is faith. At first this realization can feel disappointing because it means the past cannot simply be recovered. Over time, however, it often becomes a source of hope. The goal is no longer recovering a faith untouched by suffering. The goal is discovering a faith capable of surviving suffering. Those are profoundly different aspirations, and the second ultimately proves far more resilient than the first.

Parker Palmer has written about living an undivided life, a life in which reality is embraced rather than denied. Theological injury often pushes people toward precisely that kind of honesty. They stop separating painful experiences from their spiritual lives. Instead, they bring the whole story before God—the questions, the disappointments, the anger, the grief, the gratitude, and the hope. Nothing is hidden because nothing needs to be hidden.

That integration often becomes one of the clearest signs of healing. Faith grows less compartmentalized, less fragile, and more capable of engaging the realities of everyday life. People no longer feel compelled to protect God from their questions or protect themselves from their disappointments. They simply bring the whole truth into the presence of the One who already knows it.

One of the unexpected gifts of growing older has been becoming increasingly comfortable saying, "I don't know." Earlier in ministry, I often felt responsible for providing answers whenever people sought guidance or reassurance. I assumed that faithful leadership required certainty. Years later, I have discovered that honesty is often far more helpful than certainty. Sometimes the most faithful response is simply admitting that a mystery remains a mystery.

That realization has brought an unexpected freedom. I no longer feel responsible for explaining everything. Instead, I feel responsible for being present, for listening carefully, and for walking beside people when answers remain unavailable. In many ways, this has become one of the most enduring lessons theological injury has taught me. Presence frequently accomplishes what explanation cannot, and companionship often becomes more healing than certainty.

Perhaps the most encouraging change I have observed over the years is that many people who experience theological injury eventually become remarkably compassionate toward others. They understand what it means to struggle. They know what it feels like to question, to doubt, and to live with uncertainty. As a result, they often become safer pastors, safer caregivers, safer friends, and safer spiritual guides. Their faith has been softened by experience, not weakened. There is a profound difference between those two realities.

The apostle Paul speaks of living with a persistent thorn in the flesh, something never fully removed despite repeated prayer. Yet within that continuing limitation he discovers that God's grace remains sufficient. That image has always seemed deeply relevant to theological injury. Some questions receive satisfying answers. Others never do. Some wounds heal completely. Others leave lasting scars. Yet faith continues nonetheless. It learns to live not because every limitation has disappeared, but because grace proves greater than the limitations themselves.

Theological injury often removes harshness. It lessens the need to possess every answer. It increases patience, deepens empathy, and nurtures humility. These are not small achievements. They are among the clearest marks of mature faith. The faith that emerges after the rupture is rarely the faith people expected to have. It is often quieter, less certain, more compassionate, and more deeply rooted in God. It focuses less on explanation and more on presence, less on appearing strong and more on being honest.

Such faith does not eliminate struggle. Instead, it changes the way people move through struggle. The rupture remains part of the story, but it no longer defines the whole story. Something larger has emerged: a faith that knows suffering, a faith that knows grace, a faith that has learned to trust God while carrying unanswered questions, and a faith that continues moving forward one faithful step at a time.

One question remains as this journey through theological injury draws toward its conclusion: What does enduring faith actually look like? Not idealized faith, not theoretical faith, and not the faith we imagine we might possess under perfect circumstances, but real faith—the kind of faith that survives disappointment, unanswered prayer, grief, uncertainty, betrayal, and loss. After years of ministry, disaster response, and conversations with people whose lives have been shaped by suffering, I have come to believe that enduring faith is often much quieter than we expect. It is rarely dramatic, rarely triumphant, and rarely certain. More often, it looks like persistence. A person continues praying. A congregation continues worshiping. A caregiver continues serving. A responder continues deploying. A survivor continues rebuilding. One faithful act follows another, and over time those ordinary acts become the visible expression of extraordinary trust.

Enduring faith often appears so ordinary that it is easy to overlook. We expect faith to reveal itself through remarkable experiences or dramatic spiritual victories. More often, it reveals itself through simple acts of faithfulness sustained over many years. A widow continues attending worship after the loss of her spouse. A parent continues praying for an adult child whose life has taken painful turns. A volunteer quietly shows up week after week without recognition. A disaster survivor continues taking the next step toward rebuilding even when the future remains uncertain. None of these actions attract much attention, yet each bears witness to something profound. Faith remains.

One of the lessons theological injury teaches is that faith is not measured primarily by certainty but by perseverance. The person who continues trusting despite unanswered questions often demonstrates a deeper faith than the person who has never encountered such questions. The individual who continues loving despite disappointment may reveal greater spiritual maturity than the one who has never known heartbreak. Likewise, the person who continues hoping despite uncertainty often bears witness to a stronger faith than someone whose circumstances have consistently reinforced belief. Faith becomes visible through endurance rather than explanation.

The writer of Hebrews describes a great cloud of witnesses who continued moving forward despite hardship, uncertainty, and suffering. Their lives were not defined by perfect understanding but by steadfast perseverance. That same pattern continues today. I have seen it in congregations struggling through seasons of conflict, in disaster shelters filled with uncertainty, in hospital rooms where families waited through long nights, in recovery centers where survivors faced impossible decisions, at funeral homes where grief settled heavily over every conversation, and around kitchen tables where painful truths were spoken with remarkable honesty.

Over the years I have spent countless hours in funeral homes with grieving families. In those sacred and difficult spaces, theological explanations rarely occupy center stage. What matters is presence, prayer, shared memories, tears, and quiet acts of kindness. Again and again I have been struck by how faith reveals itself in those moments. It does not appear as certainty or as confidence that every question has been answered. Instead, it appears as the willingness to gather, to remember, to grieve honestly, and somehow to continue moving forward together. Time after time I have witnessed faith expressing itself not through explanation but through endurance.

That persistence should never be mistaken for weakness. It is a particular kind of strength, though not the loud or dramatic strength our culture often celebrates. It is quiet strength, developed slowly over many years and refined through hardship rather than protected from it. It is the strength of people who have learned that faithfulness is often measured in ordinary decisions repeated faithfully over a lifetime.

As I reflect upon my own journey, I realize that faith looks very different from what I once expected. Earlier in life I assumed that maturity would bring greater certainty. I imagined that years of ministry, study, and experience would answer many of the questions that troubled me. Some questions were answered. Others were not. What changed most was not the quantity of answers I possessed but the depth of trust that gradually emerged.

I no longer expect faith to eliminate mystery. I no longer expect theology to resolve every tension or prayer to produce predictable outcomes. What I have come to expect instead is that God remains faithful. That expectation has become the foundation of my faith. It rests not upon certainty but upon God's faithfulness, not upon explanations but upon God's presence, not upon control but upon trust. Those convictions did not emerge quickly. They were formed gradually through years of ministry, caregiving, disaster response, disappointment, and grace.

Looking back, I can see that theological injury changed my faith in ways I never anticipated. More importantly, I can also see that it deepened my faith. This was not because the injury itself was good. I would never describe suffering in those terms. Rather, it was because God continued working patiently within those experiences. The rupture became part of my story, but it never became the whole story. That distinction has become increasingly important to me.

Some of the people who have taught me the most about enduring faith never attended seminary, never wrote books, and never stood behind pulpits. They were disaster survivors, caregivers, widows, volunteers, neighbors, and ordinary people whose lives had been disrupted by circumstances they never would have chosen. Watching them continue moving forward taught me more about resilient faith than many of the books I studied during my theological education.

Many people experiencing theological injury fear they have reached the end of faith. In reality, they may be standing at the beginning of a different kind of faith—a faith less dependent upon certainty and more dependent upon trust, less concerned with defending explanations and more concerned with remaining in relationship, less focused on avoiding questions and more willing to live faithfully alongside them. At first this faith may feel unfamiliar, but over time it often becomes home.

One disaster survivor, whose life had been marked by losses most people would consider overwhelming, shaped my understanding of this reality more than she probably ever realized. During one conversation I asked what had sustained her through so many difficult years. She reflected quietly before answering. "I stopped asking whether everything would make sense," she said. Then she smiled gently and added, "I started asking whether God would still be with me if it didn't."

Her words captured something I had witnessed repeatedly but struggled to articulate. Faith after the rupture is not confidence that life will always make sense. It is confidence that God remains present even when it does not. That confidence changes everything. It does not remove grief, eliminate uncertainty, or answer every question. What it does provide is a place to stand when everything else seems uncertain, and sometimes that is enough.

Paul Tillich's understanding of faith as ultimate concern, Karl Rahner's insistence that God always remains mystery, Henri Nouwen's emphasis upon presence, and Jürgen Moltmann's vision of hope all point toward a remarkably similar conclusion. Mature faith is not the absence of struggle. It is the decision to remain engaged with God amid struggle. That is the faith that often emerges after theological injury—not perfect faith, not untroubled faith, but faithful faith. It is the kind of faith that has learned to walk with a limp, that carries scars without surrendering to them, and that knows suffering is real while refusing to believe suffering has the final word.

If I am honest, there are still questions I cannot answer. There are disasters I cannot explain, prayers I wish had been answered differently, losses that continue to grieve me, and moments I still do not fully understand. Yet I find myself trusting God more deeply than I did when I believed I understood much more. That may be one of the strangest gifts theological injury has given me.

As this journey comes to an end, I find myself returning to one simple conviction. The goal was never to recover the faith we once had. The goal was to discover whether faith could survive the rupture. Again and again, through decades of ministry, disaster response, and the lives of countless people I have been privileged to accompany, I have watched it do exactly that. The faith that emerged was not unchanged, untouched, or uncomplicated. It was alive. It was still trusting, still hoping, still growing, and still reaching toward God.

Faith after the rupture is not the end of the story. It is what remains when everything unnecessary falls away. It is quieter than before, humbler than before, and perhaps less certain than before. Yet it is also deeper, more compassionate, and more resilient. It has learned that God's faithfulness does not depend upon our understanding, that grace remains even when certainty disappears, and that love continues long after explanations have failed. In the end, that enduring faith may be one of God's greatest gifts to wounded people—a faith that bears the marks of struggle, carries the memory of grace, and continues walking forward because it has discovered that, whatever else may change, God remains.

# Chapter 16

# What Remains

Every journey eventually reaches a point where we look back. We do not do so in order to relive old wounds or become trapped in nostalgia, but because looking back allows us to understand what has endured. Distance has a way of revealing what urgency once concealed. Experiences that once seemed isolated begin to form patterns. Questions that once felt overwhelming become part of a larger story. We begin to see not only where we have been, but also who we have become along the way.

As I write these closing pages, I find myself looking back across more than three decades of ministry and many years of disaster response. I think about hospital rooms where families waited through long nights, funeral homes filled with quiet grief, congregations navigating seasons of conflict and change, disaster shelters where strangers slowly became neighbors, and recovery centers where people struggled to imagine a future beyond devastating loss. I think about conversations that lasted only a few minutes and others that continued over many years. Together they have shaped nearly everything I now believe about faith.

What surprises me is not how much I remember but what I remember.

I remember very few sermons in detail. I do not remember every deployment, every committee meeting, every pastoral visit, or every difficult decision. Those moments were important at the time, but many of their details have faded.

What remains are people.

I remember faces more readily than events. I remember conversations more vividly than schedules. I remember the quiet courage of survivors sorting through debris where homes once stood. I remember exhausted caregivers who somehow found enough strength to care for one more person before finally resting themselves. I remember disaster responders sharing coffee before sunrise as another demanding day began, and volunteers quietly cleaning mud from homes they had never seen before and would never visit again.

I remember families gathered around hospital beds, saying things they wished they had spoken years earlier. I remember congregations singing hymns through tears after tragedies that defied explanation. I remember children laughing in disaster shelters despite the uncertainty surrounding them. I remember older couples holding hands after losing nearly everything they owned because, as one man quietly told me, "We still have each other."

Those memories have shaped my theology far more than I expected they would.

When I first entered ministry, I imagined that theological understanding would emerge primarily through study. I loved books, ideas, history, doctrine, and careful reflection. I still do. The church needs thoughtful theology, careful scholarship, and faithful teaching. Yet somewhere along the way I discovered that theology is also formed by listening to people whose lives have been interrupted by suffering.

The questions that emerge beside hospital beds are different from the questions discussed in classrooms. The questions asked in disaster shelters are different from those debated in theological journals. They are not abstract questions. They are deeply personal ones.

Where is God?

How do I pray now?

Can I still trust when I no longer understand?

What does faith look like after this?

Those questions rarely have simple answers. In fact, one of the defining characteristics of theological injury is that familiar answers often lose their ability to satisfy. Assumptions that once felt secure begin to shift. Explanations that once seemed complete reveal their limitations. Beliefs that had never been tested by profound suffering suddenly encounter realities they cannot easily explain.

For many people, including myself, that experience feels like unraveling.

What once appeared solid begins to loosen. Long-held certainties become less certain. Confidence gives way to humility. Questions multiply faster than answers. For a season, it may seem as though everything is being dismantled at once.

When that happens, our attention naturally turns toward what has been lost. We mourn the certainty that once comforted us. We grieve the simplicity that once characterized our faith. We miss the confidence with which we once spoke about God, prayer, providence, and suffering. Loss deserves our attention because something real has been wounded. Honest grief is not a sign of weak faith. It is often evidence that something precious mattered deeply.

I know this because I have experienced it myself, and because I have walked beside countless others who have as well.

Over the years I have listened to pastors who quietly admitted that they no longer knew how to answer questions they once addressed confidently from the pulpit. I have sat with disaster responders whose repeated exposure to suffering had altered how they understood prayer. I have accompanied caregivers who wondered whether years of heartbreak had permanently changed their relationship with God. I have spoken with survivors who struggled to reconcile the God they had trusted with the world they now inhabited.

Again and again, the conversation began with loss.

Eventually, however, another question always seemed to emerge.

Not simply, "What has been taken from me?"

But, "What remains?"

Looking back now, I believe that question changed everything.

Earlier in life, I tended to think about spiritual growth as a process of accumulation. Faith meant acquiring greater knowledge, deeper understanding, stronger convictions, and increasing confidence. More years would bring more answers. More study would produce more certainty. More experience would create greater clarity.

Theological injury challenged that entire framework.

Instead of accumulation, it introduced subtraction.

Certain explanations fell away because they no longer reflected the complexity of life. Some assumptions disappeared because experience revealed their inadequacy. Expectations about how God should act became more tentative. Confidence in my own ability to understand everything gradually gave way to a deeper appreciation for mystery.

At first, those losses felt frightening.

Later, they became revealing.

There is something profoundly clarifying about subtraction. When enough unnecessary things fall away, what truly matters becomes easier to recognize. In some ways, theological injury performs that difficult work. It strips away the illusion that faith depends upon having every answer. It exposes the limits of explanations that once seemed sufficient. It removes the false confidence that often accompanies untested belief.

What remains after that stripping away is often quieter than before.

It is less dramatic, less certain, and less interested in defending itself.

Yet it is also more durable because it is no longer resting upon assumptions that could never carry the full weight of faith.

Disaster response has repeatedly reinforced this lesson for me. After a tornado, flood, or wildfire, survivors often stand in neighborhoods that no longer resemble the places they once called home. Buildings have disappeared. Possessions have been scattered or destroyed. Familiar landmarks have vanished. Looking across such devastation, it is natural to focus first on what has been lost.

Yet over time another reality begins to emerge.

Relationships remain.

Memories remain.

Acts of kindness remain.

Communities begin gathering again.

Neighbors continue helping one another.

Love refuses to disappear.

Again and again I have watched people discover that some of life's most important realities survive even extraordinary catastrophe.

I have come to believe that theological injury often reveals a similar truth. Not everything survives. Certain assumptions are permanently changed. Some explanations never return. A measure of innocence may be lost forever.

But not everything is lost.

Some things endure precisely because they are deeper than the beliefs that surrounded them.

That discovery became one of the central reasons I wanted to write this book.

One of the deepest hopes I have for this book is that it will reach people who quietly fear that their questions have somehow disqualified them from faith. Throughout the years I have met pastors, disaster responders, physicians, nurses, caregivers, volunteers, and thoughtful believers who carried a hidden anxiety. They wondered whether their doubts meant they had failed spiritually, whether their inability to reconcile suffering with earlier beliefs meant they had somehow disappointed God, or whether the simple act of asking difficult questions revealed an absence of faith rather than its presence.

Those fears are understandable.

I have carried some of them myself.

There have been seasons when I questioned not only particular theological ideas but also my own ability to continue trusting God when so much no longer fit together as neatly as it once had. There were moments after difficult deployments when I found myself replaying conversations with survivors long after returning home. I remembered prayers offered in hospital rooms, families searching through what remained of their homes, and responders carrying burdens they rarely discussed with anyone. Those memories did not destroy my faith, but they certainly changed it. They forced me to acknowledge that many of the answers I once offered with confidence were no longer sufficient for the realities I had witnessed.

Looking back now, I do not regret those questions.

I regret only the years I believed I should not have asked them.

Experience has convinced me that theological injury does not automatically destroy faith. Questions do not inevitably lead to unbelief. Disappointment does not necessarily end trust. Unanswered prayer does not force people to abandon God. These experiences certainly change faith, sometimes profoundly, but change should not automatically be mistaken for collapse. In many lives, including my own, the disruption becomes the beginning of a different kind of relationship with God—one marked less by certainty and more by trust, less by explanation and more by presence.

As I think back over the many people whose stories have shaped these pages, I am struck by how rarely they arrived at complete theological certainty. Few received satisfying answers to every question they carried. Many continued living with mysteries they could neither resolve nor ignore. Yet something remarkable happened. They continued praying. They continued serving. They continued loving their families, supporting their communities, and caring for neighbors whose burdens were often as heavy as their own. Their questions remained, but the questions no longer determined the direction of their lives.

That quiet persistence taught me something seminary never could.

Faith is sustained by relationship far more than it is sustained by explanation.

This realization unfolded slowly over many years. It emerged through countless conversations rather than a single dramatic insight. I remember sitting with disaster survivors who freely admitted they no longer understood why certain things had happened. They were honest about their disappointments with God. Some confessed that prayer felt different than it once had. Others acknowledged that particular Bible passages now raised more questions than comfort.

Yet when I asked whether they still prayed, many quietly answered yes.

When I asked whether they still believed God cared for them, many paused before nodding.

When I asked what kept them moving forward, they rarely pointed toward explanations.

Instead, they spoke about God's faithfulness, about people who had remained beside them, about moments of unexpected kindness, and about a quiet conviction that, although they understood far less than they once hoped to understand, they had never been abandoned.

Those conversations gradually reshaped my own understanding of faith.

Earlier in life, I often assumed that confidence grew primarily through accumulating knowledge. If I studied hard enough, read enough theology, and gained enough experience, many of life's difficult questions would eventually become manageable. Some did. Many did not.

What changed most was not the quantity of answers I possessed.

It was the growing realization that God's faithfulness had never depended upon my ability to explain God.

There are theological frameworks I once held with considerable confidence that I now hold more gently. There are questions I once believed would eventually yield satisfying answers that now seem destined to remain mysteries. There are passages of Scripture I understand differently than I did when I entered ministry, and there are experiences from disaster response that permanently altered how I think about suffering, prayer, and providence.

Yet through all those changes, one thing has become increasingly clear.

My trust in God has not diminished.

If anything, it has become steadier because it no longer depends upon the illusion that I can understand everything. Instead, it rests upon the repeated discovery that God remains faithful even when my understanding remains incomplete. That realization did not emerge through abstract theological reflection alone. It was forged through funeral services, disaster deployments, congregational crises, hospital visits, difficult conversations, and countless moments when I discovered that God's presence continued long after my explanations had reached their limits.

Over time I began noticing a pattern that became impossible to ignore. Whenever certainty weakened, God's presence somehow remained. Whenever explanations proved inadequate, God's presence remained. Whenever confidence faltered beneath the weight of suffering or disappointment, God's presence remained.

Those experiences never removed every question.

They did something better.

They revealed Someone who could be trusted even when many of the questions remained unanswered.

Perhaps that is where the long journey of theological injury ultimately leads. It does not lead to possessing complete certainty or recovering every explanation that once seemed convincing. Instead, it leads toward a relationship that has survived disappointment, endured uncertainty, and discovered that God's faithfulness extends far beyond the limits of human understanding.

That discovery does not solve every problem.

It does, however, provide a place to stand.

And after years spent accompanying people through suffering, I have come to believe that such a place is one of God's greatest gifts.

As I have reflected on the experiences described throughout this book, I have become increasingly convinced that theological injury is not ultimately a story about what has been taken away. Loss is undeniably part of the journey, and to ignore it would be both dishonest and unkind. The wounds are real. The grief is real. The disappointment is real. Questions arise that cannot easily be dismissed, and assumptions that once seemed unshakable may no longer provide the security they once did. Every person who has traveled this road knows something about the ache of discovering that faith is more vulnerable than they imagined.

Yet if we look only at what has been lost, we risk overlooking what has endured.

That realization did not come quickly for me. For many years I measured seasons of struggle primarily by what seemed to be disappearing. I noticed confidence slipping away. I noticed familiar explanations becoming less convincing. I noticed prayers becoming more tentative and my willingness to speak with certainty becoming increasingly restrained. It would have been easy to conclude that faith itself was steadily diminishing.

Instead, something quieter was taking place.

While some forms of certainty were fading, other qualities were quietly becoming stronger. Compassion deepened. Patience expanded. Humility grew. My appreciation for mystery increased, and my confidence shifted away from my own understanding toward the faithfulness of God. What initially felt like subtraction slowly became an invitation to discover what could not be taken away.

One of the first things many people eventually discover remains is God.

That statement may sound almost self-evident to someone who has not experienced theological injury, but for many who have, it is anything but obvious. Seasons of profound questioning often include moments when God seems silent, distant, or painfully absent. Prayer may feel hollow. Worship may seem strangely disconnected from everyday experience. Scriptures that once brought immediate comfort may suddenly raise difficult questions instead. In those seasons, many sincere believers wonder whether God has withdrawn or whether they themselves have somehow wandered beyond God's reach.

Those questions deserve respect rather than quick correction.

The Bible itself gives them generous space. The psalmists ask them repeatedly. Job refuses to suppress them. Jeremiah voices them with remarkable honesty. Even Jesus cries from the cross with words that echo the lament of Psalm 22. Scripture never portrays such questions as evidence that faith has ended. Instead, it presents them as part of what faithful people sometimes experience when life becomes more painful than their understanding can adequately contain.

Again and again, the biblical story reveals something remarkable.

The questions remain.

God remains as well.

Years of disaster response reinforced that truth in ways I never expected. I rarely witnessed dramatic miracles that removed suffering overnight or restored shattered communities in an instant. What I witnessed instead were countless ordinary moments through which God's presence quietly became visible. A volunteer stayed long after the workday had ended to listen to someone who needed to tell their story. Neighbors cleared debris from one another's yards before attending to their own. Churches opened their doors to strangers. Families, themselves overwhelmed by loss, somehow found the strength to encourage one another. None of these moments explained why suffering had occurred. None eliminated grief.

They did reveal something else.

God was still present.

Not always through dramatic intervention.

More often through ordinary compassion.

I remember sitting in a disaster shelter one evening after an especially difficult day. Survivors had spent hours navigating paperwork, uncertainty, and exhaustion. Volunteers looked equally tired. Nothing about the situation suggested easy optimism. Homes were still damaged. Insurance questions remained unanswered. No one knew exactly what the coming weeks would bring.

Yet as the evening unfolded, I watched people quietly caring for one another. Someone shared food with a family that had arrived late. A volunteer sat beside an elderly survivor who simply needed company. Children began playing together while exhausted parents exchanged stories about the neighborhoods they hoped someday to return to. No one pretended everything was fine. No one claimed to understand why the disaster had happened.

Still, compassion flourished.

As I watched those ordinary acts of kindness, I found myself wondering whether I had spent too many years expecting God's presence to appear primarily through explanation. Perhaps the deeper evidence of divine faithfulness was often found somewhere else—in the quiet refusal of people to abandon one another when life became difficult. Perhaps God was not absent because suffering remained. Perhaps God was already present wherever compassion persisted despite suffering.

That realization gradually changed the way I thought about faith.

Earlier in ministry, I often expected God's presence to become clearer as my understanding increased. If I could make sense of what had happened, I felt reassured. Theological injury slowly dismantled that assumption. There were many situations I simply could not explain, no matter how carefully I studied or prayed. Understanding remained incomplete.

Presence did not.

Henri Nouwen devoted much of his life to reminding the church that presence itself possesses healing power. Looking back across decades of ministry, I believe he recognized something that many caregivers eventually discover through experience. The deepest evidence of God's faithfulness is often not found in answers that eliminate mystery but in companionship that refuses to abandon people within it.

Alongside God's presence, I also discovered that faith itself often remains.

Not unchanged.

Not untouched by suffering.

Not untouched by questions.

But unmistakably alive.

Many people enter seasons of theological injury fearing that faith itself will disappear. Sometimes cherished beliefs do change. Certain theological formulations no longer satisfy. Spiritual practices evolve. Prayer takes on a different character. Yet beneath those changes, something surprisingly durable often continues. Trust remains. Relationship remains. A quiet desire to continue seeking God remains.

The faith that emerges may appear smaller than the faith that preceded it. It is usually less interested in certainty, less eager to defend every position, and more willing to acknowledge mystery. Yet it is also stronger in important ways. It has survived disappointment. It has survived unanswered prayer. It has survived the collapse of assumptions that once seemed indispensable. Because it has endured those experiences, it often possesses a resilience that earlier faith never needed to develop.

I have seen this pattern repeatedly among survivors, responders, clergy, caregivers, and ordinary people whose lives were unexpectedly interrupted by suffering. Their faith no longer depended upon having every answer. Instead, it rested upon continuing the relationship. That distinction changed not only the way they understood God but also the way they understood themselves.

Paul writes that we walk by faith rather than by sight. For years I understood those words primarily as an invitation to trust what could not yet be seen. Today they also remind me that faith has never depended upon complete understanding. It has always involved continuing the journey with God even when the path ahead remains only partially visible.

That is what remained for so many people I have known.

And, by God's grace, it is what remained for me as well.

Hope also remains.

We explored hope in the previous chapter, yet it belongs here as well because faith and hope are never far apart. Indeed, many of the people who have taught me the most about faith have also taught me the deepest lessons about hope. They were not people whose lives had unfolded according to plan. They had buried loved ones, rebuilt homes after disasters, endured illness, lived through disappointment, and carried questions that never found complete answers. Yet they continued moving toward the future with a quiet determination that could not be explained simply by favorable circumstances.

Again and again, I found myself asking what sustained them.

The answer was rarely certainty.

It was hope.

Not hope that every problem would be solved exactly as they wished. Not hope that every prayer would receive the answer they desired. Rather, it was hope that life remained meaningful, that love remained worthwhile, and that God's faithfulness extended beyond what they could presently understand. That kind of hope proved remarkably resilient because it was no longer anchored primarily in circumstances. Circumstances had already disappointed them. Instead, their hope had become rooted in relationship—with God, with one another, and with the conviction that suffering would not have the final word.

Jürgen Moltmann famously argued that Christian hope is not wishful thinking but confidence in God's future. That insight has become increasingly important to me over the years. Hope is not optimism dressed in religious language. Optimism rises and falls with circumstances. Hope survives circumstances because it rests upon the character of God rather than upon the predictability of life.

Theological injury often strips away hopes that were tied too closely to control, certainty, or specific outcomes. At first, that experience feels devastating. People realize they cannot guarantee the future, explain every tragedy, or predict how life will unfold. Yet after that painful stripping away, many discover a quieter hope that proves much harder to destroy. It has already survived disappointment. It has already endured unanswered prayer. It has already lived through uncertainty. Because it has been tested, it becomes more durable than the hope that preceded it.

One of the most encouraging discoveries people make after theological injury is that faith and hope can coexist with uncertainty. Neither requires complete understanding. Both require trust. That realization creates space for genuine healing—not healing that erases every wound, but healing that allows people to continue living faithfully despite those wounds.

When enough falls away, certain realities become easier to recognize.

God remains.

Faith remains.

Hope remains.

Those discoveries naturally lead toward another truth that has become increasingly important to me over the years.

Love remains.

If there is one conviction that has grown stronger with age, it is that love endures in ways few other things do. Circumstances change. Institutions change. Communities sometimes change. Even our understanding of God may mature and deepen. Yet love possesses an astonishing capacity to survive upheaval. The apostle Paul concluded his great reflection on love by writing that faith, hope, and love remain, and that the greatest of these is love. The older I become, the more persuasive those words appear.

Theological injury often strips away assumptions and challenges beliefs that once seemed immovable. Yet even amid those disruptions, love frequently becomes more visible rather than less. When explanations fail, people continue caring for one another. When certainty weakens, compassion continues to bind communities together. When answers prove inadequate, simple acts of kindness quietly bear witness to God's presence.

I have witnessed this repeatedly throughout ministry. I have seen it in hospital rooms where families sat together through long nights of uncertainty. I have seen it in disaster shelters where strangers shared meals, blankets, and encouragement with people they had met only hours earlier. I have seen it in congregations quietly surrounding grieving members with meals, prayers, and companionship. I have seen it in volunteers who returned day after day because they simply refused to leave suffering people alone.

Again and again, I have been reminded that love often becomes most visible precisely when life is most difficult.

Theological injury may challenge what people believe.

It rarely diminishes the importance of loving well.

In fact, many people emerge from theological injury with a deeper appreciation for love than they possessed before. Their experiences often make them more patient, more compassionate, slower to judge, and more willing to extend grace. Their confidence in easy answers decreases, but their willingness to accompany another person's pain often increases.

Suffering, of course, does not automatically produce compassion. It can just as easily produce bitterness or withdrawal if the wounds remain unattended. Yet when healing begins, suffering often enlarges a person's capacity for empathy. Those who have known grief recognize grief more quickly in others. Those who have wrestled with unanswered questions become safer companions for those who are asking similar questions. Those who have discovered how desperately they needed grace frequently become more generous in extending grace.

I have seen this among disaster survivors, caregivers, responders, pastors, and ordinary people whose lives have been reshaped by hardship. Some of the most compassionate individuals I know are not people who escaped suffering but people who endured it and, by God's grace, emerged without allowing it to harden their hearts. They know what it means to hurt. They know what it means to wonder. They know what it means to wait. Because they know those realities personally, they often become extraordinary companions for others walking similar roads.

That observation leads naturally to another answer to the question of what remains.

Community remains.

Not every community survives theological injury intact. Some relationships fracture under the weight of disappointment. Some churches struggle to make room for difficult questions. Some institutions respond poorly to honest doubt. Those painful realities should neither be ignored nor minimized.

Yet healthy community remains one of God's greatest gifts.

Throughout both ministry and disaster response, I have learned repeatedly that no one survives life's deepest struggles entirely alone. Even the strongest people eventually discover the limits of self-sufficiency. We all need companions. We all need people who can lend us hope when our own hope grows thin. We all need those who are willing to sit beside us when explanations are unavailable and silence is the most faithful response.

There have been seasons in my own life when others carried hope for me. Friends listened when I needed someone simply to hear my questions. Colleagues quietly checked in after difficult deployments. Congregations prayed for me when I found it difficult to pray for myself. Small gestures—a handwritten note, an unexpected phone call, a shared meal, a thoughtful conversation—often arrived at precisely the moment they were needed most.

Those moments mattered far more than I realized at the time.

Theological injury teaches us that human beings were never intended to carry every burden alone. We need companions who remind us that we are not abandoned, communities that create space for honesty, and relationships that sustain us when our own strength begins to fail. Over the years I have become increasingly convinced that many of the most significant moments of healing occur not through explanation but through companionship. A friend listens. A caregiver remains. A volunteer shows up. A congregation refuses to abandon someone whose faith has become fragile.

These moments rarely appear dramatic.

They almost always prove unforgettable.

They remind us that love remains.

Community remains.

And because they remain, grace continues finding ways to reach us through the ordinary faithfulness of one another.

# Appendix A

## *Practicing Lament*

### LIVING FAITHFULLY WITH UNANSWERED QUESTIONS

By the time many people reach this appendix, they are no longer asking what lament is. They are asking something more practical.

How do I live this way?

How do I continue moving forward when the questions remain unanswered? How do I keep praying when prayer feels difficult? How do I maintain faith when certainty has disappeared? How do I remain honest without becoming cynical? How do I continue trusting God when life no longer makes sense?

These are the questions of people living with theological injury. They are also the questions of people learning to practice lament.

Lament is not merely something we do during moments of crisis. For many people, lament becomes a way of living faithfully in a world where not everything can be explained, fixed, or understood. It becomes a spiritual discipline, a habit of honesty, and a way of remaining in relationship with God even when the relationship feels strained.

The purpose of this appendix is not to explain lament. We have already explored that throughout the book. The purpose of this appendix is to help you practice it.

## LAMENT IS NOT A MOMENT. IT IS A PRACTICE

Many people imagine lament as a temporary response to a particular loss. Sometimes it is. But some losses remain. Some questions remain. Some wounds heal slowly. Some disappointments continue shaping our lives for years.

In those situations, lament becomes less of an event and more of a practice. Like prayer, worship, or forgiveness, it becomes something we return to again and again—not because we enjoy it, but because it tells the truth.

One of the most important lessons I learned in ministry and disaster response is that healing rarely begins with explanation. Healing often begins with honesty. People do not need permission to have answers. They need permission to tell the truth.

Lament provides that permission.

## TELL THE TRUTH DAILY

One of the simplest ways to practice lament is also one of the hardest: tell the truth.

Tell the truth about what hurts. Tell the truth about what you fear. Tell the truth about what you miss. Tell the truth about what you cannot understand. Tell the truth about your disappointment, your anger, and your grief.

Many people spend enormous energy pretending they are doing better than they actually are. Lament invites a different path.

Each day, ask yourself:

- What hurts today?
- What am I carrying today?
- What am I afraid to say aloud?

Then bring those realities before God—not after they are resolved, but now, exactly as they are.

## PRAY WITHOUT EDITING YOURSELF

One of the hidden effects of theological injury is self-censorship. People become afraid of their own prayers. They worry that their questions are inappropriate, their doubts unacceptable, or their anger unfaithful. As a result, they begin offering God carefully filtered versions of what they actually feel.

Lament rejects that approach.

The psalmists did not edit themselves. Jeremiah did not edit himself. Job did not edit himself. Even Jesus cried out from the cross.

Practice praying honestly rather than eloquently. Some days your prayer may consist of a single sentence:

"God, I do not understand."

That is enough.

Some days it may be:

"God, I am angry."

That is enough too.

The goal is not polished prayer. The goal is an honest relationship.

Read the Psalms of Lament as Companions

When people experience theological injury, they often assume they are alone. The Psalms remind us otherwise.

Generations of believers have walked similar roads. Spend time with Psalms 13, 22, 42, 73, 88, and 130. Read them slowly. Read them repeatedly. Do not rush to study them. Instead, allow them to become companions.

Notice how often the writers speak honestly. Notice how often they ask difficult questions. Notice how often they refuse to pretend.

The Psalms give us permission to do the same.

## ALLOW QUESTIONS TO REMAIN QUESTIONS

One of the most difficult practices of lament is resisting the urge to force closure. We want answers. We want certainty. We want resolution.

Sometimes those things come.

Sometimes they do not.

One of the marks of mature faith is learning that not every question can be answered. Some questions become lifelong companions. The goal is not to eliminate every mystery. The goal is to remain faithful within mystery.

Over the years, I have discovered that some questions have shaped me more than their answers ever could have. They taught humility, patience, compassion, and dependence upon God. Sometimes unanswered questions continue doing important work within us.

## FIND PEOPLE WHO CAN SIT WITH PAIN

Lament was never intended to be entirely solitary.

We need companions. We need people who can listen without fixing, remain present without offering easy explanations, and tolerate uncertainty without rushing toward resolution.

In ministry, I have often discovered that the most helpful people are not those with the best answers. They are those who remain present.

Find those people.

And whenever possible, become one of those people for others.

## PRACTICE LAMENT IN COMMUNITY

Congregations often know how to celebrate. They are less certain how to grieve. Yet churches, care teams, disaster-response organizations, and families all need lament.

Healthy communities create space for loss, disappointment, grief, and unanswered questions. This may involve reading lament psalms, lighting candles, holding memorial services, sharing stories, observing silence, naming losses, and praying honestly.

Communities that make room for lament become safer places for wounded people.

## KEEP SHOWING UP

This may be the most important practice of all.

Keep showing up.

Keep praying.

Keep worshiping.

Keep serving.

Keep loving.

Keep participating in community.

Keep taking the next step.

Not because everything has been resolved, but because faithfulness often precedes understanding.

I have seen this repeatedly among survivors, responders, caregivers, and grieving families. They continue moving forward one day at a time, one conversation at a time, one prayer at a time, and one act of kindness at a time.

This is not denial.

It is perseverance.

## LAMENT IN DISASTER RESPONSE

Years of disaster response taught me that people rarely need immediate explanations. They need witnesses. They need listeners. They need companions. They need someone willing to remain present in the midst of suffering.

I have sat in shelters where answers were unavailable. I have listened to survivors whose lives changed in a single afternoon. I have spoken with responders carrying grief they could not easily describe.

Again and again, I learned that lament is not weakness.

It is honesty.

And honesty often becomes the first step toward healing.

Disaster survivors taught me that people can grieve deeply and remain hopeful. Responders taught me that people can continue serving even when their hearts are heavy.

Both taught me that lament and courage frequently coexist.

## THE QUIET HOPE WITHIN LAMENT

Some people assume lament and hope are opposites. Scripture suggests otherwise.

Lament exists because hope has not completely disappeared. The person who laments is still speaking to God, still listening, still reaching, and still hoping—however faintly—that grace has not abandoned them.

That is why lament remains one of the most profound acts of faith. It refuses both denial and despair. It tells the truth about suffering while refusing to surrender the relationship.

Theological injury may leave questions unanswered. Lament allows us to carry those questions honestly. Theological injury may leave scars. Lament allows us to acknowledge them. Theological injury may change faith. Lament allows faith to remain alive during the change.

In the end, practicing lament is not about learning how to suffer well. It is about learning how to remain in conversation with God when suffering becomes part of the story.

Sometimes faith is nothing more—and nothing less—than continuing that conversation until we discover that God has been listening all along.

# Appendix B

## *Recognizing Theological Injury*

### NAMING WHAT HAS BEEN WOUNDED

Many people experience theological injury long before they have language for it.

They know something has changed. Prayer feels different. Faith feels more difficult. Questions have become heavier. Certainty has weakened. Beliefs that once felt secure no longer seem adequate.

Yet they often struggle to describe what is happening.

Some assume they are simply tired. Others assume they are losing faith. Some worry they are becoming cynical. Others wonder whether they have failed spiritually.

In reality, they may be experiencing theological injury.

One of the challenges of theological injury is that it is often mistaken for other experiences. It can resemble burnout, compassion fatigue, grief, depression, moral injury, or a crisis of faith. While it may overlap with those realities, theological injury involves something distinctive.

At its core, theological injury occurs when experiences of suffering, loss, betrayal, catastrophe, unanswered prayer, or prolonged exposure to human pain significantly disrupt a person's understanding of God, faith, prayer, meaning, or the way the world is supposed to work.

The injury is not merely emotional.

It is theological.

The questions are not only, "Why am I hurting?" They become:

- Where is God in this?
- What do I believe now?
- How do I pray after this?
- Can I still trust what I once trusted?

Recognizing theological injury is often the first step toward healing.

## COMMON EXPERIENCES OF THEOLOGICAL INJURY

Not everyone experiences theological injury in the same way. Some symptoms appear immediately. Others emerge gradually over months or years.

Common experiences include:

- Feeling spiritually disoriented
- Struggling with unanswered prayer
- Increased difficulty trusting God
- Feeling distant from God
- Loss of theological certainty
- Persistent questions about suffering
- Difficulty engaging in worship
- Feeling disconnected from previous beliefs
- Frustration with simplistic religious answers
- Anger toward God, religious institutions, or spiritual leaders
- A sense that faith no longer functions the way it once did

Experiencing these reactions does not mean faith has disappeared. Often it means faith is struggling to adapt to realities it did not previously have to confront.

## EMOTIONAL INDICATORS

Theological injury frequently affects emotional life as well.

You may notice sadness, grief, frustration, anger, helplessness, emotional exhaustion, numbness, disappointment, loneliness, or anxiety about spiritual questions.

These reactions are not necessarily signs of weakness. They are often normal responses to significant disruption.

Many people feel guilty about these emotions, particularly if they believe faith should protect them from such struggles. Scripture suggests otherwise. The Bible contains abundant examples of faithful people expressing grief, confusion, fear, disappointment, and anger.

Emotional struggle is not evidence that faith has failed.

## SPIRITUAL INDICATORS

Because theological injury affects faith itself, spiritual indicators are often especially significant.

You may find yourself:

- Praying less
- Praying differently
- Feeling uncertain whether prayer matters
- Avoiding worship
- Struggling with Scripture passages that once brought comfort
- Questioning long-held beliefs
- Feeling disconnected from spiritual practices
- Experiencing doubt more frequently
- Wondering whether God is present
- Feeling spiritually exhausted

Some people become alarmed by these changes. In many cases, they are part of a larger process of reconstruction.

Faith is not necessarily disappearing.

It may be changing.

## RELATIONAL INDICATORS

Theological injury often affects relationships as well.

Some people withdraw from faith communities. Others become frustrated with religious conversations. Some find themselves feeling isolated from people who appear certain. Others struggle with resentment toward religious leaders or institutions.

Common indicators include:

- Withdrawal from community
- Difficulty discussing faith
- Increased sensitivity to spiritual clichés
- Frustration with easy answers
- Distrust of institutions
- Reluctance to share doubts
- Feeling misunderstood by fellow believers

These reactions are common. They often reflect a desire for honesty rather than a rejection of faith.

## THEOLOGICAL INJURY AND UNANSWERED PRAYER

One of the most common pathways into theological injury involves unanswered prayer.

A loved one dies despite fervent prayer. A disaster occurs despite prayer. Healing does not come. Protection does not arrive. The hoped-for outcome never materializes.

The struggle is not simply disappointment.

It is theological.

People begin asking:

- What does prayer mean?
- Was God listening?
- Did I misunderstand faith?
- How should I pray now?

These questions are not signs of spiritual failure. They are signs that faith is wrestling with reality.

## THEOLOGICAL INJURY AMONG CAREGIVERS AND RESPONDERS

Over the years, I have encountered theological injury frequently among clergy, chaplains, disaster responders, healthcare workers, caregivers, and others whose lives involve repeated exposure to suffering.

These individuals repeatedly encounter tragedy, grief, injustice, loss, trauma, and death. Over time, such experiences can challenge theological assumptions that once seemed secure.

Many discover that suffering affects theology as much as it affects emotions.

Sometimes more.

One of the observations that eventually shaped this book is that disaster work often wounds theology before it wounds emotional functioning. The questions emerge before the symptoms. The struggle begins in belief before it becomes visible elsewhere.

Theological Injury Is Not the End of Faith

Perhaps the most important thing to remember is this:

Theological injury is not evidence that faith has failed.

It is evidence that faith has been challenged.

There is a difference.

Throughout Scripture, faithful people wrestle with disappointment, confusion, suffering, and unanswered questions. Job wrestles. Jeremiah wrestles. The psalmists wrestle. The disciples wrestle.

Faithful people have always wrestled.

Theological injury places us within that long tradition.

Recognizing the injury does not solve it, but naming it often brings relief. When we finally have language for what we are experiencing, we discover that we are not alone. Others have walked this road before us. Others continue walking it today.

While the journey may be difficult, it remains possible to move through theological injury without abandoning faith. Indeed, many people discover that faith eventually emerges deeper, humbler, and more resilient than before.

Recognition is not the end of the journey.

It is the beginning.

# Appendix C
## *Questions for Reflection and Discussion*

The purpose of these questions is not to produce correct answers.

They are intended to encourage reflection, conversation, honesty, and deeper engagement with the themes explored throughout this book.

Some questions may be most helpful for personal reflection. Others may work well in small groups, clergy cohorts, seminary classes, disaster-response teams, spiritual-care groups, or congregational settings.

You do not need to answer every question.

Begin with the ones that seem most important to you.

### REFLECTING ON YOUR OWN STORY

1. Can you identify a season in your life when your understanding of God, faith, or prayer was significantly challenged?
2. What experiences have most shaped your theology?
3. Have there been moments when suffering, loss, disappointment, or unanswered prayer altered what you believed?
4. What theological assumptions have become stronger over time?
5. What theological assumptions have become less certain?
6. What questions do you carry today that you did not carry ten years ago?
7. How have those questions affected your faith?

## RECOGNIZING THEOLOGICAL INJURY

1. Which descriptions of theological injury resonated most strongly with you?
2. Have you ever experienced a period of spiritual disorientation?
3. How did you respond?
4. Were there people who helped you during that season?
5. Were there responses from others that proved unhelpful?
6. What signs of theological injury do you recognize in yourself?
7. What signs do you recognize in people around you?

## FAITH AND UNANSWERED PRAYER

1. How do you understand prayer today?
2. Has your understanding of prayer changed over time?
3. Can you recall a prayer that seemed unanswered?
4. How did that experience affect your faith?
5. What have you learned about prayer through disappointment?
6. What role does trust play when outcomes differ from what we hoped for?

## SUFFERING AND THE PRESENCE OF GOD

1. When have you felt most aware of God's presence?
2. When have you felt least aware of God's presence?
3. How do you respond when God seems silent?
4. What role does the ministry of presence play in your understanding of faith?
5. How have other people helped make God's presence visible during difficult seasons?
6. How might you offer that same presence to others?

## PRACTICING LAMENT

1. What emotions are most difficult for you to bring before God?
2. How comfortable are you with expressing grief, disappointment, or anger in prayer?
3. What role has lament played in your spiritual life?
4. Which lament psalms speak most powerfully to you?
5. What losses are you currently carrying?
6. What might it look like to practice lament more intentionally?

## HOPE AFTER DISAPPOINTMENT

1. How would you define hope?
2. How has your understanding of hope changed over time?
3. Have you ever confused hope with certainty?
4. What helps sustain hope during difficult seasons?
5. Who has modeled hope for you?
6. What role does hope play in your faith today?

## COMMUNITY AND COMPANIONSHIP

1. Who has accompanied you through difficult seasons?
2. What qualities made them helpful?
3. How well does your faith community make space for questions and uncertainty?
4. What prevents communities from practicing honest conversation?
5. How can churches become safer places for people experiencing theological injury?
6. How can you become a better companion to others?

## CAREGIVING, MINISTRY, AND SERVICE

1. Have you ever experienced theological injury while caring for others?
2. How has caregiving affected your faith?
3. What have you learned about suffering through ministry or service?
4. Have you ever felt spiritually exhausted by the needs of others?
5. What practices help sustain you?
6. What boundaries help protect your well-being?

## DISASTER RESPONSE AND HUMAN SUFFERING

1. How does repeated exposure to suffering affect belief?
2. What have disasters, crises, or tragedies taught you about human resilience?
3. What have they taught you about faith?
4. How do responders and caregivers remain compassionate amid repeated exposure to pain?
5. What lessons from disaster response apply to everyday life?
6. What does it mean to remain human in the presence of suffering?

## FAITH AFTER THE RUPTURE

1. How has your faith changed over the years?
2. What aspects of your faith feel stronger today?
3. What aspects feel more uncertain?
4. What role does humility play in mature faith?
5. What questions remain unresolved?
6. Can faith and uncertainty coexist?
7. What does faithfulness look like in this season of your life?

## LOOKING FORWARD

1. What remains after certainty falls away?
2. What remains after disappointment?
3. What remains after loss?
4. What remains after theological injury?
5. What gives your life meaning today?
6. What do you hope readers will remember from this book?
7. If you were to summarize your current faith in a few sentences, what would you say?

## A FINAL QUESTION

The final chapter asks a simple question:

What remains?

Take a few moments to answer that question for yourself.

Write your response.

Sit with it.

Return to it from time to time.

Your answer may change.

That is part of the journey.

# Appendix D

## *Practices That Sustain Faith During Seasons of Theological Injury*

Theological injury is rarely resolved quickly.

For many people, it unfolds over months or years. Questions linger. Certain wounds heal slowly. Some losses never completely disappear. Even when faith remains, it may feel different than it once did.

In those seasons, people often ask what they should do.

The answer is not a technique.

It is a collection of practices.

Over the years, I have learned that faith is sustained less by dramatic breakthroughs than by ordinary habits repeated faithfully over time. These practices will not eliminate every question or remove every struggle. They can, however, help create space for faith to remain alive while healing unfolds.

### CONTINUE THE CONVERSATION

One of the greatest temptations during theological injury is to stop talking to God.

Prayer feels difficult. Answers seem absent. Silence feels discouraging. Many people gradually withdraw from prayer because they assume the conversation is no longer accomplishing anything.

Yet some of the most faithful prayers in Scripture emerge from seasons of confusion and disappointment.

Continue the conversation.

Pray when prayer feels meaningful.

Pray when it does not.

Speak honestly.

Speak simply.

Some days your prayer may be eloquent. Other days it may consist of only a few words.

Keep speaking.

The goal is not perfect prayer.

The goal is relationship.

## PRACTICE HONEST SCRIPTURE READING

During theological injury, certain passages of Scripture may become difficult to read. Familiar verses may no longer provide the comfort they once offered.

That is normal.

Rather than forcing yourself toward texts that feel disconnected from your experience, spend time with passages that reflect honesty. The Psalms are particularly helpful, as are Job, Lamentations, Jeremiah, Habakkuk, and portions of the Gospels that reveal suffering, grief, and uncertainty.

Read Scripture as a companion rather than a problem to solve.

Allow it to speak honestly.

Allow yourself to do the same.

## MAINTAIN CONNECTION TO COMMUNITY

Theological injury often encourages withdrawal. People become tired of conversations, frustrated with easy answers, and reluctant to discuss their questions.

While temporary retreat can sometimes be healthy, prolonged isolation rarely is.

Faith is difficult to sustain entirely alone.

Maintain connection to trusted people. Find individuals who can listen without fixing. Seek companions who can tolerate uncertainty. Participate in communities where honesty is welcomed.

You do not need a large number of people.

A few trustworthy companions can make a profound difference.

## EMBRACE LAMENT

Lament is not merely a response to theological injury.

It is one of the ways people survive it.

Continue naming losses, expressing disappointment, acknowledging grief, and bringing questions before God.

Lament prevents suffering from becoming hidden. It allows honesty and faith to coexist. Many people discover that lament becomes one of the most important spiritual disciplines of their lives.

## PRACTICE SABBATH

Theological injury can be exhausting.

Questions require energy.

Grief requires energy.

Disappointment requires energy.

Many people attempt to solve spiritual struggles through constant effort. Sometimes the most faithful response is rest.

Sabbath reminds us that we are not responsible for holding the entire world together.

God remains God while we rest.

Take time away from constant striving. Create space for renewal. Allow yourself to receive rather than produce.

## PAY ATTENTION TO SMALL GRACES

When people are struggling, they understandably focus on what has been lost.

An important spiritual practice involves noticing what remains.

Pay attention to small signs of grace:

- A conversation
- A friendship
- A shared meal
- A moment of laughter
- A sunrise
- An unexpected kindness
- A sense of peace that arrives without explanation

These experiences do not erase suffering.

They remind us that suffering is not the whole story.

## SERVE OTHERS

This recommendation may seem surprising.

People experiencing theological injury sometimes assume they should wait until everything is resolved before helping others.

Life rarely works that way.

Service often becomes one of the places where healing occurs.

Helping others does not eliminate our questions. It does remind us that meaning, compassion, and love remain possible even while questions persist.

Many caregivers, responders, clergy, and volunteers discover that acts of service help reconnect them with hope.

## SEEK WISE COMPANIONS

Some questions require companions.

Consider seeking a trusted pastor, spiritual director, chaplain, counselor, therapist, support group, or mature friend.

The goal is not finding someone who possesses every answer.

The goal is finding someone willing to walk with you.

Healing often occurs through companionship rather than explanation.

## REMEMBER THAT FAITH CHANGES

One of the most important lessons theological injury teaches is that faith can change without disappearing.

Many people become frightened when faith begins to look different than it once did. Questions increase. Certainty decreases. Assumptions shift.

This does not necessarily mean faith is dying.

It may mean faith is maturing.

A faith that has endured suffering often looks different from a faith that has not. The difference is not failure.

It is growth.

## REMAIN OPEN TO HOPE

Hope after theological injury rarely resembles optimism.

It is quieter.

More realistic.

More durable.

Hope does not require certainty.

It requires trust.

The people who have taught me the most about hope are rarely those who avoided suffering. They are people who experienced suffering and continued moving forward—one day at a time, one prayer at a time, and one act of faithfulness at a time.

Hope often grows in exactly the same way.

## A FINAL ENCOURAGEMENT

If you are experiencing theological injury, remember this:

You do not need to resolve every question immediately.

You do not need to force certainty.

You do not need to pretend.

Your task is not to eliminate every struggle.

Your task is to remain faithful within it.

Continue the conversation.

Stay connected.

Practice lament.

Receive grace.

Notice hope.

Trust that God remains present even when understanding feels incomplete.

Faith has survived difficult seasons before.

It can survive this one as well.

# Appendix E

## *Guidance for Clergy, Chaplains, and Spiritual Care Providers*

### CARING FOR PEOPLE LIVING WITH THEOLOGICAL INJURY

Many clergy, chaplains, spiritual care providers, and caregivers receive little formal training in theological injury. They are trained to provide care, listen well, and support people through crisis. Yet they are often less prepared for situations in which suffering has damaged a person's understanding of God, faith, prayer, meaning, or trust.

People experiencing theological injury frequently arrive carrying questions that cannot be answered quickly:

- Why did this happen?
- Where was God?
- Why were my prayers not answered?
- What do I believe now?
- How do I trust again?

These questions often emerge from grief, catastrophe, betrayal, trauma, caregiving, disaster response, or prolonged exposure to suffering. The caregiver's role is not to eliminate these questions. The caregiver's role is to accompany people as they live with them.

## BEGIN WITH PRESENCE

One of the most important lessons I have learned through ministry and disaster response is that people rarely need immediate explanations.

They need presence.

When individuals are struggling with theological injury, they often feel isolated. Some fear judgment. Others fear being misunderstood. Many have already heard simplistic answers that failed to address the depth of their pain.

Before offering guidance, offer presence.

Listen carefully. Remain attentive. Allow silence. Resist the urge to solve what may not be solvable.

The ministry of presence is not the absence of care.

It is often the deepest form of care.

## LISTEN FOR THE THEOLOGY BENEATH THE STORY

People do not always describe theological injury directly. Instead, they tell stories.

A loved one died.

A disaster destroyed a home.

A ministry ended painfully.

A child suffered.

A prayer remained unanswered.

As caregivers, we must learn to listen beneath the story. What assumptions have been disrupted? What beliefs have been challenged? What expectations have collapsed? What image of God is struggling?

The visible wound is not always the deepest wound.

Theological injury often resides beneath the surface.

## AVOID THE TEMPTATION TO FIX

Caregivers frequently feel pressure to provide answers. The pressure is understandable. We want to help. We want to relieve suffering. We want to restore hope.

Yet theological injury rarely responds well to quick explanations.

Statements such as:

- Everything happens for a reason.
- God must have a plan.
- You just need more faith.
- God never gives us more than we can handle.

may be intended as comfort. Often they create additional pain.

People experiencing theological injury usually need companions more than explanations. They need someone willing to remain present when answers are unavailable.

## RESPECT HONEST QUESTIONS

Some faith communities unintentionally communicate that questions are dangerous.

Scripture suggests otherwise.

The Bible contains questions from Job, Jeremiah, Habakkuk, the psalmists, the disciples, and even Jesus.

Questions are not necessarily evidence of unbelief. They are often evidence of engagement. People who continue asking questions have not abandoned the conversation.

They are still participating in it.

Allow room for honest questions.

Do not rush toward closure.

## NORMALIZE LAMENT

Many people have never been taught how to lament. As a result, they assume grief, anger, disappointment, and confusion are spiritual failures.

Help them discover otherwise.

Introduce lament psalms. Discuss biblical examples of lament. Model honest prayer. Create space for sorrow.

Lament allows wounded people to remain connected to God while speaking truthfully about their experience.

That is a gift.

## DISTINGUISH THEOLOGICAL INJURY FROM OTHER STRUGGLES

Theological injury often overlaps with other forms of distress.

A person may simultaneously experience:

- Grief
- Depression
- Burnout
- Compassion fatigue
- Secondary trauma
- Moral injury
- Anxiety

All of these realities deserve attention. Yet theological injury specifically involves disruption of meaning, belief, trust, prayer, or one's understanding of God.

Recognizing this distinction can help caregivers provide more effective support.

## CARE FOR CAREGIVERS

One of the lessons disaster response taught me is that caregivers are not immune to theological injury.

In fact, they may be particularly vulnerable.

Clergy, chaplains, disaster responders, healthcare workers, counselors, volunteers, and caregivers repeatedly encounter suffering. Over time, exposure to grief, tragedy, injustice, and unanswered questions can affect their own faith.

Caregivers need care.

They need places where they can speak honestly.

They need permission to acknowledge struggle.

They need companions as well.

Do not assume that because someone is providing care they are unaffected by suffering.

## OFFER HOPE WITHOUT FALSE REASSURANCE

Hope is important.

False reassurance is not.

Theological injury often develops when reality contradicts expectations. Caregivers should therefore be cautious about making promises they cannot keep.

Avoid guaranteeing outcomes. Avoid minimizing pain. Avoid suggesting that healing follows a predictable timeline.

Instead, offer realistic hope:

- Hope that God remains present.
- Hope that people do not walk alone.
- Hope that faith can survive difficult seasons.
- Hope that healing is possible even when answers remain incomplete.

Such hope is both honest and sustaining.

## TRUST THE LONG WORK

One of the most important lessons caregivers can learn is patience.

Theological injury is rarely resolved in a single conversation. Healing often unfolds slowly. Questions return. New experiences reshape understanding. Faith develops gradually.

Trust the long work.

Remain present.

Listen well.

Offer compassion.

Allow room for mystery.

Many people eventually discover that faith emerges from theological injury not weaker, but deeper, humbler, and more resilient.

Our task is not to force that outcome.

Our task is to accompany people faithfully while the journey unfolds.

## A FINAL WORD TO CAREGIVERS

If you serve others in ministry, chaplaincy, spiritual care, healthcare, disaster response, counseling, or caregiving, remember this:

You do not need to have every answer.

You do not need to resolve every question.

You do not need to fix every wound.

You do need to remain present.

Again and again, I have witnessed the healing power of a compassionate listener, a faithful companion, a quiet presence, or a simple act of kindness. Never underestimate the significance of showing up.

In a world eager to explain suffering, the ministry of presence remains one of the most profound gifts we can offer.

And often, it is enough.

# Appendix F

## *Theological Injury in Disaster Response*

### WHEN CATASTROPHE CHANGES FAITH

Disaster response changes people.

Most responders expect that. They anticipate fatigue, stress, long hours, difficult decisions, and exposure to suffering. Organizations increasingly recognize the emotional consequences of disaster work and provide training related to resilience, burnout, compassion fatigue, and secondary trauma.

These conversations matter.

Yet there is another consequence of disaster work that receives far less attention.

Disaster response can affect theology.

It can alter how people understand God, prayer, suffering, justice, hope, and the nature of the world itself. In other words, disaster work can produce theological injury.

For some responders, the changes are subtle. For others, they are profound. Many discover that repeated exposure to catastrophe affects faith as deeply as it affects emotional well-being.

### THE QUESTIONS THAT EMERGE

One of the realities of disaster response is that responders encounter suffering repeatedly. Homes are destroyed. Lives are disrupted. Families are displaced. Communities experience profound loss.

Again and again, responders stand in places where people ask questions that have no easy answers:

- Why did this happen?
- Where was God?
- Why were our prayers not answered?
- How do we rebuild after this?

Over time, responders often begin asking some of these same questions themselves.

Theological injury frequently begins here—not with disbelief, but with questions; not with rejection of faith, but with the collision between faith and reality.

Many responders discover that assumptions they once held comfortably become more difficult to maintain after years of exposure to suffering.

## WHEN PRAYER BECOMES COMPLICATED

Disaster settings often complicate prayer.

Responders pray with survivors whose homes have been destroyed. They pray with grieving families. They pray with people facing uncertain futures. They pray for safety, healing, recovery, and protection.

Sometimes those prayers appear to be answered.

Sometimes they do not.

Over time, many responders begin wrestling with difficult questions about prayer itself. What does prayer accomplish? How should we understand unanswered prayer? How do we continue praying when outcomes remain uncertain?

These questions do not necessarily weaken faith.

They often deepen it.

But the process can be unsettling. Theology that once seemed straightforward may no longer feel adequate.

## EXPOSURE TO HUMAN SUFFERING

Most people encounter tragedy occasionally.

Responders encounter it repeatedly.

A single disaster may involve hundreds or thousands of stories of loss. Responders often move from one deployment to another, carrying memories from previous events into the next response.

For many responders, deployments eventually blur together into airports, briefing rooms, shelters, recovery centers, damage assessments, and long operational periods measured more by exhaustion than calendar dates.

Exposure accumulates.

Stories accumulate.

Questions accumulate.

Some responders discover that the cumulative effect is not simply emotional fatigue.

It is theological fatigue.

They become less certain, less confident in easy explanations, more aware of mystery, and more aware of how limited human understanding can be.

## THEOLOGICAL INJURY AND MORAL INJURY

Although related, theological injury and moral injury are not identical.

Moral injury often involves violations of deeply held moral beliefs, experiences of betrayal, impossible choices, or actions that conflict with one's values. Theological injury focuses on disruptions in faith, meaning, trust, prayer, and one's understanding of God.

In disaster response, the two frequently overlap.

A responder may witness institutional failures, resource limitations, preventable suffering, or circumstances in which every available option carries consequences. Such experiences can challenge both moral convictions and theological assumptions.

Many responders find themselves wrestling with both forms of injury simultaneously.

Recognizing the distinction can be helpful, but separating them completely is often impossible.

## THE HIDDEN LONELINESS OF RESPONDERS

One of the most significant challenges facing responders is that many feel unable to discuss these struggles openly.

Disaster culture often emphasizes competence, resilience, and operational effectiveness. These are important values, but they can unintentionally discourage vulnerability.

Responders may hesitate to discuss questions about faith. They may fear appearing weak. They may assume others are not experiencing similar struggles. They may conclude they should simply push through.

As a result, theological injury often remains hidden.

Questions remain private.

Doubts remain unspoken.

Wounds remain unnamed.

This isolation can intensify suffering.

One of the most important lessons I have learned is that responders need safe places for honest conversation. They need permission to acknowledge what disaster work does to the soul.

## WHAT RESPONDERS HAVE TAUGHT ME

Some of the most important lessons I have learned about faith have come from disaster responders.

I have watched volunteers continue serving despite exhaustion. I have watched caregivers offer compassion in heartbreaking circumstances. I have watched responders return repeatedly to difficult work because they believed helping others mattered.

Their example has taught me that faith is often less about certainty than faithfulness, less about explanation than presence, and less about having answers than continuing to show up.

Again and again, responders have demonstrated extraordinary resilience, kindness, generosity, and courage. They have also reminded me that even strong people need care.

## CARING FOR THE SPIRITUAL LIVES OF RESPONDERS

Organizations increasingly recognize the importance of emotional well-being.

The spiritual well-being of responders deserves similar attention.

Responders need opportunities to:

- Reflect on their experiences
- Discuss difficult questions
- Practice lament
- Receive spiritual care
- Connect with supportive communities
- Process grief and loss
- Explore changes in belief and understanding

These practices do not eliminate theological injury.

They help prevent responders from carrying it alone.

## HOPE AFTER THE DISASTER

One of the surprising realities of disaster work is that responders witness not only suffering but also resilience.

Communities rebuild. Neighbors help one another. Volunteers serve. Acts of kindness emerge in unexpected places.

Hope appears.

Not as optimism.

Not as denial.

As persistence.

Responders see people continue moving forward despite profound loss. That reality matters because it reminds us that catastrophe is never the whole story.

Neither is theological injury.

## A FINAL REFLECTION

Years of disaster response have convinced me that disaster work often wounds theology before it wounds emotional functioning. The questions emerge first. The struggle begins in belief. The search for meaning intensifies.

Yet I have also learned something else.

Faith can survive these questions.

Prayer can survive uncertainty.

Hope can survive disappointment.

And God remains present even in places where explanations fail.

Responders know better than most people that the world can change in a single day. Many have also learned that faith can endure far more than they once imagined.

That may be one of the most important lessons disaster work has to teach.

# Appendix G

## *Continuing the Journey*

### BOOKS AND RESOURCES FOR FURTHER EXPLORATION

No single book can answer every question.

Theological injury is a complex and deeply personal experience. For some readers, this book may simply provide language for struggles they have carried for years. For others, it may mark the beginning of a longer journey of reflection, healing, and growth.

If you have found this book helpful, I encourage you to continue reading, reflecting, learning, and engaging in conversation with others. The resources below have shaped my own thinking and may prove helpful as you continue exploring questions related to suffering, faith, lament, hope, caregiving, disaster response, moral injury, and spiritual formation.

The goal is not to find a single author who possesses all the answers.

The goal is to find trustworthy companions for the journey.

### RELATED WORKS BY GC SMITH (ALL AVAILABLE THROUGH WIPF AND STOCK OR AMAZON)

Many of the themes explored in Theological Injury are developed more fully in other books within the broader Moral Injury Project.

## Faith Without Explanation

A theological reflection on what disaster response has taught me about God, suffering, unanswered prayer, and faith after certainty.

## Staying Human in Disaster Work

A practical guide for responders, caregivers, clergy, chaplains, and volunteers seeking to remain compassionate and healthy amid repeated exposure to suffering.

## What the Work Asks

An exploration of the emotional, moral, and spiritual demands placed upon disaster responders and caregivers.

## Bearing the Unbearable

Stories and reflections from disaster response that explore suffering, resilience, compassion, and the human search for meaning.

## Beyond Burnout

A guide for clergy, caregivers, and helping professionals seeking to understand the deeper spiritual and moral dimensions of exhaustion.

## Wounded Shepherds

An examination of moral injury among pastors, church leaders, chaplains, and others engaged in ministry.

## The Beatitudes After Betrayal

A theological exploration of Jesus' Beatitudes through the lens of suffering, disappointment, moral injury, and grace.

### Blessed Are the Broken

Stories of moral injury, faith, loss, healing, and unfinished grace.

## BIBLICAL AND THEOLOGICAL VOICES

### Walter Brueggemann

Brueggemann's work on lament, the Psalms, exile, prophetic imagination, and the life of faith has profoundly influenced contemporary conversations about suffering and hope. Readers interested in lament should begin here.

### Jürgen Moltmann

Moltmann's theology of hope emerged from profound personal suffering and remains one of the most important theological resources for those seeking faith beyond despair.

### Nicholas Wolterstorff

His reflections on grief, loss, and Christian faith offer some of the most honest writing available on suffering and mourning.

### Henri J. M. Nouwen

Nouwen's work on presence, woundedness, caregiving, and spiritual formation continues to help readers understand how vulnerability can become a source of ministry rather than a barrier to it.

### Paul Tillich

Tillich's writings on courage, doubt, faith, anxiety, and meaning provide valuable resources for readers wrestling with uncertainty.

### Karl Rahner

Rahner's emphasis on mystery, grace, and the hiddenness of God offers important insights for those learning to live with unanswered questions.

### Richard Rohr

Rohr's work frequently explores transformation through suffering, loss, and spiritual growth, helping readers understand how disruption can become a pathway toward deeper faith.

### Thomas Merton

Merton's writings on contemplation, silence, prayer, and the inner life remain valuable companions for those navigating spiritual uncertainty.

### Frederick Buechner

Buechner's reflections on grace, vocation, suffering, and faith combine theological depth with literary beauty.

### Parker J. Palmer

Palmer's work on vocation, identity, community, leadership, and the inner life has helped countless readers navigate seasons of struggle and transformation.

## FAITH DEVELOPMENT AND SPIRITUAL GROWTH

### James W. Fowler

Fowler's work on stages of faith development provides a helpful framework for understanding how faith changes and matures throughout life.

While not every aspect of his model is universally accepted, many readers find it useful when reflecting on their own spiritual journeys.

Meaning, Suffering, and Human Resilience

### Viktor E. Frankl

Frankl's reflections on meaning, suffering, resilience, and human dignity continue to offer important insights for people seeking hope amid adversity.

His work reminds us that meaning often remains possible even in difficult circumstances.

## RESOURCES FOR CLERGY, CHAPLAINS, AND CAREGIVERS

Readers serving in ministry, chaplaincy, disaster response, healthcare, counseling, education, social services, and other helping professions may find it helpful to continue exploring:

- Moral injury
- Compassion fatigue
- Secondary trauma
- Resilience
- Caregiver well-being
- Spiritual formation
- Ministry of presence
- Reflective practice
- Grief care
- Disaster spiritual care

These subjects are increasingly important as helping professionals seek ways to remain healthy while caring for others.

## RESOURCES FOR DISASTER RESPONDERS

Disaster responders often face unique emotional, moral, and spiritual challenges.

Additional study in the following areas may prove beneficial:

- Disaster spiritual care

- Psychological first aid
- Moral injury
- Compassion fatigue
- Volunteer care
- Trauma-informed response
- Community resilience
- Long-term recovery
- Care for caregivers

Responders spend significant time caring for others.

They deserve care as well.

## A FINAL RECOMMENDATION

Read widely.

Read thoughtfully.

Read humbly.

No single author, tradition, denomination, or perspective possesses every answer.

Theological injury teaches many of us that faith grows not through certainty alone, but through honest engagement with difficult questions.

Seek wisdom wherever you find it.

Remain curious.

Remain teachable.

Remain hopeful.

Most importantly, remember that you do not need to walk this journey alone.

Others have walked it before you.

Others are walking it now.

And many faithful companions remain available for the road ahead.

# Appendix H

## *A Letter to Those Living with Unanswered Questions*

Dear Friend,

If you have read this far, there is a good chance that some part of this book felt familiar. Perhaps you recognized your own questions in these pages. Perhaps you recognized your own disappointments, your own struggles, or a season when faith became more difficult than it once seemed.

Or perhaps you are still living in that season.

If so, I want to say something simple: you are not alone.

One of the great challenges of theological injury is that it often feels isolating. People frequently assume they are the only ones carrying certain questions. They worry that their doubts indicate spiritual weakness. They fear that their struggles place them outside the boundaries of faith.

Yet throughout Scripture, faithful people wrestle with questions. Job wrestled. Jeremiah wrestled. The psalmists wrestled. The disciples wrestled. Even those closest to God often found themselves struggling to understand what God was doing.

You stand within a long tradition.

A very long tradition.

If suffering has complicated your faith, you are not unusual. If unanswered prayer has left you disappointed, you are not unusual. If tragedy has disrupted your theology, you are not unusual. If certainty has become more difficult, you are not unusual.

You are human.

And you are in good company.

Over the years, I have sat with disaster survivors, grieving families, exhausted responders, caregivers, clergy, and ordinary people trying to make sense of experiences that seemed impossible to explain. Again and again, I have discovered that many of us carry similar questions:

Where was God?

Why did this happen?

Why were our prayers not answered?

How do we trust now?

I wish I could tell you that every question eventually receives a satisfying answer.

I cannot.

Some questions remain. Some mysteries remain. Some losses remain.

Yet I have also discovered something else.

God remains.

Not always in ways we expect. Not always in ways we recognize immediately. But again and again, I have witnessed the quiet persistence of grace. I have seen it in hospital rooms, shelters, funeral homes, congregations, disaster operations, and ordinary acts of kindness. I have seen it in people who continued showing up for one another despite their own grief, in responders who returned to serve despite exhaustion, in caregivers who remained present when nothing could be fixed, and in survivors who somehow found the strength to begin again.

These experiences have not eliminated my questions. They have simply convinced me that questions are not the whole story.

Faith does not require certainty.

Faith requires relationship.

And relationships often survive questions.

Perhaps that is where you find yourself today—not certain, not finished, not fully healed, yet still searching, still hoping, still praying, still wondering.

If so, I encourage you to keep going.

Continue the conversation.

Continue asking questions.

Continue practicing lament.

Continue seeking companions.

Continue paying attention to moments of grace.

Most importantly, do not confuse unanswered questions with God's absence.

They are not the same thing.

The road may be longer than you expected. The journey may be different than you imagined. But you do not walk it alone.

Others have walked this road before you.

Others are walking it now.

And God remains present on the journey.

May you find courage for the questions, patience for the uncertainty, companions for the road, and hope sufficient for the next step.

Grace and peace,

Greg

# Appendix I

## *About The Moral Injury Project*

The Moral Injury Project emerged from a simple observation: many people carry wounds that are difficult to name.

Some of those wounds are emotional. Some are psychological. Some are moral. Some are spiritual. Many exist at the intersection of all four.

For years, I encountered individuals whose experiences did not fit neatly into traditional categories such as burnout, stress, grief, trauma, or compassion fatigue. They were carrying burdens related to betrayal, impossible choices, exposure to suffering, institutional failure, caregiving, ministry, disaster response, and the struggle to remain human in difficult circumstances.

Increasingly, I found myself drawn to the concept of moral injury. The more I explored the subject, the more convinced I became that moral injury provided an important framework for understanding many experiences that had previously remained unnamed.

Over time, however, another pattern began to emerge.

Some wounds were not merely moral.

They were theological.

People were not only struggling with what had happened. They were struggling with what those experiences meant for faith. They were questioning prayer, questioning assumptions about God, questioning long-held beliefs, and questioning the explanations that had once sustained them.

Theological injury became one way of describing those experiences.

This book is part of a much larger conversation.

The Moral Injury Project exists to explore the moral, emotional, and spiritual consequences of suffering, caregiving, public service, ministry, disaster response, leadership, and life in a wounded world. Its goals are straightforward:

- To provide language for difficult experiences
- To encourage honest conversation
- To support caregivers and helping professionals
- To bridge theology and lived experience
- To promote healing, resilience, and hope
- To create resources for individuals, communities, and organizations
- To foster deeper understanding of moral and theological injury

The project includes books, articles, training events, workshops, presentations, community conversations, and educational resources.

Areas of particular focus include:

- Moral injury
- Theological injury
- Disaster response
- Disaster spiritual care
- Caregiving
- Clergy well-being
- Chaplaincy
- Public service
- Ministry of presence
- Lament
- Faith after suffering
- Hope and resilience

At its heart, The Moral Injury Project is rooted in a simple conviction:

People need language for what they are carrying.

When experiences remain unnamed, they often remain isolated. When experiences are named, conversations become possible. And when conversations become possible, healing often becomes more possible as well.

My hope is that this project will help create those conversations—not because every question can be answered and not because every wound can be eliminated, but because people should not have to carry these burdens alone.

If this book has helped you better understand your own experience—or the experience of someone you love—then it has accomplished its purpose.

The conversation continues.

For additional books, articles, speaking engagements, training opportunities, and project resources, visit:

TheMoralInjuryProject.org

Thank you for being part of the journey.

# Appendix J

## *Building Communities That Make Room for Theological Injury*

One of the great challenges facing many people who experience theological injury is isolation.

They often assume they are the only ones asking difficult questions. They worry that their doubts are unusual. They fear that speaking honestly may lead to judgment, misunderstanding, or exclusion.

As a result, many suffer quietly.

Theological injury may be experienced individually, but it rarely heals entirely in isolation. Healthy communities can play an important role in helping people navigate seasons of spiritual struggle.

The question is not whether people in our congregations, organizations, ministry teams, disaster-response groups, and communities are experiencing theological injury.

They are.

The question is whether those communities are prepared to respond well.

### CREATE SPACE FOR HONEST CONVERSATION

Many faith communities unintentionally communicate that certain questions are unacceptable. People quickly learn which subjects are welcomed and which subjects are avoided. As a result, difficult questions often remain hidden.

Healthy communities create room for honest conversation.

This does not require agreement on every issue.

It does require respect.

People need opportunities to discuss suffering, unanswered prayer, doubt, grief, disappointment, faith struggles, questions about God, and the moral or theological concerns that arise from lived experience.

Communities become healthier when honesty is welcomed rather than feared.

## NORMALIZE SPIRITUAL STRUGGLE

One of the most powerful gifts leaders can offer is the normalization of struggle.

Scripture is filled with examples of faithful people wrestling with God. Job wrestled. Jeremiah wrestled. The psalmists wrestled. The disciples wrestled.

Faithful people have always wrestled.

Communities should communicate that spiritual struggle is not a sign of failure.

It is often part of growth.

When people understand this, they are less likely to interpret their questions as evidence that something is wrong with them.

## TEACH LAMENT

Many congregations know how to celebrate.

Far fewer know how to lament.

Yet communities need practices that help people respond faithfully to grief and loss.

Consider incorporating lament psalms, times of silence, memorial services, prayer vigils, story-sharing, and public acknowledgment of loss. Such practices create space for honesty and remind people that faith does not require pretending.

Communities that know how to lament are often better equipped to support wounded people.

## VALUE PRESENCE OVER EXPLANATIONS

When people experience theological injury, they rarely need immediate answers.

They need companions.

Leaders, caregivers, and fellow community members can provide profound support simply by listening, remaining present, and resisting the urge to explain away suffering.

The ministry of presence is not passive.

It is active compassion.

One of the most important lessons of caregiving, chaplaincy, and disaster spiritual care is that people often remember who stayed with them long after they forget what was said.

## CARE FOR CAREGIVERS

Every community depends upon caregivers.

Pastors.

Chaplains.

Responders.

Teachers.

Healthcare workers.

Volunteers.

Yet caregivers often receive little care themselves.

Communities should intentionally support those who spend their lives supporting others. They need opportunities for rest, reflection, encouragement, and honest conversation about the burdens they carry.

Healthy caregivers contribute to healthy communities.

## ENCOURAGE PATIENCE

Healing rarely follows a predictable timeline.

Some questions remain for years.

Some wounds heal slowly.

Some losses continue shaping lives long after the initial event has passed.

Communities should avoid pressuring people toward premature resolution. Patience is one of the most important forms of care we can offer.

People need room to grieve, wrestle, question, and heal at their own pace.

## A COMMUNITY OF GRACE

Ultimately, communities that respond well to theological injury become communities of grace.

They make room for questions. They welcome honesty. They practice lament. They value presence. They extend compassion. They trust that God remains at work even when certainty is difficult to find.

Such communities will never eliminate suffering.

They cannot remove every question.

They cannot prevent every wound.

They can, however, ensure that people do not face those realities alone.

And sometimes that is one of the greatest gifts a community can offer.

A community willing to stay.

# Acknowledgements

Books are often attributed to a single author, but no book is ever truly written alone.

This one certainly was not.

Over the years, I have been shaped by countless people whose lives, questions, struggles, faith, and companionship helped make this book possible. Some appear in these pages directly. Many more are present indirectly through the lessons they taught me.

I am grateful to the survivors, responders, caregivers, clergy, chaplains, healthcare workers, volunteers, and ordinary people whose stories have shaped my understanding of suffering, faith, hope, and the human spirit. Again and again, I have witnessed remarkable courage in the midst of loss and extraordinary compassion in the presence of pain. Much of what I know about resilience, lament, grace, and faithfulness has been learned from them.

I am especially grateful to my colleagues in disaster response. Through the American Red Cross, Presbyterian Disaster Assistance, the Iowa Disaster Human Resource Council, Iowa VOAD, and many other partners, I have had the privilege of serving alongside people whose dedication to helping others continues to inspire me. They have taught me that compassion is not merely a feeling. It is a practice. It is something we choose, day after day, even when the work is difficult.

My thanks also extend to the many members of Disaster Spiritual Care teams, Interdisciplinary Care and Condolence Teams, care teams, chaplaincy groups, and congregations who have shared their wisdom, experiences, and questions over the years. Their insights helped me recognize that theological injury is far more common than many of us realize.

I am grateful to the authors, theologians, pastors, scholars, and spiritual writers whose work has informed my own thinking. While this book reflects my conclusions, it has been enriched by the wisdom of many others who have wrestled honestly with suffering, faith, grief, hope, and the mystery of God.

Special thanks to my editor and copy editor, Hannah, whose careful attention, thoughtful suggestions, and encouragement helped strengthen this manuscript in countless ways.

I am grateful to the team at Wipf and Stock Publishers and to everyone who has encouraged, supported, and believed in the broader vision of The Moral Injury Project. This book is one part of a much larger conversation about suffering, meaning, faith, caregiving, and what it means to remain human in difficult circumstances.

Most importantly, I am grateful to the people who have trusted me with their stories. Whether in churches, shelters, hospitals, funeral homes, disaster operations, care teams, or quiet conversations over coffee, they have allowed me to glimpse both the fragility and resilience of the human spirit. Their willingness to share honestly has shaped me more than they know.

Finally, I give thanks to God.

Not because every question has been answered.

Not because every mystery has been resolved.

But because through years of ministry, caregiving, disaster response, and theological struggle, I have repeatedly discovered that God's presence remains.

That conviction made this book possible.

And it remains one of the gifts for which I am most grateful.

Rev. GC Smith, PhD

# About the Author

Rev. GC Smith, PhD is a pastor, disaster spiritual care provider, author, and speaker whose work focuses on moral injury, theological injury, caregiving, faith after suffering, and the spiritual dimensions of disaster response.

For more than three decades, he has served in pastoral ministry and has spent many years accompanying individuals and communities through disaster, loss, grief, and recovery. Since 2011, he has served with the American Red Cross and has deployed to numerous disaster responses as a Disaster Spiritual Care provider. He has also served with Presbyterian Disaster Assistance's National Response Team and has worked alongside responders, caregivers, chaplains, clergy, and volunteers across a wide range of disaster settings.

Dr. Smith is the founder of The Moral Injury Project, an ongoing initiative exploring the moral, emotional, and spiritual consequences of suffering, caregiving, public service, ministry, and disaster response. His writing seeks to create language for experiences that often remain unspoken and to help readers navigate questions of meaning, faith, hope, and human resilience.

He is the author of numerous books on moral injury, disaster response, caregiving, faith, and spiritual formation, including Faith Without Explanation, Staying Human in Disaster Work, What the Work Asks, Bearing the Unbearable, Beyond Burnout, Wounded Shepherds, The Beatitudes After Betrayal, and Blessed Are the Broken.

Throughout his ministry and disaster-response work, he has become increasingly interested in the ways suffering reshapes theology. Theological Injury emerges from years of listening to survivors, responders, clergy, caregivers, and ordinary people struggling to make sense of faith after loss, disappointment, catastrophe, and unanswered prayer.

He lives in Iowa and continues to write, teach, speak, and serve in disaster response and spiritual care.

Learn more at TheMoralInjuryProject.org.

www.ingramcontent.com/pod-product-compliance
Lightning Source LLC
LaVergne TN
LVHW050804061126
851857LV00012B/671